MULTINATIONAL INSTITUTIONS AND THE THIRD WORLD

MULTINATIONAL INSTITUTIONS AND THE THIRD WORLD

Management, Debt, and Trade Conflicts in the International Economic Order

Robert Henriques Girling

PRAEGER SPECIAL STUDIES • PRAEGER SCIENTIFIC

New York • Philadelphia • Eastbourne, UK
Toronto • Hong Kong • Tokyo • Sydney

Library of Congress Cataloging in Publication Data

Girling, Robert Henriques.
  Multinational institutions and the Third World.

  Bibliography: p.
  Includes index.
  1. Developing countries—Foreign economic relations.
2. International economic relations. 3. Debt
External—Developing countries. 4. Banks and banking,
International—Developing countries. 5. International
business enterprises—Developing countries. I. Title.
HF1413.G57 1985   337'.09172'4   84-18131
ISBN 0-03-001003-9 (alk. paper)
ISBN 0-03-001004-7 (pbk. : alk. paper)

Published and Distributed by the
Praeger Publishers Division
(ISBN Prefix 0-275)
of Greenwood Press, Inc.,
Westport, Connecticut

Published in 1985 by Praeger Publishers
CBS Educational and Professional Publishing
a Division of CBS Inc.
521 Fifth Avenue, New York, NY 10175 USA
Printed in the United States of America
on acid-free paper

ACKNOWLEDGMENTS

I am indebted to many friends who have directly and indirectly helped in the shaping of my ideas about multinational institutions. To former students in Latin America and the Caribbean, as well as in the United States, I owe particular appreciation for their thoughtful and probing questions.

Several colleagues and friends, including Richard Feinberg, Richard Sack, Frank Bonilla, John Weeks, Carmen Diana Deere, Beatriz Nofal, Pierre Ewanczyk, and Richard Fagan, read parts of the manuscript. In addition, Barbara Koeppel, Benecio Schmidt, Jorge Werthein, Maria Valeria Junho Pena, Alan Riding, Richard Fletcher, Claudia Johnson, Reggie Dale, Joe Eldridge, Mayra Buvinic, DeLisle Worrell, Luin Goldring, David Morawetz, Delmar Valleau, Helen Safa, Alain de Janvry, Horace Levy, Liz Dore, Dave Reed, Robin Hahnel, and Sheldon and Barbara Annis were among those who provided encouragement at vital moments. Connie Winnie assisted me with the research for chapter 9. Gladstone Bonnick provided an important opportunity for me to work with and learn about the World Bank. Anne Salda of the World Bank-IMF library was particularly helpful during two years of library research. The International Center for Research on Women provided an additional opportunity to view the situation of women in the Third World while working on its Socioeconomic Participation of Women in the Third World Project.

The Washington Office on Latin America gave me the chance to understand the impact of U.S. policy in Central America. Ron Weber provided invaluable editorial assistance, challenging me at all points to express my ideas more clearly and forcefully. Gabriela Fort provided excellent secretarial assistance, patiently typing and retyping numerous drafts. Leslie Barham lent her artistic eye to assist me with graphics.

My greatest debt, however, is to Sherry Keith, who furnished encouragement, support, and intellectual stimulation at all times. Her incisive mind provided me with the intellectual inspiration to persevere in trying circumstances. My daughter, Chalyn, provided a refreshing source of distraction at appropriate moments.

CONTENTS

LIST OF TABLES

LIST OF FIGURES

LIST OF BOXES

LIST OF ACRONYMS

ACC advanced capitalist countries
AIC advanced industrial countries
ASP American Selling Price

BDC beneficiary developing countries

CVD countervailing duty

EEC European Economic Community
EFF extended fund facility
EFTA European Free Trade Association
EPZ export processing zone

FRBNY Federal Reserve Bank of New York

G-10 Group of Ten
GATT General Agreement on Tariffs and Trade
GDP gross domestic product
GNP gross national product
GSP generalized system of preferences

IBRD International Bank for Reconstruction and Development
ICB international competitive bidding
IDA International Development Agency
IDB Inter-American Development Bank
IRR internal rate of return
IFAD International Fund for Agricultural Development
IFC International Finance Corporation
IFI international financial institutions
ILO International Labour Organisation
IMF International Monetary Fund
IPR investment performance requirement
ITO International Trade Organization

LDC less-developed country

MDB multilateral development bank
MNC multinational corporation
MNI multinational institution

MTN multilateral trade negotiation

NIC newly industrialized country
NIEO New International Economic Order

OECD Organization for Economic Cooperation and Development
OMA orderly marketing agreement
OPEC Organization of Petroleum Exporting Countries

SAL structural adjustment loan
SDR special drawing right

TNC transnational corporation

UNCTAD United Nations Conference on Trade and Development
UNDP United Nations Development Program

VER voluntary export restraint

INTRODUCTION

In 1968 I took my first job in the field of economic development, as an economic planner for the Jamaican government. This proved to be a good place to begin to learn about the problems of underdevelopment. I was placed in charge of constructing an input-output model of the national economy that could be used to forecast its future performance. I soon learned that Jamaica's economy was a small dot in the sea of the international economy, and that the large tides of that sea defined shorelines and sometimes threatened to erode meaningful growth.

For example, one study pointed to the unintended consequences of investment incentive legislation. The government had instituted ten-year "tax holidays" to encourage foreign investors to build factories in Jamaica, thereby creating jobs for the large number of unemployed workers. However, our study showed that many foreign investors used small amounts of their own risk capital to leverage domestic finance. Profits tended to be repatriated rather than reinvested locally. One enterprising capitalist earned a tax-free 3,800 percent return by producing for export. Even when profits were predicted for the long term, the owners of these enterprises still packed up and left once their "tax holiday" had expired.

Another experience that influenced my view was my contact with Jamaica's peasantry. I lived in a rural village outside of Kingston among many subsistence farmers. We often talked about how our lives and the lives of our families had changed. I was surprised to find that despite the country's considerable industrial progress, the quality of everyday life for most of those people was only marginally affected. (They often complained about how food was less plentiful, although they seemed to be better dressed than before.) Such trade-offs in the basic necessities of life led me to question whether Jamaica's economic development was in fact "trickling down," as conventional economic wisdom suggested it should. I decided to undertake research in the theory of economic development, which I did at Stanford University.

When I returned to Jamaica after completing my studies in 1974, I became the deputy director for regional planning. Much more development assistance was available then than when I had left. Development banks were lending to finance port construction, new housing, schools, and tourist facilities. One day the project officer of an international lending agency met with me to discuss a proposed loan for a study of "urban growth management" in Kingston. Soon the organization sent a consultant who, we soon discovered, knew very little about our particular situation and had no prior experience in any underdeveloped country. He produced a highly sophisticated, computer-assisted model and research project for deciding where new schools, police stations, and hospitals should be built.

Unfortunately, the model required reams of data. Moreover, it called for Jamaica to take out a loan of over $1 million, to be repaid at the prevailing market rate of interest. The analysis of my department indicated that scarce resources might be better spent on upgrading and developing small towns, which were increasingly dilapidated and possessed few sources of employment or amusement. If rural employment, culture, and housing were improved, migration to the cities and the swamping of urban services might be prevented.

I shared these views with the representative of the development bank. He replied that there was no money available for such a harebrained scheme; furthermore, a new study would take time, and he had no time to waste. In the end, our department's analysis was ignored. The loan was signed; the contracted study was completed, filed, and forgotten.

Several years later I found myself in Washington, D.C. Here I was able to follow up on the perplexing events in Jamaica. I could not understand why the representative of the development bank had been so insistent on funding a study when we had been so skeptical. In Washington I discovered the "ins and outs" of international banking and its relationship to economic development. I learned, for example, that employees of the private banks, as well as of the World Bank and other development banks, have quotas to meet. Their career prospects are, in part, tied to their making loans and the volume of those loans. The eventual benefit, if any, to the borrowing country is not considered in evaluating the employees' or the bank's performance. Strangely enough, in this world of "bottom lines," there is rarely time to consider the merits of a project, either theoretically or morally, or nontraditional alternatives. The emphasis is on keeping the mill turning.

While discussing these concerns with a senior official at the development bank, I was told that employees are counseled not to preach development: "The very worst thing you can do is to let on that you are an advocate of development or are personally concerned about the welfare of your country." The recipe for success was to "be cold-hearted in your assessments and don't contradict your superiors."

I also learned that the cavalier approach to foreign lending by the private banks was encouraged by the extensive profits; a week's debt negotiation can net several million dollars in service fees. And careful analysis was often considered to be "negative thinking." Loans to Third World governments and public corporations were "sovereign risks"; governments, unlike private businesses, cannot declare bankruptcy. In Wonderland, risk is a fantasy.

Working as a private consultant in several developing countries, I discovered that public officials often regard loans as handouts or political plums to be negotiated quickly. I was disturbed by the apparent profligacy and lack of responsibility in the handling of large sums. (In Brazil $100 million was "small change.") I was forced to conclude that the international debt crisis promoted and grew out of shared irresponsibilities by a cast of actors: Third World and industrial world governments searching for easy, tax-free solutions; international banks and corporations seeking high profits; development bankers seeking power and prestige; and politicians finding pots of gold to finance their careers.

This book grew out of that insight and is an attempt to pare away the rhetoric that passes for analysis. What is clearly lacking in the international arena is the ability to view the long-term interests of the whole. No actor is prepared to view the welfare of the world economy as its concern. In particular, the industrial capitalist countries as a group have been particularly unwilling to make the short-term sacrifices that can provide long-term gains for both themselves and the developing world. In lieu of concrete actions to place the world economy on a new and sound footing, there has been an elaborate dance in endless meetings that reiterate the status quo. Real and separate interests lie behind the pieties that divide the developed and the developing worlds. More important, the sense of crisis that accentuates those divergences has a silver lining. We are becoming more interdependent, and the basic value of mutual survival, once it is considered, can lay the groundwork for constructive action.

The economic health of the Third World has, for centuries, depended upon the vitality of markets in the developed, industrial capitalist economies. The Third World still depends on the United States, Western Europe, and Japan to buy raw materials. However, something new is occurring. The Third World is an increasingly important market for products and financial services from the advanced capitalist countries. Developing nations purchase 30 percent of the European Economic Community's exports, 46 percent of Japan's exports, and a surprising 36 percent of U.S. exports. In 1978 the industrialized capitalist countries recorded a surplus of $34.5 billion in trade with the Third World. The World Bank noted, "The developing countries increasingly act as an 'engine of growth' for the rest of the world" (1981, p. 11). A study of middle-income countries (such as Brazil, Mexico, Malaysia, and the Philippines) showed that substantial imports by these countries during the 1970s "prevented the recession in the industrial world from becoming worse than it was" (World Bank 1981, p. 112).

Perhaps the key actors in this process were the private banks and the multinational financial institutions. The extensive financial interdependence that emerged during the 1970s became the central factor in the performance, if not the survival, of the world economy. During the decade, balance of payments deficits recorded by Third World oil importers reached record levels as commodity prices tumbled, petroleum imports soared, and interest rates skyrocketed. Private banks around the world expanded their activities remarkably, increasing their loans to the underdeveloped world sixfold. This extension of credit was justified by the expectation that the Third World could handle heavy interest costs by producing and selling more exports. The World Bank commented (1981) that "The health of international banking, with its growing exposure in middle-income countries, depends on the countries' export prospects to a far greater degree than it did a decade ago."

But by the early 1980s exports were sitting unsold on the piers while the balance of payments deficits were ballooning. Third World debt, which at the beginning of the 1970s stood at $70 billion, reached over $800 billion by 1984. Country after country began to face economic and social crises as a mountain of debt crushed earlier hopes for rapid growth. In short, the "development gap" between the industrial countries and the Third World was as wide as ever (see Figure A). The Third World crisis was in full swing, and there was time to avert a catastrophe.

This book explores the genesis and implications of these events. It begins with a brief history of the origins, development, and breakdown of the postwar Bretton Woods system. Part I analyzes the source of Third World debt, examining its causes and future implications. It includes comprehensive institutional surveys of the World Bank and the International Monetary Fund and of the private international banking network. Part II examines the trade problems that have bedeviled the Third World's development, focusing on the erratic ups and downs of commodity prices. It contains a detailed history of the General Agree-

FIGURE A. The Development Gap

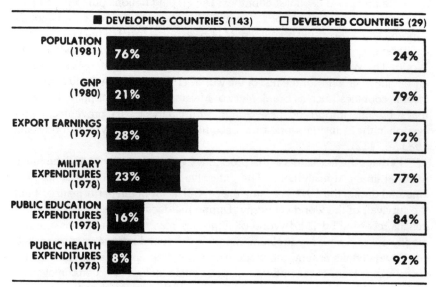

	DEVELOPING COUNTRIES (143)	DEVELOPED COUNTRIES (29)
POPULATION (1981)	76%	24%
GNP (1980)	21%	79%
EXPORT EARNINGS (1979)	28%	72%
MILITARY EXPENDITURES (1978)	23%	77%
PUBLIC EDUCATION EXPENDITURES (1978)	16%	84%
PUBLIC HEALTH EXPENDITURES (1978)	8%	92%

Source: Overseas Development Council. Reprinted with ODC permission.

ment on Tariffs and Trade and a look at the emergence of the multinational corporation. Part III provides an agenda for reform – a discussion of the various approaches and proposals to resolving the Third World's debt and trade problems, including the New International Economic Order. In particular, countertrade is examined as a possible step toward constructing a more stable and equitable economic order.

Two-thirds of the world's population lives in poverty. Piped water and sanitary facilities are a luxury in Nepal, where this woman is washing her clothes. Third World countries borrow money for finance of urban development projects.

Source: Mary M. Hill, World Bank. Reproduced with permission.

MULTINATIONAL INSTITUTIONS AND THE THIRD WORLD

1

GENESIS OF THE POST WAR MULTINATIONAL ECONOMIC SYSTEM

There are more than 300 international institutions that deal with multilateral trade and financial issues. Together, they form a network of bridges connecting the economies of the Third World with the First World. Traffic does not always flow smoothly or in both directions across those bridges. Since national economies are becoming increasingly interdependent, the problems of developing countries cannot be properly understood in isolation. This chapter will explore how and why a range of multinational institutions (MNIs) has evolved to regulate the international economy. Later chapters will describe the makeup and specific purpose of each major MNI and how the operations of those institutions affect the social welfare and economic development of Third World nations.

Despite the proliferation of international organizations since the mid-1940s, only a few factors are powerful enough to affect the overall system of finance and trade. This book focuses on the roles of the following institutions: the International Monetary Fund (IMF); the International Bank for Reconstruction and Development (IBRD), commonly called the World Bank; the General Agreement on Tariffs and Trade (GATT); and the U.N. Conference on Trade and Development (UNCTAD). The increasingly important parts played by the private international banking system and multinational corporations (MNCs) in the operations of the world's economy are also examined.

Bit actors whose parts are unessential to understanding international financial and trade flows have been excluded. The activities of some of these institutions may be vital at the microeconomic or political level, but they do not mediate between nations. For example, the operations of the London Futures Market helps determine world commodity prices, but it does not regulate intergovernmental relationships. (For an excellent, comprehensive discussion of the microeconomics of international trade and finance, see Rodríguez and Carter, 1979.)

1

It is important to study these international institutions for two fundamental reasons. First, by learning how each actor plays his part, insight is gained into how the actors, together as a cast, enact the international economic system. Second, to the extent that knowledge contains the seed of power, the character and the history that formed a particular character must be understood before roles can be rewritten to meet the challenges of new realities and meet desired social goals.

THE EFFECTS OF TWO WORLD WARS ON THE INTERNATIONAL ECONOMY

It may seem ironic that after six years of destabilizing conflict, World War II ended as a system for global economic management was being born. The new system was deliberately planned to avoid the errors of policy that had followed the end of World War I and had eventually led to the Great Depression of the 1930s and to renewed global conflict. For Europe, World War I had been a disaster of tidal wave proportions, and as the wave receded, the economic and political landscapes seemed permanently altered. Empires had fallen; a revolution had swept across Russia and threatened to spread westward; new nations arose in Central Europe; the seeds of national independence movements were being planted in far-flung colonies such as India and French Indochina; treasuries were emptied; and a generation of young men lay dead. Two kinds of attempts were made to order this chaos. Neither succeeded.

Politically, the League of Nations was founded in 1919 to guarantee the peace. However, the United States, one of the principal architects of the organization, failed to join because ratification was rejected by the Senate. Although its absence weakened the League, the U.S. refusal to participate was symptomatic of a larger problem. Member nation-states never ceded substantive power to the League, and it was unable to prevent or halt Italy's invasion of Ethiopia in the 1930s or the rise of a rearmed and aggresive Germany.

Economically, World War I had closed a period of imperialist expansion in trade and investment. That era had been underpinned by an international gold standard. The British and U.S. governments minted gold coins that circulated freely, and most other countries backed their currencies with the metal. Gold flows between nations reflected balance of payments deficits and surpluses, expanding or contracting domestic money supplies and stabilizing domestic prices through deflation or inflation. It was a time of severe fluctuations, with booms as fragile as balloons. For the system to work and to prevent total collapse, the world's strongest national economy had to absorb, at least in large part, the costs of adjustments in international trade.

Between 1870 and 1914, Great Britain was the hub of the wheel of international trade. It was the industrial workshop of the world, and manufactured goods and raw materials flowed in and out without tariff restrictions. British bankers served as the final guarantors of the international financial system, providing credit as needed. Domestic economic policy was subordinated to that requirement, and England was able and willing to tolerate times of high unemployment or to run balance of payments deficits to stabilize the system.

However, as the Great War began, Britain moved away from free-trade policies and imposed duties on imports to raise revenues and conserve foreign exchange. Instead of tariffs being reduced after the war, new duties were levied to protect a range of strategic industries. Wartime trade interruptions had spurred local industrialization in several traditional foreign markets – such as India – and British manufacturers were hard pressed to maintain their advantages. Reduced overseas profits and a growing demand for investments to re-equip domestic industries devastated by the war limited the supply of export capital and eroded Britain's role as the leading international banker. The relative decline of the national economy led to "tied loans," which linked foreign access to capital to the purchase of British goods.

Dislocations in the British economy were magnified in the rest of Europe. A general climate of political instability reduced capital flows to a trickle as investors hoarded gold. Increasing defaults on overseas loans further undermined investor confidence. Massive postwar inflation racked the German economy, where prices rose by over 1,000 percent. By 1923 one copy of a daily newspaper cost 200 billion marks.

The war had left in its wake a host of unresolved economic problems. The trickiest and most divisive issue was also first and foremost: who would pay for the war? The answer to that question had two separate but interrelated parts: the repayment of Allies' war debts to each other and the payment of German war reparations. Both Britain and the United States had helped finance the war efforts of their allies. After the armistice England proposed the cancellation of those outstanding bills in order to stimulate world trade, while the Americans demanded full repayment. That demand, however, proved to be a practical impossibility, since U.S. tariff policies prevented debtor nations from earning enough dollars through exports to repay their obligations. The United States could recover only one-quarter of its claims.

Although the British policy of canceling debts owed by its allies seemed generous, the flip side of this policy was stamped with retribution. The Treaty of Versailles in 1919 had imposed a stiff schedule of reparations on Germany, and now the loser on the battlefield would have to carry almost the full weight of the financial costs of the war. When multilateral commissions and institutions were formed, it was not to facilitate general reconstruction and the revival of European trade, but to supervise the German payment of damages. For a time British and French troops occupied the Ruhr Basin, holding the center of German heavy industry as a hostage to ensure compliance. High tariff barriers in most Allied countries not only dampened the general growth of trade but also made it virtually impossible for Germany to export enough goods and earn enough foreign exchange to pay reparations. As a result, during the 1920s Germany experienced periods of hyperinflation that fueled political unrest and threatened the country's first democratic government. To help revitalize its economy and finance the war debt, short-term loans were eventually arranged through a variety of foreign banks. As interest costs mounted, the German economy became trapped on an accelerating treadmill of payments. (See Box 1.)

In effect, the Treaty of Versailles distorted the world economy by linking large international payments to a fixed schedule unrelated to shifting levels of production or trade, and helped to disguise the fact that Britain was no longer the undisputed leading economic power. England continued to play its role as political broker in the European balance of power, but in financial circles the emperor was losing his clothes. As the British economy shuttered, the United States experienced rapid growth: production during the 1920s increased by 31 percent. Private U.S. banks replaced British banks as makers of foreign loans. The Americans, however, were less experienced at managing international portfolios, and many of the loans, particularly to Central Europe and Latin America, were soft. Lending often financed imports rather than productive projects that would enable debtor countries to increase exports to repay their loans. Loans that were made to stimulate production were usually designed to boost the output of commodities, such as coffee, that were already in oversupply. Moreover, loans were mostly short-term, while capital improvement projects were long-term. That is, loans fell due before projects could generate sufficient profits to cover their costs. As private banks extended their vistas, the international financial structure began to resemble a house of cards, vulnerable to the slightest breeze.

In 1931 the inevitable happened. When outstanding Central European loans were defaulted, the Austrian Credit Anstalt Bank collapsed, triggering a worldwide banking crisis. During the previous decade expanding international trade had made national economies more interdependent and increased systemic risks to such a degree that no single country could prop up the structure. When a deflationary cycle took hold and balance of payments deficits grew, the affected nations rushed to devalue their currencies. This action produced equal and opposite reactions as other countries responded in kind. High tariffs, which already impeded the flow of trade, were raised to protect domestic industries when currency devaluations threatened to reduce the price of imports.

First Great Britain and then the United States abandoned the gold standard in order to insulate their internal economies – which were already severely deflated – from the general collapse. (Dollars could be redeemed for gold only by central banks or foreign governments at the assigned official rate of $35 per ounce.) By 1933 U.S. spending and lending had plunged to one-third of the 1927–29 level. World trade had shrunk by one-third. When the London Economic Conference met in 1933 to restore international confidence, it broke up

BOX 1. The German Reparations Problem

During the interwar period Germany was saddled with a formidable debt burden, similar in some respects to that of many developing nations. As the penalty for losing World War I, Germany was forced to pay reparations to the victorious allied nations. Germany's struggle to meet the onerous payments had a crippling effect on its economy, exacerbating social instability and contributing to the rise of Nazism. According to economic historian W. A. Brown, "The conviction that Germany would eventually develop with the aid of foreign borrowing, export surpluses sufficient to provide real and ultimate payment of reparation . . . was one of the greatest of all post-war illusions" (1940, p. 485).

J. W. Angell (1929), writing midstream in the German crisis, said, "It is extremely unlikely that a lasting surplus of the necessary size [to meet reparation and loan repayments] can be developed in the near future. A transition of 20 or even 30 years . . . must intervene. This seems all the more probable when one recalls that Germany's exports, and indeed her production in general, are dependent to an unusually high degree on prior imports of raw materials and foodstuffs."

German repayments could be made only by recourse to continued borrowing. But new loans were drying up. As companies failed to secure credit, projects were curtailed and workers were dismissed. Imports were cut back, but still Germany could not break out of its downward spiral. A coal strike in Britain in 1925 led to a brief recovery as demand for German coal exports picked up. But the interlude was as short-lived as dew in the summer sunshine, and by 1928 – because of large short-term indebtedness – the economy once again took a nose dive.

This was followed by the Great Depression. Debt repayment and transfers exerted a powerful deflationary impact on the whole economy, and the once admirable German standard of living began to plummet. Intensified German competition for export markets was of no avail. Moreover, the dependence of German banks on foreign capital produced a contradiction. Additional capital imports were needed to develop the economy to the point at which debt payments could be made, while reduction of capital imports was necessary to preserve the solvency of the German banks against sudden withdrawals by foreign depositors. This led to a second contradiction: foreign funds could not be retained unless Germany continued to pay its war debts. But it could not do this without aggravating fiscal difficulties and further provoking social instability. Meanwhile, the United States, and to a lesser extent the Allies, demanded prompt repayment of the war debt. The result: economic conditions deteriorated, social conflict intensified, and together these factors produced a fertile breeding ground for Hitler's rise.

amid mutual suspicions and animosities; the rest of the decade would offer an endless replay of "beggar thy neighbor" economic policies. As political unrest spread and the shadow of an impending war loomed, there were widespread flights of "hot money" in search of safe havens. Most of that money came to roost in the United States. At the start of the decade, U.S. foreign investments totaled $15 billion; at the end, repatriation of those investments and capital inflows reduced the total to $2 billion. (Significantly, foreign deposits in U.S. banks did not stimulate the U.S. economy: banks did not relend overseas capital for productive projects, since it could be withdrawn at a moment's notice.) The desolation seemed complete – and the war had not even begun.

As that next war was ending, the Western democracies began to plan for the coming peace. Politically, a new and more effective international body – the United Nations – would replace the defunct League of Nations. Most important, the United States was emerging as the world's leading economic and military power, and its leadership was determined that the country could not afford to retrench into isolationism if the mistakes made following World War I were to be avoided. Although American leadership seemed necessary, it was not clear that it would be sufficient. Neither Great Britain nor the United States had been able to single-handedly prevent the worldwide depression of the 1930s. A set of multilateral institutions was needed to rebuild, to provide a safety net for, and to structure the postwar world economy. That vision led to the meeting of nations at Bretton Woods, New Hampshire, in July 1944.

The Bretton Woods system was anchored with three institutional cornerstones. The IMF would provide short-term financial assistance – usually for no more than five years – to help countries running balance of payments deficits. It was hoped that access to such support capital would prevent the destructive cycle of currency devaluations that had aggravated the depression of the 1930s. The IBRD, later called the World Bank, was set up to provide long-term development loans for major projects with gestation periods in excess of five years. The International Trade Organization (ITO) would negotiate reductions of tariffs and other discriminatory practices that had first bottlenecked, then throttled, world trade.*

Despite the best-laid plans, the newborn international system might have died prematurely without a mechanism for pumping dollars into the struggling national economies of Europe. Although the Marshall Plan was originally justified as a necessary measure to curb Soviet expansion into Western Europe, the plan was an exercise in "enlightened self-interest." After the war a series of U.S. payments surpluses depleted U.S. dollar reserves in Europe and threatened to undercut U.S. exports. This, in turn, would have depressed the U.S.

---

*The ITO was, in effect, stillborn. It was, however, replaced by GATT, which has held seven negotiating meetings since 1948 on reducing national barriers to trade.

economy and increased unemployment. The Marshall Plan provided loans to avoid the crisis; it was central to the success of multilateralism and the avoidance of another depression (Block 1977).

While the Marshall Plan laid the groundwork for European reconstruction by channeling massive, indeed unprecedented, quantities of capital to Europe, it was only a first step. That and successive steps were spelled out in the U.S. government's Gray Report – published in November 1950 – which advocated private investment by U.S. firms as the most desirable way to promote European reconstruction. To succeed, private investment required three conditions. First, adequate infrastructure (such as ports, roads, and power grids) had to be built for a modern economy to work, and that construction had to be financed by the public sector. Since the return on capital invested in infrastructure is low and it takes a long time to recoup the initial outlay, these projects are not attractive to private capital. Consequently, aid from the Marshall Plan, channeled through the IBRD, should concentrate on constructing the infrastructure needed to make private ventures profitable.

The other two conditions focused especially on the needs of private firms. First, treaties must be negotiated to protect investors against nationalization, expropriation, or possible nonconvertibility of profits. This was a clear recognition of the political conflict inherent in the foreign investment process. Finally, the Gray Report recommended that U.S. corporate income tax concessions be granted to encourage foreign investment by U.S. firms by increasing the relative profitability of successful overseas activities.

Immediately after the publication of the Gray Report, Nelson Rockefeller was asked by President Truman to find channels for speeding the flow of private foreign investment to Europe. Rockefeller offered three main recommendations, each of which was subsequently implemented. First, since Europe lacked enough dollars to buy the machinery and technology it needed from U.S. corporations, a government fund of $500 million should be set aside for direct loans to finance those purchases. Second, the profits American firms earned overseas should be exempt from U.S. income taxes. Third, bilateral treaties must be established to guarantee U.S. capital investments against nationalization, expropriation, or nonconvertibility. Among the major aims of the World Bank and IMF was the establishment of conditions necessary for private foreign investment.

THE EMERGENCE OF A NEW FINANCIAL CRISIS

In many respects the 1950s was a decade of fair weather and clear sailing for the new international economic system. Public capital from the Marshall Plan and private investment capital flowed into Europe at a steady pace. Several billion dollars in loans was funneled through the World Bank to finance reconstruction. Special efforts were made to incorporate the western half of a divided Germany in this retooling process, and treaties (including some for coal and steel) were concluded between France and the Federal Republic of Germany. The West Germans were also partners in the new European Economic Community (EEC), which was trying to integrate the national economies of Western Europe in order to minimize future political and military conflicts and to lower the trade barriers that had stifled economic growth after World War I. Bilateral aid agreements between Japan and the United States were restructuring and rebuilding that economy. Meanwhile, there was little demand on the IMF for balance of payments support, with the exception of the Suez crisis of 1956, when France and Britain negotiated precautionary standby credits. There was only one puff of smoke on the horizon: in 1958 the United States ran its first postwar trade deficit.

One decade later that puff of smoke looked like it belonged to a freight train. Three pistons were working the engine that had begun to undermine U.S. economic predominance. First, the postwar blueprint for economic reconstruction had worked, and the West Europeans and Japanese were competing on an equal footing with U.S. firms in a variety of markets, from tools and toys to electronics and automobiles.

Second, nationalism had swept through the English and French colonial empires in Africa and Asia, and new states with neutral, if not anti-U.S., foreign policies were redrawing the political and geographical maps throughout the late 1950s and early 1960s. In 1965 the United States intervened massively and directly in the Vietnamese civil war, which was in many respects an anticolonial war. That intervention was financed by a massive infusion of U.S. dollars, which sparked inflation in the United States and, eventually, abroad. In the face of stiff economic competition from Japan and the EEC countries, the dollar – which was the cornerstone of international exchange rates – seemed overvalued, and U.S. balance of payment deficits grew steadily.

Finally, the new world economy encouraged multinational capital and monetary transfers and led to the expansion of a new hybrid, the MNC. Operating bases of production and distribution in a variety of national markets, these new businesses developed their own economic logic and interests. Those interests could, and did, overlap state boundaries, engaging in activities that transcended national economic management. As John Kenneth Galbraith noted in his presidential address to the American Economic Association: "When the modern corporation acquires power over markets, power in the community, power over the state, power over belief, it is a political instrument different in form and degree, but not in kind from the state itself."

By the early 1970s these three factors were of increasing importance. Two events showed that the international economy was the freight train, and no one was driving it. On August 15, 1971, President Richard Nixon announced that the United States was unilaterally jettisoning the official gold standard. Since 1934 the U.S. government had agreed to convert dollars into gold for foreign central banks and governments at a rate of $35 per ounce. That policy was formalized at Bretton Woods, and the IMF had used the dollar's tie to gold to administer and stabilize exchange rates among the world's capitalist nations. The new policy in effect devalued the dollar and improved the U.S. balance of payments in the short run. However, it appeared that the United States was jumping off the train to save itself, and international financial markets reflected the confusion. By September 1971 the three-month Eurodollar rate – a benchmark for international interest rates – had almost doubled, to 11.5 percent. Since that time interest rates on international transactions have swung wildly, only briefly dipping below 10 percent.

That first shock was more than doubled by a series of aftershocks. In October 1973 the previously anonymous Organization of Petroleum Exporting Countries (OPEC), which had been formed in 1960, boosted its prices from $2 to $5 per barrel of oil. By March 1974, following an OPEC embargo on shipments to Western countries during the latest Arab-Israeli war, the price of oil doubled again, to over $10 per barrel. The price jumped to $24 by the end of 1979 and by 1982 was $34 per barrel. OPEC could become an effective price-setting cartel because U.S. fields were running dry and both the United States and the other major capitalist countries were increasingly dependent on oil imported from Third World countries. (Although OPEC set the price structure, it should be noted that the private multinational oil companies collaborated in administering prices, using their control of petroleum refining and distribution networks. Corporate policies and interests often flew in the face of the interests of the economies of the nations that housed the corporations' headquarters.) The dramatic rise in oil prices translated into a tidal shift of economic power from the United States to the OPEC bloc. OPEC countries rapidly amassed financial reserves, nearly $300 billion between 1974 and 1979.

After the United States abandoned the gold standard, international currencies were allowed to float against each other. Originally it was assumed that the central banks of the various industrial democracies could intervene to stabilize that market. However, the huge OPEC reserves, coupled with the reserves of national currencies accumulated by multinational corporations and banks, dwarfed the ability of governments to control the market. In effect, a tractor-trailer had broken loose and was rolling wildly about the pitching deck of international finance. Speculation against all currencies was rife, and all economies, including that of the United States, were suddenly vulnerable.

THE CRISIS IN TRADE

Meanwhile, the new pressure on national economies was straining world trading relationships. From the end of World War II until the late 1960s, GATT provided a framework for negotiating massive reductions of tariffs among the advanced industrial countries (AICs). The one outstanding exception was in textile and agricultural products, which were subject to powerful domestic political pressures in Japan and the EEC. However, the opening up of most domestic markets to international competition sparked the growth of world trade and rapid economic growth in the AICs. By the late 1960s that growth was extending to the industrializing countries of the Third World.

As economic growth slowed from the oil shocks of the 1970s, world trade assumed a Jekyll-Hyde nature. Countries competed fiercely to increase exports, thereby keeping workers employed and "exporting" unemployment to less competitive nations. Trade negotiations, which previously were focused on complex "technical" issues, suddenly became newsworthy. In an era of stagflation (slow economic growth and high inflation) new cries for protectionism were heard as industries, such as the U.S. steel and auto producers, began to erode as a result of poor management and the internationalization of capital. Social conflicts appeared in the industrial capitalist nations. The loss of jobs to "foreign" labor fueled a resurgence of trade protectionism in the same AICs that had benefited from the reduction of tariffs under GATT. The period from the mid-1970s until the early 1980s was punctuated by a series of increasingly acrimonious public meetings of representatives from the major trading nations.

At first the calamity that struck the nonoil-exporting nations seemed a sidebar to the stresses in the international system. Soon, however, those nations accumulated debts that matched the reserves accumulated by the oil-exporting countries. This debt took on increased importance as AICs tried to expand exports to pay for their oil imports. This was one key explanation for the wholesale expansion in foreign lending during the 1970s: to maintain existing Third World markets and expand them whenever possible. As the rising price of oil cut into Third World export earnings, it threatened to reduce the Third World's imports from the AICs. The obvious solution was to augment the Third World's export earnings with loan capital. Nevertheless, this strategy could only postpone the inevitable day of reckoning, tying together trade-debt conflicts and increasing the potential for an even greater problem in the 1980s. Once again, the international economy resembled a house of cards, and everyone was tiptoeing around that house. Chapter 2 and later chapters will examine this new instability, and look at how multilateral institutions that were designed in a different age contribute as they try to cope with new uncertainties.

TABLE 1.1. Historical Developments in the International Economic System, 1914-84

Developments in the Financial System		Historical Benchmarks		Developments in the Trading System	
		1914-1939			
1914-1920	Britain leaves gold standard	1914-1918	World War I	1914	Britain abandons free trade
1918-1923	Postwar inflation	1918	Russian Revolution		
1919-1931	German inability to repay war debt	1919	League of Nations Treaty of Versailles		
1920-1930	U.S. banks lend to Europe and Latin America	1923	France and Belgium occupy Ruhr		
1928-1929	U.S. stock market boom				
1930	Bank for International Settlements established to facilitate German war debt repayment				
1931	Worldwide bank failures			1931	World depression begins
1931-1933	Wave of Latin American defaults				
1933	U.S. leaves gold standard				
		1945-70			
		1939-1945	World War II		
1944	Bretton Woods Conference establishes agreement for founding of IMF and IBRD				
		1945	United Nations founded		

(continued)

TABLE 1.1. (*Continued*)

Developments in the Financial System		Historical Benchmarks		Developments in the Trading System	
1947	IMF and IBRD open for business			1947	GATT founded
1948	U.S. launches Marshall Plan			1948	U.S. launches Marshall Plan
		1949	Chinese revolution		
1950	European Payments Union formed	1950–1953	Korean War		
1952	IMF makes first standby loan				
1955–1959	Eurocurrency market begins				
				1958	First U.S. trade deficit
		1959	Cuban revolution		
		1960–1963	Wars of liberation in Africa	1960	OPEC formed
		1961	Nonaligned Movement's first meeting in Belgrade		
		1963	Vietnam War begins	1963	Kennedy round of GATT
				1964	UNCTAD formed
		1965	U.S. invades Dominican Republic		
		1967	Suez crisis	1967	Beginning of chronic U.S. trade deficits
1968	Sterling crisis				
1970	First IMF SDR allocation				

TABLE 1.1. (Continued)

Developments in the Financial System		Historical Benchmarks		Developments in the Trading System	
		1971–1985			
1971	U.S. closes gold window, gold price rise begins	1971	Détente	1971	General system of preferences (GSP) tariff initiated
1971	Third World debt reaches $70 billion				
1973	U.S. deficit ($20 billion) causes worry, loss of confidence	1973	Failure of Vietnam negotiations Hanoi bombed	1973	OPEC increases oil prices
1973	World Bank begins "basic needs" strategy			1973	Third World demands New International Economic Order
1973	Private banks begin rapid increase in Third World lending			1973	Tokyo round of GATT negotiations
				1974	U.N. Commission on Transnationals formed
1975–1982	IMF concludes standby agreements with Third World nations	1975	Vietnam War ends		
				1976	UNCTAD creates "common fund" for commodity purchases
		1979	Nicaraguan revolution	1979	Second oil price shock

(continued)

TABLE 1.1. (*Continued*)

Developments in the Financial System		Historical Benchmarks		Developments in the Trading System	
1980	Third World debt reaches $500 billion, triggering fear of debt crisis	1980	Central America becomes a war zone		
1980	World Bank unties "structural adjustment lending"				
1981	Cancún Conference produces no accord				
1982	Third World debt crisis; 30 nations reschedule debts	1982	Falklands Malvinas war	1982	World trade declines for first time since Depression
				1982	Third World nations increase resort to countertrade
1983	Williamsburg summit produces no substantive results	1983	U.S. invades Grenada	1983	UNCTAD VI meets in Belgrade
1984	World debt crisis worsens				

Source: Prepared by the author.

PART I

THE POLITICAL ECONOMY OF DEBT

The Christian Science Monitor

Source: Langley in *The Christian Science Monitor.* © 1983 TCSPS.

2

THE ORIGIN OF THE THIRD WORLD DEBT CRISIS

The growing external debt of the Third World during the 1970s has operated like an underground river to steadily, almost surreptitiously, undermine the foundation of the international economy. So profound has been its effect that one writer called it "the most phenomenal international event of the 1970s" (Seiber 1982). Between 1971 and 1984 the indebtedness of the less-developed countries (LDCs) swelled from $87 billion to an estimated $810 billion. The immense size and the rapid acceleration of this growth have severely strained the international economy's capacity to absorb debt; at the same time it has linked the fate of the various national economies more closely. In the past, rich nations could imagine themselves as splendid "houses on the hill." Today the economies of the wealthier nations are penthouses in a condominium. If the foundation of the building crumbles, no one's home will be spared.

THE NATURE OF THIRD WORLD DEBT

Access to finance is essential for economic development. Building factories, acquiring infrastructure (such as hydroelectric dams and roads), and improving educational systems and housing stocks requires money. Those investments expand the society's capital stock; they increase the production of goods and services so that more money can be accumulated for investments that will stimulate more production. Unlike a perpetual motion machine, however, there are sources of friction, a number of "ifs," "ands," or "buts" that accompany the process of going from initial finance to ultimate production.

Financial capital has a variety of sources: some are internal and others are external to the borrowing country. (The distinction in the literature of public finance between an internally held debt and an external debt is that an internal debt can be serviced by taxation or money creation, while the external debt must ultimately be serviced by export earnings.) Common internal sources are net profits of local enterprises, individual deposits in banks, and government taxes. These represent the domestic sources of savings that can be used to finance investments in factories, port facilities, private automobiles, or hospitals.

When available domestic savings are inadequate to undertake the level of investment desired by businesses, governments, or individuals, these groups can borrow foreign capital. Foreign capital comprises the retained profits of foreign enterprises, the individual savings deposited in foreign banking and financial networks, and the revenues foreign governments make available through bilateral or multilateral lending agencies.

During the 1970s (and this has historical precedents) Third World nations tapped this source repeatedly. The overall debt is, of course, many smaller debts, and each Third World country borrowed according to its particular economic condition. In general, however, three main tributaries flowed together to make up the massive debt accumulation of the 1970s: the massive surge in oil costs; the rising Third World balance of payments deficits; and a push to expand exports. These factors also help to explain why there was so much foreign capital available for lending and why foreign financing took the form of debt rather than equity investments (such as building factories or infrastructure), as had been typical during the 1960s.

Before the history of this new debt is detailed, and to get perspective, it is necessary to understand the dangers posed. In any thorough reading of the literature on Third World debt, several themes stand out:

1. The size of the debt is enormous compared with the gross national product (GNP) of the debtor countries and the banking systems' resources (*Wall Street Journal* 1981). This contributes to the destabilization of the international financial system, magnifying the effects of the boom-bust cycle of international trade and liquidity, and increasing the probability of borrowers defaulting and banks collapsing (Lever 1982).

2. The burden of debt service (debt interest costs and principal repayment) is getting heavier. The rise in servicing costs means that countries must export more, cut domestic consumption (and probably living standards), or borrow still more to pay past debts. (The total value of Brazil's exports in 1983 did not equal the cost of the country's debt service, necessitating a drop in living standards.)

3. The costs of borrowing involve more than economic sacrifice, as debtor countries are increasingly forced to compromise political sovereignty and remove economic management from the government while placing a good portion under the control of the IMF or the private banks.

4. The structure of debt and loan terms have changed dramatically; private commercial lending has replaced official lending as the main source of finance. Meanwhile, interest rates have risen and repayment time has shortened (Seiber

1982), raising doubts about the ability of debtor nations to make principal or interest payments and throwing a cloud over national economies and the world economy (Lever 1982). By 1980, over half of all new borrowing was to repay past debts, and debt reschedulings rose dramatically.

5. In making loans, bankers have been astonishingly imprudent, ignoring probable risks; this is particularly true of the so-called Eurobanks (Graham 1982). This left the private banks open to severe losses in the event of default by any of the major debtors, an event that would destabilize the entire world economy.

6. The impact on people. As an example, in the Brazilian northeast the conjunction of the debt crisis and the world recession resulted in thousands of workers begging for work at a "food for work" project. Workers who weren't hired broke down in sobs, facing the virtual certainty of starvation of their wives and children.

Historical Perspective

Foreign debt and financial instability are not new. History is replete with debt bubbles that have grown and burst. The Medici Bank of Florence flourished in the early fifteenth century, but sustained massive losses later in the century when unsecured loans to medieval monarchs were not repaid. The bank finally failed (Seiber 1982).

During the nineteenth century the United States defaulted on foreign loans. The level of U.S. foreign indebtedness was estimated at 40 percent of GNP throughout the 1830s. In 1841–42 the price of cotton collapsed, provoking a foreign exchange crisis when North American states suspended interest and principal payments on money borrowed overseas to build canals and railroads. And in the latter part of the century, over half of the international banks established between 1856 and 1865 went bankrupt. That experience was repeated in the 1920s, when inexperienced and imprudent management overextended lending, only to be caught short by the 1920 foreign trade crisis. Banks that blithely ignored the borrowers' abilities to repay failed (Seiber 1982, pp. 21ff).

During 1933 the debt service ratios of Latin American countries ranged from 22 to 82 percent of exports and 25 to 73 percent of government revenues. Eight Latin American republics defaulted on their foreign loans during this period (McMullen 1979).

After World War II public indebtedness in the Third World rose slowly but steadily through the 1960s. In 1950 external public debt totaled $2.1 billion; by 1961 it was $21.6 billion. Throughout the next decade outstanding Third World debt grew by an average of 17 percent per year, reaching a level of $60.9 billion in 1969. (A word of caution – these data are not as reliable as more current statistics and, moreover, different definitions of debt were used at different times. Nevertheless, the data indicate the prevalent trend. See Seiber 1982, pp. 25ff.) This was followed by an explosive growth in the late 1970s and early 1980s. By year end 1983 the World Bank estimated Third World debt at $810 billion, nearly 12 times the 1969 level – with a repayment burden that had grown far more quickly than these figures would suggest. (See Table 2.1, Figure 2.1.)

The Causes of Indebtedness

A country's indebtedness may derive from any of several sources. Some causes are primarily internal: they stem from the internal structure, resource endowment, or economic policies of the borrowing nation. Other causes are primarily external: they arise from events beyond the control of domestic policy or decisions, such as export prices. These two kinds of forces are illustrated in Table 2.2 and Figure 2.2.

TABLE 2.1. Third World Debt, 1950-83 (selected years)

	1950	1961	1971	1977	1980	1981	1982	1983
Medium- / long-term debt (total)	21.1	21.6	109.2	239.5	406.5	464.5	517.8	575.0
Latin America and the Caribbean	n.a.	8.8	43.9	100.4	170.8	206.4	233.9	n.a.
Africa[a]	n.a.	3.3	9.9	22.0	42.7	46.7	50.4	n.a.
East Asia and the Pacific	n.a.	2.2	15.8	36.4	58.1	67.9	79.3	n.a.
South Asia	n.a.	3.6	15.9	25.2	33.0	34.3	37.5	n.a.
North Africa and Middle East[a,b]	n.a.	1.4	7.9	25.9	44.3	46.9	48.9	n.a.
Southern Europe	n.a.	2.3	15.8	29.6	57.6	62.3	67.7	n.a.
Short-term debt, nonreporting countries	n.a.	n.a.	n.a.	n.a.	128.0	160.0	172.0	210.0
Total debt	n.a.	n.a.	n.a.	n.a.	535.0	624.0	689.0	810.0

Note: Columns may not add to totals due to rounding.
[a]North Africa is included in Africa for 1961.
[b]Includes small OPEC countries.
Sources: World Bank 1981b, 1984; 1982; Seiber 1982.

FIGURE 2.1. Developing World Debt (medium and long term)

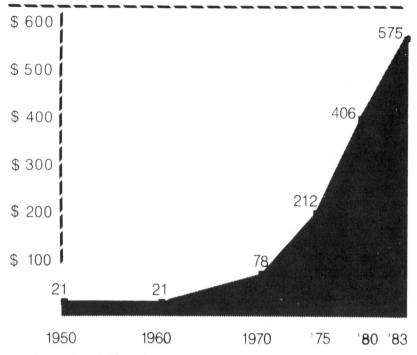

Source: Compiled by author.

External Causes of Indebtedness

External causes of indebtedness are primarily of two types: those that are related to trade conditions and lead to balance-of-trade difficulties, and those that are affected by changes in the price and availability of capital on the international financial market. In both instances the typical Third World country has little power to act decisively.

Three principal variables contribute to a deteriorating balance of trade: depressed commodity prices and depressed demand for exports reduce trade earnings, while a rise in import prices raises costs. (A dramatic example of the latter is the 15-fold jump in oil prices that boosted Latin America's annual oil import bill from $660 million in 1970 to $15.4 billion in 1980.) In practice, there need not be a depression in export earnings or steep rise in the price of imports: a relative change in import and export prices can produce deteriorating terms of trade and generate a balance-of-payments deficit.

TABLE 2.2. Internal and External Causes of Indebtedness

External Causes	Internal Causes
Depressed commodity prices	Capital-intensive growth policies
Depressed demand for exports	High energy dependence
Rise in import prices, especially of oil	High dependence on imported food-stuffs
Increased liquidity of international financial markets	Import-intensive industrialization strategies
Reduced availability of grant and concessionary aid	Public external borrowing for financing recurrent expenditures
Harder loan terms	Decline in domestic savings ratios
Growth of the unregulated Eurodollar market	Failure to tax elites

Source: Prepared by author.

Four prominent factors alleviated the outlook in the international financial market during the 1970s. The increased liquidity in the international market resulting from a flood of petrodollars entered the largely unregulated Eurodollar market and encouraged banks to expand their markets for loans to Third World countries. These supply-side factors combined with the balance-of-payments factors and a lack of concessionary and grant aid to produce a demand-side spur to borrowing. (This was particularly evident in the Latin American and Caribbean region, where concessional loans fell from 26 percent to 7.7 percent between 1971 and 1980.) Together, these resulted in harder loan terms that increased interest rates, shortened maturities, and generated further balance-of-payments deficits in need of finance. In 1971 Latin American and Caribbean loans carried an average interest rate of 7 percent and an average maturity of 13.3 years. By 1980 interest rates had risen to 11.5 percent and maturity had dropped to 10.7 years. Meanwhile, in East Asia and the Pacific interest rates repayment time had shifted from 5.6 percent and 21.2 years to 10.1 percent and 15 years between 1971 and 1980, while grants fell from 30 to 3.3 percent of total resource flows.

That is, during the 1970s, the private banking system became the largest holder of Third World debt. The number of private banks with overseas offices soared: in 1950 there were 95 overseas branches; by 1979 the figure had reached 779, and many countries of the Third World contained offices of the world's major lending institutions. The banks were receiving enormous deposits of petrodollars from OPEC nations and, in a desperate search for markets to

FIGURE 2.2. The Third World Debt System

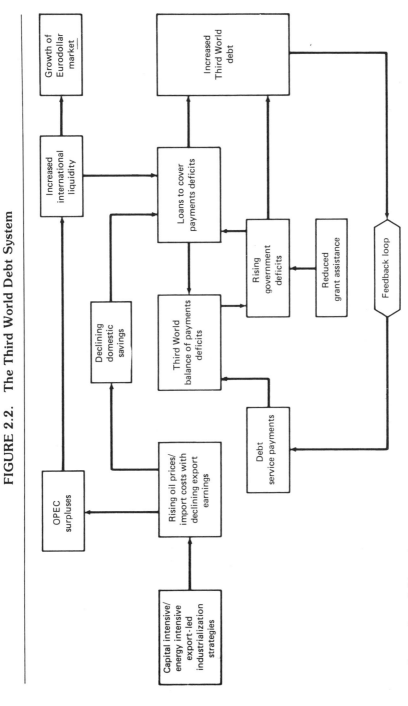

Source: Compiled by author.

25

invest these assets, eagerly turned to Third World nations. Peru's former finance minister commented at a joint meeting of the World Bank and IMF held in Washington: "I can hardly face going back to my room; there are six different banks waiting for me" (Sampson 1981, p. 16). As competition increased among banks, they began providing a host of services, from technical assistance to arrangement of complete financing packages, to win Third World loans. While the need for new capital was expanding, the international lending agencies – such as the World Bank, the IMF, and the Inter-American Development Bank (IDB) – provided only a fraction of Third World requirements, funneling borrowers toward the private banks. In 1978, a year in which the combined Third World deficit was over $70 billion, the World Bank financed a mere $2.1 billion in net transfers.

Internal Causes of Indebtedness

At least six internal factors attributable to past and present development strategies, as well as to resource limitations, contributed to the rise in Third World debt. First, the growth strategies and programs pursued by most Third World countries during the 1960s and 1970s were highly capital intensive, requiring substantial imports of capital goods. Those strategies contributed directly to balance-of-payments deficits. For example, in the late 1960s Barbados shifted its industrialization toward tourism and the share of capital imports rose by over 33 percent (from 20 percent of total imports in 1964 to 27 percent in 1970). Meanwhile, total imports were growing rapidly by 12 percent annually (Janarain 1976, pp. 212ff.). Likewise, an International Labour Organization (ILO) study of high technology industry in Colombia found that the cost (in constant pesos) to employ one worker jumped from 45,000 to 100,000 pesos between 1957 and 1966 (Barnet and Müller 1974, p. 169).

Second, this development strategy was highly dependent on imported energy. (Brazil, for example, was 90 percent reliant on imported oil.)

Third, the high dependence on imported foodstuffs is a direct result of import intensive industrialization. Mexico, until the mid-1970s, was a net food exporter; its shift toward a petroleum-based, export-oriented economy proved disastrous. In 1980 Mexico's consumer import bill grew by 142 percent, which the IDB in its 1980-81 report, *Economic and Social Progress in Latin America*, says was "mainly as a result of an almost eightfold increase in public sector purchases, mainly food imports."

Fourth, public external borrowing to finance recurrent expenditures has become common. This practice is fiscally unsound because long-term debt should be undertaken only for projects that can pay for themselves. Recurrent fiscal expenditures, by definition, do not. Governments are easily tempted to forgo short-term sacrifices by foreign borrowing rather than increased taxation (Girling 1982). International lending agencies and private banks generally and imprudently do not restrict lending in this area.

Fifth, domestic savings rates have been declining. In Latin America the growth of gross national saving dropped by nearly a fifth: from 6.3 percent between 1960 and 1970 to 5.1 percent between 1970 and 1980. Meanwhile, the demand for gross domestic capital grew by 7 percent in both decades. A 1960 savings gap of under $2 billion (in 1980 dollars) had grown to $34 billion by 1980. The shortfall in savings was aggravated by the sixth factor, the failure of governments to progressively tax elites to raise revenues.

Finally, the entire debt problem was compounded by recycling effects of prior borrowing. At the beginning of the 1970s there was little feedback in the debt system. By the late 1970s the noise was deafening. In 1979, $50 million of every $100 million borrowed by Third World countries was to repay past loans. Panama, for example, borrowed $398 million in 1979 and used $210 million to meet previous obligations (World Bank 1981).

EVOLUTION OF THE THIRD WORLD DEBT

Third World debt is firmly rooted in the misapplication of resources. Paul Baran (1956), indicates that the ability to invest the maximum potential economic surplus is the crucial variable in Third World development. (Potential economic surplus is determined by subtracting essential private and public consumption from the greatest amount of production that can be achieved with available technology and resources.) Obviously, the actual economic surplus – the difference between a country's actual output and its actual consumption – may be much less. Two implications follow. In order for a country to grow, the level of actual surplus must be pushed toward the level of the potential, and the potential surplus should be wisely invested in goods that generate further production and income.

For example, the millions of idle workers in the Third World are available resources to boost production and the potential economic surplus. Nobel Laureate Arthur Lewis (1954) has argued that using this surplus labor would provide a relatively inexpensive impetus to growth. But beyond idle workers, additional unused or unapplied resources glare, blatant as neon signs, in any Third World country. In Jamaica, Mercedes Benz autos cruise past workers waiting for buses – there is a chronic shortage – to take them to work. The headquarters of private banks are modern and palatial while, just blocks away, factories that process food or produce clothing and other consumer or industrial goods are decaying.

Surplus capital also is withdrawn from the Third World by multinational investors. This phenomenon is not new. Traditionally, most of the wealth generated through the New World production of precious metals, sugar, and spices was shipped to Europe instead of being reinvested domestically (Williams 1971). This was, of course, a major cause of the war for independence of the American colonies in 1776. Two centuries later, although colonialism is nominally dead, politically the patterns of economic hemorrhage overseas persist. A sizable portion of the profits generated within Peru, Indonesia, Namibia, and the Dominican Republic doesnot remain in those countries. For example, in 1980 Indonesia's actual surplus was $8.8 billion. Of this total $2.3 billion, over one-quarter, was remitted to foreign investors and unavailable for domestic investment.

At issue, then, is the underlying source of Third World debt. Is it merely attributable to a shortage of capital, or does it stem from a misapplication and misappropriation of existing resources? If the former is the key, then foreign borrowing will spur the generation of new wealth. If the latter is true, then foreign borrowing may affect production only marginally.

Social and Political Costs of Foreign Borrowing

The traditional development strategies that dominated the 1950s and 1960s emphasized the shortage of capital. However, in the early 1970s a growing number of critics challenged the old consensus. Several questions were raised to put the relation of foreign borrowing and development in perspective.

First, do foreign resources add to domestic savings, or do they supplement and displace domestic sources? One empirical study in the late 1960s indicated that foreign aid as loan capital actually replaces domestic investment resources and leads to reduced internal savings rates (Griffin 1970).

Second, does an influx of foreign financing drive up exchange rates, bias investment via tied-aid toward inappropriate, capital-intensive technology, and encourage imprudent financial policies? (Girling 1973). Employees of aid agencies in off-the-record comments often criticize the lack of management skills in their institutions. Too often, loans are designed and negotiated by persons with tunnel vision. The emphasis is on turnover: the speed of placement and quantity rather than the quality of loans. When the lender fails to evaluate the need for and purpose of the loan and the ability of the borrower to invest resources in a way that will facilitate payment, financial irresponsibility and a "candy store" mentality prevail. Moreover, even when lenders do undertake extensive analyses, they sometimes use the wrong criteria, judging investment projects by technological standards inappropriate to developing countries. That is, the project may be profitable but not mesh with the local economy to spur further domestic growth (Payer 1982).

Third, does readily available external capital block the institutional changes needed for reform while strengthening autocratic regimes that are more able to control their populations and promote U.S. security interests as opposed to genuine development efforts? (Payer 1975, 1982; Frank 1980). For example, between 1980 and 1983 the United States pressured the IMF and IDB to lend $232 million to El Salvador to bolster a government with a notorious record of human rights abuses. Aid to Zaire has served to support an openly corrupt but staunchly pro-Western regime.

BOX 2.   International Financial Institutions and Central America: Development or Politics?

Beginning in the late 1970s, with mounting East-West tensions, multinational economic assistance provided by the IMF, World Bank, and IDB in Central America was increasingly viewed as a tool of U.S. foreign policy. The first instance was an emergency loan authorized by the IMF to the Somoza government of Nicaragua in May 1979, just weeks before Somoza's defeat by a popular uprising. Critics claim that most of the money went into Somoza's pockets when he fled the country.

The incoming Sandinista government earned high marks for its efficient completion of urban development and education projects that had been marked by corruption and inefficiency under the Somoza government. Yet the Reagan administration, attempting to institute a credit embargo, tried to block any further loans to Nicaragua. In 1982 it applied pressure to the World Bank to stop several loans for education, water supply, and rural roads that had been recommended by the bank's technical staff. Drawing on solid European and Canadian support, Nicaragua was able to squeeze by the Reagan embargo, receiving $42 million in 1981 and 1982 for hydroelectric and forestry projects. But U.S. pressures continued into 1983 and 1984 – for example, through a U.S. veto of a $2.2 million IDB loan for construction of roads to serve small coffee farmers, which was supported by all the 42 other members of the bank.

In contrast, the United States used its muscle to push the international financial institutions (IFIs) to increase lending to El Salvador. In 1981 U.S. pressures were successful in forcing the IMF to break its own notoriously strict rules; it approved a $36 million loan from the Compensatory Financing Facility without the necessary staff approval and over the objections of all but one of the European directors. Despite the warnings of one executive director that the granting of the loan would have an adverse impact on the IMF's "reputation for objectivity," the loan was approved, marking the first time in the institution's history that a loan was granted without the approval of the staff. A subsequent $85 million IMF loan was later questioned by the House Banking Subcommittee of the U.S. Congress, which criticized the provision of "easy money to a regime that is guilty of gross human rights violations."

The charters of the IFIs stipulate that the institutions are to be neutral and nonpolitical. Yet critics contend that these instances suggest that in Central America, U.S. power in the IFIs was used to convert their mission from peaceful economic development to support for U.S. foreign policy. The result not only is detrimental to the region, which has been polarized by the questionable lending policies, but also undermines the effectiveness and future credibility of the IFIs.

Source: This information is based on material supplied by the Center for International Policy, Washington, D.C.

And finally, do foreign capital inflows just pave the way for greater out-flows, decapitalizing the debtor countries through profit and interest remittances? For example, between 1961 and 1968, $360 million in investment capital entered Latin America while $1.1 billion left through multinational profits and interest payments (Schmidt 1973). During 1972 Jamaica's cash receipts for its exports just equaled its total debt service, leaving no exchange surplus to import vital foodstuffs.

Together these factors suggest that foreign borrowing not only may not be a panacea, but also may aggravate the problem it was prescribed to cure.

PERSPECTIVES ON THE THIRD WORLD'S DEBT BURDEN

Economic and financial analysis provides tools to evaluate the ability of Third World countries to cope with given levels of external debt. There are several ways to approach the problem, and opinions vary on which is most appropriate. Perhaps the most common measure is the ratio of total unpaid debt to gross domestic product (GDP). Although the comparison provides a way to judge the magnitude of debt, it probably circumvents the central issue. Similarly, comparing the balance of your home loan to your annual income can be interesting, but not necessarily useful. It is more important to know the relationship between your monthly income and the monthly loan payment. When monthly housing costs are fixed, you can begin to estimate how much remains for food, clothing, and going to the football game, bar, or opera.

The Concept of the Debt Burden

The debt burden is more appropriately measured by comparing its annual external servicing cost with annual external income. Further perspective can be gained by distinguishing the long-term economic burden – the value of domestic resources that are lost or that must be transferred to foreigners until loans are repaid – from the short-term financial burden – the amount of foreign exchange that must be earned annually to meet interest and principal payments. According to the Federal Reserve Bank of New York:

> An economic burden results from the reduction of goods available for domestic use when interest and amortization payments are made. Financial burden refers to the need to acquire and maintain sufficient foreign exchange to make debt service payments. . . . An excessive burden in either form could result in liquidity crisis with sharp effects on [that is, restriction of] imports and consumption. (Roberts 1981)

Usually the financial burden is assumed to be paramount. That is, the significant burden can be measured by quantifying the annual debt-servicing cost as a percentage of exports of goods and services. (Capital inflows, which will later become outflows, are excluded.) The amount of foreign exchange that a country earns is crucial, because external debt usually can be repaid only in foreign currency.

In order to fully appreciate the genesis of the present debt burden, which increasingly preoccupies bankers and Third World borrowers alike as more and more loans must be juggled simultaneously, we need to distinguish two fundamental forms of finance. Reproductive finance comprises investments in projects that generate future streams of foreign exchange either by increasing exports or by replacing imports. Nonreproductive uses of foreign borrowing are those applications that neither earn nor conserve the foreign exchange that will be needed to service, and eventually retire, the loan.

Public finance theory emphasizes that this distinction also applies to publicly held debt. The government may create money to repay its domestically held debt; it may not do so with foreign debt.* This, of course, reveals yet another facet of the debt burden: the public burden. Publicly held debts must be repaid and serviced from government revenues and foreign exchange. An excessive annual public burden can squander accumulated foreign reserves or lead to significant reductions in government services (Girling 1982).

The Use and Abuse of Debt

The central issue, then, is how borrowed capital is used: does the economy of the debtor country use the new resources to generate sufficient foreign exchange to service its external debt, and will those costs ultimately be contained or reduced so that the economic burden is manageable? That question, of necessity, invites further questions. First, what constitutes effective application of debt? Second, what is a manageable burden?

Taking the second question first, some analysts argue that the economic burden can be ignored, since the debt is unlikely to be repaid. That is, as long as the financial burden is not crippling, the economic burden remains irrelevant. Walter Robischek of the IMF writes (1980, p. 2):

> The typical developing country runs a current account balance of payments deficit, which means that it is dependent on a continuous inflow of foreign savings, and with this inflow, its external indebtedness rises steadily. By definition, a country in these circumstances does not actually repay external debt. Consequently, its amortization payments cannot possibly pose a servicing

*An exception to this rule occurred when the United States financed the Vietnam War by issuing dollars to foreigners to back their own currencies. This contributed to the eventual demise of the Bretton Woods monetary system, beginning August 15, 1971, when the United States was forced to abandon the gold standard because it could not hope to redeem all the dollars issued for gold (see Block 1979).

problem for the nation, because they are financed by new external debt incurred. The only external debt service cost is the interest on this debt, and then only when the interest rate is positive in real terms.

Other analysts rejoin that this argument overlooks foreign exchange as a variable in debt service. Net income from foreign trade can rise or fall independently of how external resources are used – as was the case during the perverse price movements on the world's commodity markets between 1981 and 1983.

A more sophisticated objection to the IMF position is presented by the U.S. Federal Reserve Bank of New York (FRBNY): so long as the borrower receives more in new loans than must be paid out – that is, as long as net financial flows are positive,

> . . . the economic burden may not seem pressing. . . . If the borrower believes that this positive net inflow will continue indefinitely, it may not concern itself with the ultimate cost of external borrowing. This can be a dangerous approach. Unless external borrowing is making a net contribution, that is, unless its economic benefits exceed its costs, external debt will tend to rise much faster than gross domestic product (GDP). Borrowing to pay for interest and amortization on the debt will also accelerate. At some point realizing that borrowing is being used for consumption rather than investment, lenders will search for less risky borrowers. New loans will dry up, and the borrower will be faced with a painful cut in consumption. (Roberts 1981, p. 34)

Even if it can be agreed that foreign borrowing has limits, if it is relatively easy to say what external debt finance should not be used for, few analysts can usefully advise about how external debt should be used and how to gauge whether it is being applied effectively. The FRBNY states heroically that "GDP growth rate can be taken as a broad indicator of the return to foreign borrowing." GDP, however, is so all-encompassing that it makes any causal comparison with the growth of debt meaningless. The growth rate of GDP is influenced by a multitude of factors, including the sectoral composition of output and variation in export prices. Moreover, the returns from foreign borrowing invested in projects typically do not commence for three to seven years after the initial investment.

More fine tuning is required. Robischek suggests that the private sector, unlike the public sector, must judge its performance by the bottom line or go out of business. That finality makes private-sector indebtedness a potentially valuable indicator of how effectively a country is using its borrowed capital. That is, the larger the proportion of private unguaranteed debt, the larger the relative effectiveness of that debt. This argument had more force before the late 1970s, when the current rash of private-sector bankruptcies and near bankruptcies – including formerly gilt-edged corporations, such as International Harvester,

Chrysler, and Telefunken – began. Indeed, private corporations have been even more prone to debt problems than Third World countries, which implies that mismanagement is not confined to the public sector. The need for a more skeptical attitude is confirmed when the myriad private corporate subterfuges for misappropriation of foreign exchange are examined. For example, the "bicycle" was a ruse that involved private borrowing by domestic banks from the Argentine government for relending to the government at a higher rate of interest.

There seems to be no shortcut to measuring the impact of foreign borrowing. There has to be a project-by-project assessment of the current and potential impacts of loans on net generation of foreign exchange. Such an impact would include either a net lifetime contribution to exports, as in Taiwan's exports of video games, or net import saving, as in Nicaragua's substitution of geothermal power for imported oil. (See Girling and Keith 1977 for a suggested method.)

Thus, a concern with profound implications for the future is that too little of the borrowing by corporations operating in Third World countries is being used productively. To the extent that private borrowing finances imports for consumption, such as food and oil, rather than productive investment, the economic base of the loans and the Third World economies is undermined. The side effects of misapplication of resources increased as the rising interest burden cut into the quantity of financial resources available for investment in export production, import substitution, and infrastructure. In 1970 the 12 largest Third World debtors needed only 6 percent of their export earnings to pay interest abroad. However, by 1980 interest payments took 16 percent of those earnings, and by 1982 had reached 22 percent. Table 2.3 shows that for 14 Third World countries in 1982, service costs exceeded 25 percent of exports.

Perspectives on the Debt Burden

Mirroring the debate on the relative importance of the financial and economic burdens, two contrasting viewpoints about the destabilizing effect of debt on the international economy were articulated in the late 1970s and early 1980s. One group of observers maintained that the development of postwar institutions like the IMF, coupled with the natural market adjustments of the international financial system as countries try to maintain their credit rating, would make a large-scale breakdown virtually impossible. Other analysts argued that the unprecedented magnitude and the disquieting makeup of international debt would lead to severe consequences and repercussions.

Views of the Optimists

Although the optimists admitted that some Third World countries had excessive debts with onerous servicing costs, they believed that the debt crisis and its irregularities would be ironed out through the market. For example, invest-

TABLE 2.3. **Major Third World Debtors in 1982 (est.; in billions of dollars)**

	Total at Year-End 1982	Debt Service Payment* for 1983	Payment as Percent of Exports
Brazil	83.2	26.8	90
Mexico	90.0	43.1	126
Argentina	41.0	18.0	145
S. Korea	36.0	15.7	49
Venezuela	28.0	19.9	101
Israel	26.7	15.2	126
Egypt	19.2	6.0	46
Yugoslavia	19.0	6.0	41
Philippines	16.6	7.0	79
Peru	11.5	3.9	79
Nigeria	9.3	4.9	28
Zaire	5.1	1.2	83
Zambia	4.5	2.0	195
Bolivia	3.1	1.0	118

*Includes interest due on debt plus amortization due in 1983.
Sources: Morgan Guaranty Trust Co.; Exame (Brazil).

ment analysts at Citibank argued that as capital markets reach their capacity, lenders adjust their expectations and evaluations to prevent the overextension of credit. "The increasing wariness of lenders is a natural self-correcting device. (*Wall Street Journal* 1981). Ideally, there should be a complementary natural adjustment by debtors, who scale back their demand for imports and credit. The need to preserve credit ratings then causes Third World countries to manage their affairs more cautiously.

Citibank recognized that in certain cases a country might be unable to cut back and manage its debt, but regarded these as isolated instances, "hardly a threat to the banking system" (*Wall Street Journal* 1981). Optimists point to other compensating factors. Prior to the early 1980s, the natural force of world inflation tended to benefit debtors, since income from exports rose while interest payments stayed relatively fixed. Moreover, the IMF and World Bank can provide short-term and middle-term assistance to ride out a shortfall in export income or a period of adverse capital movement. Hence, as Mexico's economy began to fall into an abyss, the IMF bailed it out with a $4.5 billion loan in October 1982. A similar package was assembled for Brazil in December 1982.

Optimists were also encouraged because most of the outstanding debt tended to be concentrated in countries with dynamic export growth, such as Brazil. That augurs well for the future ability to service present debt levels, and the past record indicates willingness to do so. Historically, until 1982 the debt repayment record of the Third World had been excellent: for example, outstanding debt doubled in the period 1969 to 1973 without any appreciable strain, and the debt indicators for the key middle-income countries remained acceptable.

The optimists argued that the sum of all these restraints and balances meant there would be little chance of general financial collapse. A survey of bankers undertaken in 1981 for the Group of Thirty, an exclusive club of the world's most important banks, found that the majority of lenders did not expect a widespread debt crisis (Mendelsohn 1981).

Views of the Pessimists

Pessimists began by stressing the changes the debt system experienced throughout the 1970s. Perhaps most important was the growing linkage between debt and trade. By 1980 the volume of world trade was heavily dependent upon the ability of Third World countries to borrow to finance imports from the advanced capitalist world. Moreover, one-third of U.S. exports was going to the poorest non-OPEC sector of the Third World (President's Export Council 1980). Second, pessimists regarded the deficits that emerged in the 1970s as chronic rather than transient. Outstanding foreign debts are significantly larger and longer-lasting than at any time since the 1930s. For much of the decade banks ignored the growing bubble of deficits and continued making loans even as risks grew substantially. Furthermore, the growth of the large, unregulated, worldwide Eurodollar market of foreign-currency deposits, a major source of Third World loans, was pinpointed in 1982 by Lord Harold Lever, financial adviser to the British government, as "Surely . . . the largest and most remarkable house of cards ever created" (*New York Times* 1982b, p. 25).

The growth of risk led to the growth of "nonperforming assets." Banks use this term for loans that are not being repaid in an attempt to avoid declaring the loans in default, for the obvious reason that they would then have to be written off and would adversely affect the lending institutions' balance sheets. These problem loans grew by 63 percent in 1982 (*Washington Post* 1982). That trend grew concurrently with a growing rate of debt rescheduling. A study by the IMF indicated that debt reschedulings increased by 240 percent in the period 1979-83 compared with 1974-78 (Graham 1982).

Among the factors that bankers found most worrisome were the danger of short-term fluctuations in lending and the heavy reliance on interbank loans to finance overseas lending. A paper prepared by IMF staff officials found that in a case study of six countries that restructured their debt in the latter part of 1970s, private bank lending was perverse. It increased when times were good but shrank when adversity hit and loans were most needed (Atkinson and Rowe

1982). This phenomenon is the natural and expected outcome of traditional market criteria, and it explains why surveyed bankers told the Group of Thirty that their greatest worry is that there is no formal lender of the last resort (Graham 1982). A financial panic in the 1980s may well be provoked by nervous bankers, forcing even seemingly healthy economies into liquidity crises.

Pessimists construct the following scenario. The failure of exports to grow sufficiently to service debts, short-term liquidity crises, growing protectionism in the industrial export markets, and the limited growth prospects of the Third World as the advanced capitalist economies continue to stagnate are likely to produce a rash of nonperforming assets and debt rescheduling (Seiber 1982, pp. 46–48). If these factors provoke private bankers to dry up the supply of new loans and demand strict repayment of old loans, there is no lender of the last resort with sufficient capacity – not even the World Bank or IMF – to prop up the house of cards. Since banks are heavily extended in their foreign lending, their risks at the beginning of the 1980s were severe. For example, at the end of 1979 the nine largest U.S. banks had $39 billion in loans to developing countries. However, the banks' capital totaled only $21.9 billion. This meant that these banks could all be forced into insolvency if only about half of their Third World loans were thrown into default and had to be written off.

Moreover, the hardening of lending terms, shorter maturities, variable interest rates, and burdened repayment schedules make it increasingly difficult for Third World countries to meet their debt service. Private banks have been increasingly active in attempting to protect themselves by linking their loans to the World Bank and IMF through an accelerated program of cofinancing. This ensures that any default would affect not one or two nations but the more than 100 member nations of the IMF, and would merit the most serious consideration by the industrial nations that subscribe to the IMF and World Bank.

Human Dimensions of Third World Debt

It is rather simple to sit in an easy chair and view the debt crisis in abstract, impersonal terms, from the perspectives of countries, private banks, and international financial institutions. It is easy to forget that the actors in this drama are aggregations of individuals and intermediaries. The burden of debt does not fall on a "country"; it falls on people. Usually the poor, the unemployed, and middle-income workers bear the brunt of what bankers obliquely refer to as "international adjustment costs." Several points bear careful consideration.

First, external debt service requires transfers of real resources from poor debtor nations to largely rich industrial nations. In the abstract it is mere repayment of a prior contracted loan at a mutually agreed interest rate.

To meet those obligations, however, products must be delivered to and sold on the world market. If the investment decisions were poor, if the loans were misappropriated, if they were used to build factories for whose products no market could be found, they still must be repaid by the borrowing company or government, out of the foreign exchange earned by national exports. This may mean that dollars that would have been used to purchase medicines or pay teachers' salaries would have to be used for interest and other debt service charges.

Second, what Citibank analysts abstractly refer to as belt-tightening means something different when you are starving. In the Dominican Republic financial cutbacks meant no medicine in public hospitals, no milk for children living in caves under bridges, and no textbooks in the schools. The social consequences of an IMF-imposed belt-tightening program in Jamaica that called for price adjustments, the ending of price controls on basic commodities, and wage freezes were severe (Bolles 1982). The prices of such staples as sardines and chicken necks and backs doubled. Soap was unavailable. At first factories were closed temporarily because spare parts and production components could not be imported. Workers were furloughed, then lost their jobs when some businesses could not ride out the bad times.

A tragic outcome occurred in April 1984 in the Dominican Republic, when riots provoked by IMF-imposed austerity measures resulted in 55 deaths. The widespread disturbances occurred in response to conditions that produced an overnight doubling in the cost of a wide range of necessities.

The genesis of the debt burden illustrates the human inequity of the present international economic structure. On the one hand, the bananas, coffee, and sugarcane grown in the Third World fluctuate in value with the behavior of the world economy. But at the same time the costs of borrowed funds remain fixed or vary upward. Meanwhile, the spread for banks between borrowing and lending interest rates rarely becomes negative. When this occurred among U.S. savings and loans institutions, federal assistance was provided to reorganize the banks. Yet, the countries that produce sugarcane for 20 cents a pound but can sell it for only 6 or 7 cents a pound do not have this option. The result: cane workers must "tighten their belts" or go unemployed.

Debt Conflicts and the Future

Third World debt, along with its destabilizing impact on the world economy, is not a bad dream from which we will easily and miraculously awaken. The bubble will continue to grow unless pressure is released through major debt reorganization or a moratorium, or unless it bursts from a financial or currency collapse. The World Bank forecasts a continued expansion of 13 percent to 19 percent for differing groups of countries throughout the 1980s (Hope 1982). And one forecast sees the level of debt reaching $750 billion (in 1980 dollars) in 1985 (O'Brien 1981). All projections indicate that external debt will be a major issue in North-South relations throughout the 1980s.

The principal management issue, however, is not by how much debt will swell in the absence of clear counterinitiatives. That only indicates the gravity of the present situation. The fundamental issue is what the available alternatives are. The evolution of Third World debt has been complex, but cures for the debt problem must resolve one or more of three essential causes. First, concessional aid is inadequate, which results in increased private borrowing and contributes to hardening of loan terms and increased service costs.

Second, present Third World plans to increase exports are import-intensive. These industrialization strategies combine with declining export earnings to produce balance-of-payments shortfalls. A chill in the world's industrial economies can turn a cold into pneumonia; a depression can be fatal.

Finally, an overhang of debt accumulated during the 1970s that cannot be repaid on schedule and requires further borrowing, thereby initiating a vicious downward spiral.

The question, then, is which strategies are available for dealing comprehensively with these facets. Helleiner (1979) reminds us that the present debt crisis coincides with the most severe worldwide recession in 40 years – and penetrates so much deeper as to be different in kind from the rise of debt in the 1960s. Proposals or strategies that confront only one of the three fundamental issues will not suffice. (Strategies for debt management are discussed in Chapter 10.)

Mexico received $3.9 billion from the IMF, 40 percent of its 1983 requirements. Private banks agreed to provide the remainder. In 1983 unemployment rose from the official 22 percent to over 30 percent, and consumers' real incomes fell by 50 percent. The remainder of the decade promises to be difficult for Mexico. (See Box 3.)

BOX 3. Mexico: A Case Study

In January 1979 *Business Latin America* noted that "The nearest likeness to a miracle economy will be Mexico . . . all the economic indicators point to boom times in the 1980s."

By September 1982 the sweet smell of success had all but vanished: Mexico announced it could not service its $81 billion foreign debt and declared a three-month moratorium on all interest and principal payments, a 70 percent devaluation, and a nationalization of its private banks.

Why such a turnabout? It is not, as many analysts have said, simply due to the sudden drop in oil prices or the country's overambitious investment program of the 1970s. The causes are more fundamental, rooted in the three-pronged economic strategy that dates to the 1960s. First, priorities in agriculture shifted from domestic food production to export of fruits, vegetables, and livestock, which meant massive imports of grains. Second, the industrial sector focused on production of goods for the middle- and upper-income groups (which implied limited demand, since the majority of the population is poor).

And finally, there was the all-out drive to pump and refine oil, which soared from 10 percent of total exports in 1970 to 73 percent by 1982 – creating a dangerous dependence on a single commodity.

These three legs collapsed one after the other. Mexico's agricultural workers, for whom the income gap widened as inflation soared, fled the farms, seeking work in the new industries. But these industries failed to produce the jobs needed – either for the displaced peasants or for the spiraling population (46 percent of which is under 15; 1 million new jobs are needed each year just to keep unemployment and underemployment at the current 40 percent rate).

At the same time, the oil dependency fueled an enormous growth in imports of drilling and refining equipment and provided ample opportunities for corruption, which increased the cost of doing business, since large amounts were siphoned off for commissions and bribes.

Finally, the key ingredient was capital flight. Although foreign banks continued to pour in funds, wealthy Mexicans came to view their economy as fundamentally unstable, since they could see that the new policies required ever-increasing infusions of foreign capital to finance both industry and balance-of-payments deficits. So they rushed to find safe havens for their dollars in U.S. real estate or banks, which were offering the highest interest rates ever. What began as a modest outflow in 1979 became a torrent by 1982.

The loss of capital, desperately needed for domestic industry and development, was aggravated by the high cost of servicing the foreign debt, which had soared in 1981-82: payments on interest and principal were equal to 85 percent of expected import earnings, leaving only 15 percent for essential imports and investment. This, of course, was exaggerated as a worldwide recession reduced demand and the price of oil plummeted: instead of an expected $20 billion in oil revenues, the country received only $14 billion.

As a result the peso, which had traded at 26 to the dollar in December 1981, fell to over 100 by September 1982, and the cost of imports, critical to the economy, skyrocketed. The swollen foreign debt, most of which was owed to private banks (with 40 percent due in one year or less) simply could not be met, since the cost of debt service exceeded the value of oil profits.

As the boom collapsed, Mexicans awoke to discover that while a slow escape from poverty (based on reform of the economy) is hard, the consequences of the failed debt-financed development strategy will be worse. In December 1982 Mexico's newly elected president, Miguel de la Madrid Hurtado, announced an agreement with the IMF. Mexico would impose a strict austerity program. First, the peso was devalued a further 53 percent. Government expenditures were slashed over 15 percent, with massive cuts in public subsidies for foodstuffs (beans and tortillas) and gasoline. Prices for public services and taxes were increased. Major construction projects were canceled or suspended. Labor received a 25 percent wage increase, less than half the rate of inflation.

full-scale international debt crisis in 1982, spotlighting the dangers to the future health of the world economy.

GROWTH OF MULTINATIONAL BANKING: 1930-80

During the Depression and World War II, international banking was at a nadir. Both war and depression interrupted the flow of trade and finance. It was not until the 1950s that international banking began to pick up as a natural outgrowth of the postwar resurgence in world trade and investment. Part of that boom was the spread of MNCs, which until recently have been the banks' principal overseas customers. Naturally, as these prime borrowers moved abroad, the banks moved with them to maintain their markets. A large portion of this business has been geared to financing major investment projects – from North Sea oil and Australian minerals to the Siberian pipeline. The MNCs provide technology, managerial know-how, and investment capital all over the world, and the banks provide the long-term credits.

By the early 1960s banks were in full migration. The number of private banks with overseas branches and subsidiaries increased at an unprecedented rate. Between 1918 and 1960 the number of U.S. overseas subsidiaries doubled; since 1960 it has multiplied eightfold, rising from 124 branches in 1960 to nearly 1,000 in 1984. In 1960 eight U.S. banks had overseas subsidiaries; by 1975 the number stood at 125. Meanwhile, total overseas assets rose from $3.5 billion in 1960 to $483 billion by 1981 (Bartlett 1981; Griffith-Jones, 1980.)

Two developments in Europe during the late 1950s stimulated that flight. One was Europe's return to currency convertibility. The resurrection of European markets following the war stimulated a surge in investment. Banks opened offices to serve corporate clients, particularly U.S. MNCs that rushed into Europe in the 1960s.

The second was the development of a Eurocurrency market. Eurocurrencies are deposits of money (about 80 percent are U.S. dollars) outside the country of origin, for example, deposits of Canadian dollars in a Swiss bank. Originally based in London, the phenomenon is now global, with centers from Bahrain to Singapore to the Cayman Islands, and includes most of the world's strong currencies. This market is unregulated; the standard reserve requirements that require banks operating, say, in the United States to keep a certain portion of deposits on hand against the risk of withdrawal or default, do not apply.

Financing through the Eurocurrency market is usually handled by syndicated loans, which are loans to governments or corporations that are too large or risky for one bank's assets to cover and are extended by a group of banks. The potential network includes hundreds of private lenders, and packages are put together through worldwide telex and telephone contacts. The larger international banks not only play a dominant role in underwriting these loans but also are beginning to manage the investments.

All of this had fairly modest origins. The Eurocurrency market began in 1949, when the Soviet government deposited its dollars in London in order to avoid transferring them to the United States, where they were subject to expropriation. The Soviet deposits remained in Europe, to be borrowed and loaned by banks and commercial users who needed dollars for import or export operations. The pool was augmented in the 1960s by large U.S. payments deficits as dollars were sent abroad and held in other countries. Later, OPEC surpluses were deposited in the Eurocurrency market, leading to a quantum leap in the supply of lending capital. From an estimated $17 billion in 1964, these deposits mushroomed to about $550 billion by the end of 1979.

U.S. efforts to curb balance-of-payments deficits in the 1960s also played a part in boosting international banking. In 1964 the interest equalization tax was enacted to stem the export of U.S. capital. Instead of repatriating profits, U.S. MNCs began depositing their earnings abroad to avoid taxation. Mandatory controls on capital exports in 1968, enacted as the Vietnam war produced worsening of the balance of payments, had a similar effect. U.S. MNCs and U.S. banks responded by shifting a full range of transactions overseas. One observer summarized the situation thus: "The American attempt to stop the export of capital in the sixties led to the export of the American banking system instead" (Griffith-Jones 1980, p. 206).

Indeed, U.S. banks found their international operations to be especially lucrative. Between 1970 and 1975 international earnings accounted for 95 percent of the total increase in income for 13 major U.S. banks. In 1976 the profit margin on foreign assets of the 10 largest U.S. private lenders was 30 percent higher than on domestic assets; for Citicorp, the largest overseas financer, it was double (Porzecanski 1981). As a result, by 1976, 21 percent of total U.S. banking assets were abroad, compared with 8.5 percent in 1970 (Rodríguez and Carter 1979, p. 539).

In one sense the banks have simply been following the rainbow to a richer pot of gold. For example, the majority of international banks in the United States are domestically owned and their activities rigidly regulated. Specified reserve requirements compel them to keep a significant portion of their assets tied up in noninterest-earning securities, thereby cutting into profits. By locating in the Third World – perhaps in small Caribbean banking centers like Anguilla, the Bahamas, and the Cayman Islands – banks can escape governmental oversight and taxation.

Although the initial thrust abroad was led by U.S. lending institutions, others have followed. Of the world's top 10 banks, four are French, one is German, two are English, and one is Japanese. Further, over 100 foreign banks were competing in the U.S. market by 1980. And all of these banks were diversifying their activities. The frontier between commercial banking and project investment was beginning to blur. According to Alfred Brittain III, chairman of Bankers Trust of New York:

> We now assist in mergers and acquisitions. We serve as advisors or agents in private placement and provide debt and equity for purchases and acquisitions. We also act as underwriters for security issues abroad through foreign-based subsidiaries. . . . it is clear that wholesale bankers cannot meet customer needs simply by lending money. (1981, p. 61)

Banks unable to provide as wide a range of services as this will find it increasingly difficult to compete.

Initially, international banking was handled through correspondent banks. In this relationship a domestic bank contracts with a foreign bank to handle the affairs of its customers in the correspondent's country. It is the least costly and least encumbered form of external operation. However, it is also the least flexible and profitable.

A more advanced method of operation involves establishing a representative office in a foreign country. Although these offices do not operate as banks – they do not directly accept deposits or place loans – they assist customers in dealing with foreign financial institutions. Representative offices sell bank services and solicit deposits for their parent bank, and are often precursors for branch bank operations. In the 1960s, for example, several U.S. banks stationed representative officers in Beirut, Lebanon, to attract deposits from oil sheiks. Their success paved the way for the branch banks that followed (Wolff 1971).

Branch banks are now the principal vehicle for international finance. They generally provide the full range of services offered by the parent institution. During the 1960s the number of U.S. subsidiaries sprouted from 124 to 460, with the major growth concentrated in Latin America, Europe, and the Far East (see Table 3.1). During the 1970s rapid expansion occurred in Africa, the Caribbean, and the Middle East. (The latter was an effort to acquire OPEC deposits.)

Multinational banks also use foreign subsidiary banks. That is, a bank in one country largely owns or controls an independently chartered bank in another country. For example, Jamaica Citizen's Bank was founded in 1970 by the Citizen Southern Bank of Atlanta (Georgia). Citizen Southern provided 51 percent of the capital of the new bank and raised the remainder from Jamaican investors. Banca d'America e d'Italia – Italy's eleventh largest commercial bank, with over 100 branches – is 17 percent owned by Bank of America. The Chase Manhattan Bank owns 49 percent of Venezuela's third largest bank, Banco Mercantil y Agrícola.

Beyond branch and subsidiary banks are the Edge corporations. Section 25(A) of the Federal Revenue Act, passed shortly after World War I, helps U.S.

TABLE 3.1. Growth of Multinational Banking in the Third World

	1918	1939	1950	1960	1969	1979[a]	1979[b]
U.S. branch banks outside the U.S.	61	89	95	124	460	779	1,616[c]
Latin America and the Caribbean	31	47	49	55	235	198	371
Africa	0	0	0	1	1	151	257
Near East	0	0	0	4	6	59	188
Far East	0	18	19	23	77	164	496
Europe and other	30	24	27	41	141	207	304[c]
Assets ($ billion)	0	0	0	3.5	41	364	n.a.

n.a. = not available.
[a] U.S. branches, subsidiaries, and affiliates.
[b] All foreign branches, subsidiaries, and affiliates.
[c] Third World only; excludes Europe.
Sources: *Federal Reserve Bulletin*, various issues; Wolff, 1971, p. 22; Thorn et al. 1979.

lenders compete with more diversified foreign banks. This provision permitted U.S. banks to establish overseas subsidiaries that could undertake any activity authorized by those countries' laws. U.S. banks could do overseas what they were prohibited from doing at home – own and operate businesses – although in practice subsidiaries are confined to finance-related activities (Rodríguez and Carter 1979). For example, during the 1960s Edge corporations provided Chase Manhattan with access to African markets through its investments in London's Standard Bank, without the expense of setting up its own branches (Wolff 1979).

Finally, investment banking subsidiaries became a rage during the 1970s. Established by U.S. and European banks, these institutions provided expertise in underwriting, placing, and syndicating the loans that were in heavy demand because of the chronic balance-of-payments deficits in the Third World and the competition among private banks to capture and "recycle" OPEC surpluses. The private banks used this specialized instrument to tap into the high earnings available from charging fixed percentages for management of international financial operations. "With declining spreads in a highly competitive market, the income generated from the management function becomes of vital importance to the lending operation." (Rodríguez and Carter 1979).

BANKING AND THE THIRD WORLD: 1850-1980

The recent surge in private bank lending to the Third World is not unique. During the latter half of the nineteenth century, various expatriate banks in colonial territories, principally British, grew phenomenally. For instance, the Standard Bank was set up to finance the South African wool trade, and the Bank of London and South America underwrote commercial shipments of beef and wheat. The Hong Kong and Shanghai Banking Corporation, founded in 1865, sat at the hub of the China trade, exchanging opium, tea, and silk for silver. Investment banks in the 1850s and 1860s served as brokers for capital-importing countries such as Egypt, Spain, Russia, and the Latin American republics. The banks competed intensely to earn generous underwriting and placement fees from the sale of foreign bonds above their discounted purchase price. One observer noted that "Any government which claimed sovereignty over a bit of the earth's surface and a fraction of its inhabitants could find a financial agent in London and a purchaser for his bonds" (Jenkes 1927). When economic instability followed the 1856-65 boom, as many as half of the banks collapsed when governments defaulted on their loans (Baster 1935).

A similar banking debacle was repeated in the 1920s and 1930s in Latin America. During the early phase, dollar acceptances and letters of credit were widely used for the first time by the U.S. banks to finance trade and investment in a Latin American commodity boom. But a recession in 1921 stunted demands and led to credit losses, bankruptcies, and consolidation. U.S. banks responded to this rap on the knuckles by seeking more secure clients and focusing on sovereign governments. Bolivia, Brazil, Chile, Colombia, Peru, and the various Central American countries were prime customers. Then came the Great Depression. Between 1930 and 1933 almost every Latin American government except Haiti and Argentina went into default (Lewis 1938; McMullen 1979). After World War II the face value of many Latin bonds was unilaterally reduced. The principal of many Brazilian bonds was reduced by 20 to 50 percent, and the nominal value of Mexican debt plummeted by 80 percent (United Nations 1955).

The U.S. and European governments reacted by imposing stringent restrictions on buying and selling foreign bonds. Banks in Europe and Japan were required to obtain authorization from their home governments, and U.S. banks were effectively prohibited from brokering Third World bonds: complex regulations drawn by the U.S. Securities and Exchange Commission barred the market to subsequent issues. As a result Latin American bonds were virtually extinct between 1930 and 1970 (Stallings 1979).

For almost 40 years Third World borrowers were largely cut off from the private international financial market. Bilateral loans, grants, and direct foreign investment were the only major sources of long-term external financing. Between 1968 and 1970 private bank loans to the nonoil-producing developing

TABLE 3.2. The World's Top 10 Banks

Bank	Headquarters	Balance Sheet 1980 (billion $)
Citicorp	New York	109.6
Bank America Corporation	San Francisco	106.8
Caisse Nationale de Crédit Agricole	Paris	105.0
Banque Nationale de Paris	Paris	98.9
Crédit Lyonnais	Paris	98.5
Société Générale	Paris	90.0
Deutsche Bank	Frankfurt (Main)	89.2
Barclays Bank Group	London	87.2
National Westminster Bank Group	London	81.8
Fuji Bank	Tokyo	75.6

Source: Prepared by author.

countries amounted to only 4 percent of their combined current-account deficit, while loans from official sources amounted to 32 percent, and grants 22 percent, of the deficit. As of 1971, two-thirds of the Third World's medium- and long-term debt was owed to official sources, and the remaining third was held by a combination of banks, private bondholders, and suppliers. The incidence of private credit was so low that the Bank for International Settlements did not even collect data on loans to Third World nations until the mid-1970s (de Vries 1983).

However, 1973 proved to be a watershed. A chain of events began that restored a central role to private banks in Third World financing. During a flare-up of the Arab-Israeli war, an embargo on oil shipments to the West by Middle Eastern producers sparked the first of a series of jumps in petroleum prices, turning the desert green with dollars. The magnitude of those profits dwarfed the capacity of OPEC countries to absorb offsetting levels of technology, infrastructure, or consumer imports, so enormous sums of durable funds were deposited in private banks in the United States and Europe. In the aftermath of the embargo, the world economy went into a tailspin. A recession dampened investment demand in the advanced industrial countries (AICs) as their economies absorbed the oil shock.

Third World economies were less resilient, however, and financing was desparately needed to pay for vital industrial energy and agricultural imports. The nonoil-exporting Third World saw its current-account deficit quadrupled, rising from $11.5 billion in 1973 to $46.5 billion in 1975. As OPEC, the AICs, and the MNIs could not agree on who would bear the brunt of a bailout, private banks were encouraged to recycle the surpluses to the Third World in order to forestall any additional deflationary impact on the international economy. That is, a significant decline in Third World imports could turn the recession into a depression in the AICs. One indication of that increased vulnerability was that by 1973 over 30 percent of U.S. exports were shipped to the Third World (Matheison 1982).

Not that the banks were motivated by altruism. Their profits would decline if productive outlets were not found for the OPEC deposits. The banks discovered several promising borrowers: newly industrialized countries – such as Mexico, Brazil, and South Korea – with open economies and few restrictions on capital flows. Moreover, these nations were either ineligible for subsidized credit from the multilateral development banks (MDBs) or were unwilling to submit to austerity programs that were a prerequisite for IMF lending. The export outlook for these countries seemed excellent. Perhaps borrowing had a silver lining: in producing their way out of debt, countries could speed up their economic development.

In 1974 U.S. foreign lending was stimulated by the removal of restrictions on capital outflows that had been in effect since 1968. Subsequently, from the mid-1970s to the end of the decade, private bank lending to 21 Third World exporters grew by over 30 percent annually (de Vries 1983). Most of the borrowing took place in the Eurodollar market. Since 1976 a sizable portion of the lending was in collaboration with the World Bank via cofinancing arrangements. MDBs had to share risks and keep the wheel greased so that private banks would continue to recycle debt. A default on any of these loans would be tantamount to a default against the World Bank, which seemed unthinkable.

In fact, the levels of risk were steadily mounting. Table 3.3 indicates the growing momentum. Between 1968 and 1981 long-term lending by private banks rose from less than $1 billion to over $35 billion. The good news was that these loans patched over the widening gaps in the Third World's current-account deficits that were left by a slower growth of official lending and the marginal lending activity of the IMF. The bad news was that by 1976 the stitches began breaking, and each new patching required more cloth and thread. Prior to the OPEC price rise, the private banks supplied loans covering 3.8 percent of the Third World's deficit. Between 1973 and 1975 the figure somersaulted to 35.2 percent and then soared to 60.6 percent between 1976 and 1978, when bailouts became common. After another quantum price jump by OPEC in 1979, the banks continued to supply 40.1 percent of dollars borrowed by the nonoil exporters, and no end was in sight.

TABLE 3.3. Financing the Third World's Balance-of-Payments Deficits

	1960-67	1968-70	1971-72	1973-75	1976-78	1979-81
Balance-of-payments deficit (current account, billions of dollars)		$25.9	$25.1	$95.1	$99.5	$244.1
Percentage of total financing provided by official flows						
Grants		22.0%	17.9%	20.4%	24.7%	14.8%
Loans		32.0	29.0	27.4	37.8	23.0
SDRs		—	—	.5	3.2	1.8
Direct foreign investment		14.2	15.5	15.7	17.0	13.4
Private borrowing						
From banks		3.8	13.1	35.2	60.6	40.1
Other[a]		n.a.	n.a.	5.0	10.1	1.5
Short-term borrowing						
Private[b]		25.1	32.3	44.8	18.6	17.2
IMF		—	—	4.6	4.8	2.7
Accumulation of reserves		18.1	30.7	10.7	42.2	7.7

[a]Largely government bond issues.
[b]Includes long-term supplier credits, short-term bank credits to government, private-sector credits, errors, and omissions.

Note: columns do not add to 100 percent. Each figure is the average for the specified time period.
Sources: Gisselquist 1981; International Monetary Fund 1982.

THE NEW INTERVENTION: CONVERGING TRENDS

Certainly the repeated shocks of OPEC price rises in the 1970s provided the occasion for renewed private lending to the Third World. Another measure of the size of that shift is provided by the proportion of their total external foreign debt that developing countries owed to private banks. In 1970 the figure was 8 percent. By 1976 it had risen to 26 percent, and by 1982 private banks held almost half of the Third World's public debt.* (Griffith-Jones 1980; World Bank 1984).

Marcel Sarmet, senior vice-president of Crédit Lyonnais, a Paris-based global bank, puts it this way:

> Borrowers believe that banks may take some political risks more evenly than they can, that these risks will affect them less, and that this type of financing lessens the consequences of these risks for the project. Borrowers are increasingly seeking financing structure which allows them to shift to the banks the political risks involved in a project. This is one of the major reasons for the progress in international project financing. In some cases, borrowers who would not have resorted to a domestic project financing looked to international project financing only to cover political risks and are prepared to bear the technological and commercial risks themselves. (1981, p. 133)

As a result the banks began to accumulate experience in Third World operations. The expanding Eurocurrency market of the 1960s accelerated competition among banks to expand their portfolios to new markets. Their previous contacts through MNC finance, coupled with the high commodity price increases of the early 1970s that produced trade surpluses, made a large number of developing countries into attractive potential clients. That is, international banks were already expanding their activities and had developed a network of operatives even as the first oil shock hit. Meanwhile, the banks' experience in syndicating loans to MNCs through the Eurocurrency market seemed to pro-

---

*These and most statistics on debt are based on World Bank data. World Bank debt statistics are considered to be the most comprehensive series available for the Third World. Nevertheless, they are subject to limitations that cause them to understate the debt to private sources, particularly to private banks. First, countries are only asked to report public and publicly guaranteed debt with a maturity of one year or more, thereby excluding short-term credits and nonguaranteed medium- and long-term private borrowing, which is quite sizable in the cases of Brazil and Mexico. Second, only nations that have borrowed from the World Bank must file reports. Nonmembers, such as Cuba, which had a debt of about $3 billion in 1984, are omitted. Finally, governments may not know how much they owe. As part of a World Bank mission to the Dominican Republic to calculate the country's debt, I discovered how little the government knew about its obligations and those of its national corporations. In its 1983-84 *World Debt Tables*, the World Bank attempted to correct these oversights. Officially reported debt was estimated at $575 billion, while total external liabilities of all developing nations was estimated to be $810 billion.

vide the necessary vehicle for recycling the subsequent OPEC surplus to Third World borrowers.

With banks eager to lend, Third World governments soon were eager to borrow. Increased energy costs and ambitious public investment programs required additional foreign exchange. That need merged with increased skepticism about direct private investment. Private foreign loans seemed to offer greater national independence than either investment by MNCs, bilateral aid from a superpower, or officially supervised credit from the IMF or IBRD.

The rest of the 1970s made this "opportunity" look like fool's gold. The banks moved to protect themselves from the effects of inflation by developing rollover credits for long-term loans. That is, interest rates are adjusted periodically – usually every three to six months – shifting the risk of fluctuating interest rates from the bank to the borrower. As a result, the burden of financing a continuing series of trade deficits during the world recession of the early 1980s is matched by the danger of a simultaneous increase of previously incurred debt. To illustrate what this means for developing countries, in April 1984 the U.S. Federal Reserve raised the prime rate by 1 percentage point. That action raised Brazil's annual interest payment by just under $1 billion, wiping out one-third of an anticipated balance-of-trade surplus – the result of severe reduction in imports, substitution of alcohol for petroleum, and promotion of Brazilian exports.

In fact, most of the factors that seemed to make the banks suitable candidates for mediating the financial crisis of the mid-1970s appear increasingly makeshift. For one thing, it is difficult to translate knowledge about the political situation in a country into an effective loan policy. For example, the rate of takeovers of foreign enterprises more than doubled during the 1970s. Twice as many enterprises were nationalized in the first half of the 1970s as in all of the 1960s, according to a report issued by the Dutch government. Several leading banks have set up country-risk management groups employing former State Department and CIA officers.

One of these banks was Chase Manhattan. An insight into the operation of its country-risk committee is provided by Anthony Sampson:

> "If you sat in a meeting of the country risk committee," said the Chase chief economist, Robert Slighton, who also worked for the CIA, "I think you would be impressed by how much they knew but appalled by the difficulty of transferring that knowledge into policies for loans. . . . Operational banking consists in a constant war, a continuous adversary process between credit officers and loan officers – it takes place at every level, and it can be very bloody. . . . In retrospect we overloaned in the seventies: there is a much more hostile environment projected for the eighties. (1981, p. 256)

Perhaps the failure of bankers trying to be political seers is slightly comic, but the failure of bankers to be responsible bankers can have grave consequences. In 1976 the return on international lending was 30 percent greater than that on domestic loans. The rush to earn short-term profits led to profligate lending. According to Rimer de Vries, senior vice-president of Morgan Guaranty Trust Company, the banks overloaned because they overestimated the capacity of Third World debtors to handle the debt burden. Moreover, lenders were drawn into competitive follow-the-leader behavior based upon a "pervasive faith in almost inevitable economic growth."

By 1979 the overexpansion of foreign lending led to reversed earning ratios; banks' returns on domestic loans became 30 percent greater than on international lending. That provided the banks with a bottom-line incentive to brake their foreign lending and impose more stringent controls. When the economic depression began in 1980, the countries were unable to service their debts (de Vries, 1983, pp. 9-10). High interest rates and a shortening of maturities caused the debt-service ratios of the 21 key borrowers to rise from 50 percent in 1979 to 75 percent in 1982. Real debt-service ratios rose from 8.7 percent in 1975-77 to 16.8 percent in 1981-82 (Cline 1983). Then political events – the failure of successive international financial conferences from Cancún to Williamsburg – combined with economic realities to shatter confidence in late 1982. In 1981 the increase in total bank exposure to the Third World rose by $47 billion; in 1982 it rose by no more than $20 billion.

When Mexico threatened to default on its loans in 1982, anxious whispers could be heard in the most curious places. The prospect of high rates of return had attracted many small regional banks in the Midwest and South (most had no experience in international markets) to join the larger international banks in underwriting loans to the Third World. The flexibility that characterized the Eurodollar market and allowed private banks to recycle the OPEC surplus suddenly seemed disquieting reminiscent of the 1920s, when countless small investors rushed to make a killing on the unregulated New York stock market.

THE IMPACT OF MULTINATIONAL BANKING ON THE THIRD WORLD

For a while it seemed that the private banks might be the unsung heroes of the 1980s. Now there is real doubt about whether they have helped resolve a crisis or only papered over it. Did the recycling of capital from the surplus countries to the debtor countries of the Third World promote long-term, viable growth, or did it initiate a self-perpetuating process of growing indebtedness?

One way to approach the problem is to ask what would have happened if private bank lending had not been available. It seems doubtful that bilateral aid or loans from MNIs would have been sufficient in quantity or speed. The international financial institutions simply lacked sufficient funds to meet Third World capital needs. Moreover, they lacked the ability to act expeditiously. Government lending requires a lengthy process of building political consensus and placating special interests, a difficulty that prevented rapid expansion of IMF lending even when the private banks reached the end of their tether in the crisis years of 1982 and 1983. Private banks suffer no such limitation and, in the case of Eurodollar lending, are exempt from reserve requirements. Thus, their initial stretching capacity was great, and when that was multiplied by additional access to a wide pool of interbank loans to protect their liquidity and by syndication of loans among a number of banks, the system had enough spring to handle increasingly gigantic loans.

Another solution might have called for governments to draw down their reserves of gold and foreign currencies. Of course, the crisis of the 1970s produced effects that were universal, particularly affecting countries with insufficient reserves. Moreover, the deficit from increased oil prices was not unique; cost increases seemed inevitable for the foreseeable future. Whose reserves were great enough for that?

Traditionally, a country in such a situation must make an internal adjustment, that is, cut back on imports. It may try to stimulate exports, but that is far more difficult, particularly when the world economy is as sluggish as it was during much of the 1970s. Imports may be reduced through tariffs or a variety of direct nontariff controls. Another strategy tries to affect both imports and exports through currency devaluation, which raises the price of imports to inhibit their demand while reducing the price of exports to reinforce their demand.

There are interesting historical precedents. During the nineteenth century economic growth and stability in the industrialized countries were preserved in large part by wide economic fluctuations and enormous cyclical currency devaluation in the Third World, chiefly Latin America. "The contrast between the 'core' countries and those of the 'periphery' can largely be explained by the cyclical pattern of capital movements and terms of trade, which contributed to stability in the first group, and to instability on the second" (Triffin 1964). Fluctuations in the economies of the Third World were used to smooth out the deficit problems in the advanced countries at the expense of the Third World (Magdoff 1969).

Gisselquist argues that a different process is at work today. Although private and public bank activities in the Third World appear benign or generous, they cause larger current-account deficits:

> It has been common to interpret bank loans to developing country governments as filling a need for foreign credit. In such an interpretation, it is implicitly assumed that current account deficits came first and bank loans are the necessary response. To argue a reverse causation – that bank loans bring current account deficits – is equally true. In the 1970s, bank loans permitted nonoil developing countries to run much larger deficits than they could have without bank loans. Had banks not been willing to lend, nonoil developing countries would have been forced to reduce their current account deficits, and the deficits [required] to balance OPEC surpluses would have been forced more on the industrial countries. (1981, p. 155)

According to this view, the effect of bank activities in the 1970s was to provide easy credit to Third World oil importers so that they could continue to import not only petroleum but also the host of consumer and producer goods manufactured in the industrial countries. Without access to easy credit between 1973 and 1981, debtor countries would have been forced to balance their imports, including oil, other intermediate products, capital goods, and consumer goods, keeping them in line with exports. The net effect would have exerted deflationary pressure on the AICs. This international economic adjustment might have occurred at a time when the required reductions in incomes were proportionately smaller.

That is, the experience of the late 1970s suggests that the financial system, with banks playing the key role, incorporated a new twist by using the Third World to maintain prosperity in the industrial trading nations. Third World markets had become increasingly important since the 1950s, so that instead of the devaluations, restricted access to credit, and depreciation that characterized an earlier era, an inflationary boost was needed in this sector of the international economy. And the private banking system, responding to the institutional imperative to expand profits and to the implicit promptings of the U.S. government's lifting of financial controls on currency exports in 1974, provided it.

However, those transactions did not usher in an era of prosperity. In March 1982, following a payment crisis in Poland, the *Washington Post* raised a warning, citing five dangers: overseas borrowers may have borrowed so much that individual countries may be "unable to service or repay foreign currency debts because of overall balance of payments problems and lack of foreign exchange, even when the individual borrower is not bankrupt"; political upheavals related to onerous debt burdens could threaten loans and investments; "sovereign risk" loans made to or guaranteed by a national government may not be secured by assets (as company or home loans are); a rise in "nonperforming assets," loans on which payment was overdue, had caught the eye of government regulators; and there is a threat that in the 1980s debtor countries may have to depress their economies to cope with less foreign money, and that will "contribute to the overall world tendency to deflate."

In effect, as the 1980s approached, there was a winnowing of alternatives for the AICs and the private international banks. The breakup of the old European empires, the domination of the U.N. General Assembly by the swelling ranks of new nations and former colonies, and the U.S. defeat in Vietnam made military intervention by the AICs unlikely (as had occurred when U.S. marines took over the Dominican Republic in 1906 for nonpayment of debt). In fact, even as the banks had to seek another way to resolve the problem of nonperforming assets, the danger of political upheaval (and implicitly the threat of unilateral debt cancellation) was rising in debtor countries along with the growing economic burden of debt servicing. Above all, there was an ironic sense of déjà vu. The private banks had been encouraged to recycle OPEC surpluses and stave off international deflation; and they had willingly done so. Now that deflation loomed nearer, and it seemed that all those loans had been feeding a monster until it had grown large enough to devour its feeders.

Distortion in Third World Economies

Economic distortion is a complex concept. It takes shape according to the eye of the beholder. The World Bank uses it to characterize any deviation in a nation's price structure from a perfectly competitive model, including those deviations that impede foreign competition in a domestic market. Thus, tariff barriers are economic distortions because they result in a higher domestic price for, say, automobiles in the Dominican Republic than if there were no tariff.

Economic distortions can also be described by the external factors, price policies, or resource flows that restrain a national economy from attaining peak performance. For example, if the Chinese economy were to be deprived of access to technology needed for mining and production of copper, its productive potential would be inhibited. If the business practices of a transnational pharmaceutical company restricted its Peruvian subsidiary from exporting medicines to France, Peru's potential for earning foreign exchange would be restrained.

Economic distortions can also be attributed to mismanagement by political elites. Thus, if mineral resources remained undeveloped because capital inflows that could have been used to build access roads were diverted to support the sumptuous life-style of the Somoza family and build up their personal fortune in Swiss banks, Nicaragua's economy would have been economically distorted.

Private banks have distorted Third World economies in various ways. Some of those effects are a direct result of policy. For instance, in the mid-1970s private banks conditioned loans to Peru on a variety of concessions to foreign investment, including the reopening of Peru's jungle and coastline to oil exploration by private companies, the promotion of private over public enterprise in the fishing industry, and changes in labor law that would favor private investors.

Other – in fact, the predominant – effects are indirect. That is, they are by-products of the cost of borrowing. The wide spreads and high service fees for these loans have produced substantial profits for the banks; they have also deprived countries of income needed for economic development and public services. The rise in interest rates from 8 percent in the early 1970s to 13 percent by 1980 added approximately $25 billion to annual interest costs of Third World debt. Regardless of who caused or was responsible for the rise in rates, that sum represents a transfer of resources from Third World countries to private banks, their stockholders, and their depositors.

The key here is not intent but effect. Certainly the banks have not set out to bankrupt their clients. However, private banks charge more to service their loans than the large MDBs do. That translates into a higher turnaround cost for the borrower: the loan has to be invested in ways that earn higher short-term yields to pay itself off. The margin for error can be slight, and during the economic stagflation of the 1970s it was practically invisible. Needed development projects, which could have been financially feasible at lower interest rates, were choked off. Funding for agricultural projects to increase domestic production took a back seat to servicing loans. Those two trends formed a pincer, and many countries found their investments producing insufficient exports to pay for themselves while foodstuffs had to be imported to feed the population.

The Multinationalization of Private Banking:
Who Will Rescue the Rescuers?

In the mid-1970s the private banks emerged as the champions of the international financial system (see Figure 3.1). Relieving the IMF of its designated role, the private banks' success in recycling OPEC surpluses as loans to cover balance-of-payments deficits was heralded as proof that "the system worked." For instance, Peru arranged loans from private U.S. banks in 1976 and was able to circumvent the drastic austerity program that would have conditioned any IMF lending and was therefore politically unacceptable. The banks agreed, according to Professor Barbara Stallings, in order to avoid the leftist politicization that might have occurred within the government as the result of an IMF-imposed plan. The banks wished to keep the centrist president Morales Bermúdez afloat and to gain concessions for foreign investment (Stallings 1978).

Despite or because of the banking package, the Peruvian economy deteriorated. As demand dropped, industrial and service-sector businesses stagnated and workers were laid off. When Peru seemed on the verge of defaulting in 1977, the banks refused to renegotiate their loans without IMF participation. Stallings attributes the banks' appeal to the IMF to three factors. First, the lenders were anxious to remove themselves from monitoring Peru's performance. Identification with an arduous stabilization program "ran the risk of becoming scapegoats from unpleasant results." Second, the banks felt that the IMF had the neutral reputation, the access to data, and the experience in surveillance to establish an effective monitoring procedure. Finally, the banks realized that a change in Peru's political climate between 1976 and 1977 precluded left-wing gains despite any IMF stringency.

Peru, which once seemed a perfect example of how private banks could act effectively in the Third World, now became a more controversial model. It seemed that private lenders willingly extended credit and earned their commissions, only to retreat to the comforting arms of the IMF when conditions got difficult.

The scenario was repeated in 1982 with Mexico and Brazil. Again poor judgment led to an overextension of credit, onerous terms, and ultimately the rescue of the private banks by the IMF. The crises of 1982, in fact, produced a new high in the degree of coordination between the IMF and the private bank-

FIGURE 3.1. Major Overseas Loans by U.S. Banks (billions of dollars, September 1981)

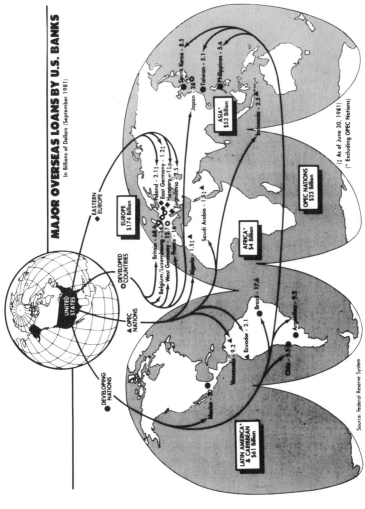

MAJOR OVERSEAS LOANS BY U.S. BANKS
In Billions of Dollars (September 1981)

EASTERN EUROPE ◆

EUROPE
$174 Billion

DEVELOPED ○ COUNTRIES

Belgium/Luxembourg - 14.5
West Germany - 13.7
France - 16
Britain - 44.5
Poland - 2.1‡
East Germany - 1.2‡
Hungary - 1‡
Yugoslavia - 2.5

Algeria - 1.5‡ ▲

Saudi Arabia - 1.5‡ ▲

Japan - 21 ○

South Korea - 8.5
Taiwan - 5.1
Philippines - 5.6

ASIA*
$53 Billion

OPEC NATIONS
$23 Billion

AFRICA*
$4 Billion

Indonesia - 2.5 ▲

(‡ As of June 30, 1981)

(* Excluding OPEC Nations)

OPEC NATIONS ▲

UNITED STATES

DEVELOPING NATIONS ●

Mexico - 20 ●

Venezuela - 9.2 ▲

Ecuador - 2.1 ▲

Brazil - 17.6 ●

Argentina - 9.1 ●

Chile - 5.9 ●

LATIN AMERICA*
& CARIBBEAN
$61 Billion

Source: Federal Reserve System

‡As of June 30, 1981.

*Excluding OPEC Nations.

Source: Federal Reserve System. Dave Cook, *Washington Post*, March 14, 1982, p. 61. © Washington Post.

57

ing system in handling the debt burden. Professor William Cline of the Institute for International Economics testified about those developments to the U.S. Senate:

> For the first time the International Monetary Fund has required private banks to increase their exposure as a precondition of lending programs, offering them the alternative of putting in new money or suffering default on the old money. This change is of historical significance. There is a well-known problem whereby each bank acting in isolation may be forced to try to take its money out [of a high-risk developing country] if it thinks the other banks will do so even if individually it would prefer to continue lending, and by acting as coordinator the IMF has reduced this problem of counterproductive action in isolation. (Cline 1983)

Other observers have different viewpoints. Conservative critics decry IMF involvement as private-sector bailouts. The IMF's defenders respond that the institution was doing precisely what it was established to do. Radicals argue that these ties demonstrate how financial institutions act in concert to enforce an "open door" to international trade and private investment, ensuring that whatever development occurs in the Third World occurs at the behest of capitalist institutions and is rooted in capitalist patterns.

What recent developments do indicate is that the private banking system does not have the capacity to sustain a mounting debt burden. A few years ago the IMF and the IBRD seemed on the verge of fossilization, their key functions taken over by heavily capitalized private lenders. Now, at a minimum, it seems that the multilateral institutions, which were founded in a different era, have a vital role to play if they can summon the will to adapt to the new challenge.

BOX 4. Poland: "A Dream Investment"

In 1980 *Fortune* magazine featured an article on Poland. Although Poland is not a Third World country, the *Fortune* article describes an almost classical case of financial distortion.

> Poland became a major consumer of Western credit during the Gierek regime. Gierek wanted to hasten development of Poland's rich coal and copper resources, and its sulfur, titanium, and lignite deposits. To build up its automobile and refrigerator industries, he developed a modern steel industry. During the 1970s, an electronics industry took shape, and Poland's shipbuilding facilities were enlarged and modernized – all with the help of Western technology and Western capital.

From $741 million in 1970, Poland's hard-currency debt rose to $10.6 billion by 1976 and to $20 billion in 1980. The Western banks, including many from the U.S., were willing to risk their money because they saw Poland as "a dream investment," in one banker's words. Besides having rich resources, particularly coal, the country was willing to pay premium interest rates, higher than those the banks could earn in financially weaker countries like, say, Brazil. Poland also had an excellent record of paying its debts, and some banks regard its credit as being assured by the Soviet "umbrella."

The bankers believed the new industries these loans were creating would generate enough exports to enable Poland to repay its hard-currency borrowings and raise its standard of living with the money left over. Why didn't that happen? One New York banker, whose institution has a modest stake in Poland, explains, "It was a vicious circle. Each company needed something from another industry, and soon there was nothing left for export. Poland has ended up like a less-developed country, selling pork bellies, ham, potatoes, and coal." Poland's financial plight also was aggravated by rising oil prices, a string of bad harvests, and the endemic inefficiency of its bureaucracy. As a result, Poland's borrowings from the West have become a millstone around its neck. According to the Central Intelligence Agency, 92 cents of every dollar of Polish export earnings go to pay interest and principal on Poland's hard-currency debt, and 85 percent of its new borrowings roll over old unpaid debts.

Far from improving Poland's economic prospects, the activities of international banks worsened the plight of the economy. Poland became mired in a "debt trap." The economic distortion and political consequences of the debt were not readily alleviated, and in 1981 contributed to the replacement of a liberal regime with an authoritarian one that enforced severe economic restrictions that reduced Western imports by 40 percent in 1982.

Source: Cameron, "A dream investment," *Fortune* pp. 26-29. © 1980 Time Inc. All rights reserved.

BOX 5. Conversation with an International Financial Consultant

Q. The international financial system has recorded some disturbing moments in the closing months of 1982. The banks seem to be very worried about the level of Third World debt and they are facing some serious losses, aren't they?

A. Not at all. The banks are making a killing off the debt crisis, just as the oil companies did in the 1974 oil crisis.

Q. That seems quite at odds with the public pronouncements and the evidence provided at U.S. congressional hearings. How could that be so?

A. The big banks are using the current opportunity. They're taking the interest payments from the Brazils and Mexicos and writing off capital. They're looking to maximize their stock prices.

Q. How does that work?

A. Well, the stockholders hardly expect them to declare positive earnings in 1983, so they won't. They will use the interest paid to reduce the outstanding debt, recording it as principal instead of interest. Next, when the interest is paid, they'll make money hand over fist, since they will be recording earnings on a lower capital base. In addition, they are making millions in up-front fees for debt renegotiation. That money is paid to the banks by poor debtor countries. For example, say Brazil owes a bank $10 billion at 15 percent interest; that's $1.5 billion. Instead of recording Brazil's payment as interest, which it is, the bank uses it to reduce its Brazil liabilities by $1.5 billion. Next year, when Brazil pays $1.5 billion, that figure is earned on $8.5 billion on the bank's books. That's an 18 percent rate of return and 21 percent for 1985. That will give a big boost to the stock prices. That's all they really care about, their share prices.

Q. What should be done?

A. They should let them go under. Take Chase Manhattan, that's just a Rockefeller outfit. Let them go under like the government did National Bank last year. The depositors wouldn't lose anything – they're protected by the FDIC – just the stockholders. Let them pay for their risky practices.

4

THE WORLD BANK AND
THE THIRD WORLD

INTRODUCTION

The World Bank has the reputation of being the world's preeminent development agency. Without doubt it has provided a financial lifeline between the advanced capitalist countries (ACC) and numerous countries in the Third World. During fiscal year 1983 the World Bank lent $15.3 billion, principally to the developing countries. Since its establishment in 1946, over $60 billion has been loaned: first for the rebuilding of Western Europe, then for long-term projects in the Third World.

A quick glance through the institution's *Annual Report* would tell a story of building infrastructure and institutions, of vast new resources being unlocked. For example, during 1983 the World Bank loaned Thailand $100 million to build roads; China $162 million to modernize its petroleum industry; Egypt $165 million to construct a steel factory; Brazil $68 million to fund rural development, land redistribution, and agricultural research programs; and Rwanda (in Central Africa) $13 million to build potable water systems for 40,000 people.

Although such a catalog of projects is intended to be, and is, impressive, a description of trees, even redwoods, does not necessarily convey a forest. A fuller examination of the bank as a central institution of the present international economic order is needed to understand how individual projects interact to promote or retard social and economic development in the Third World. This chapter discusses how the World Bank works, the sources of its finances, and the nature of its lending policies. The scope and pattern of activities are evaluated by economic function and by region. The evolution of the institution's developmental philosophy and the strategies to implement those goals are measured against the overall impact of World Bank lending on the economies of the Third World. Finally, the role of the World Bank is considered within the present international economic order as well as in relationship to the call for a new international economic order (NIEO).

The Institution

The World Bank is not the only development finance institution. Other, usually more regionally focused, bodies include the IDB (see box 6), the African Development Bank, and the Asian Development Bank. "The Bank" (as its employees call it) is, however, the largest and most influential: it channels most of the developmental assistance targeted for the Third World and specifies how those resources are to be used.

Founded in 1944 at the Bretton Woods Conference and commencing operations in 1946, the World Bank is the sister institution to the IMF. While the IMF lends to countries with essentially short-term, balance-of-payments needs, the World Bank finances long-term development projects that span from 10 to 25 years. The World Bank today comprises three institutions. The IBRD dates from 1946. It is the largest branch and lends to governments for development projects, at near market interest rates. The International Finance Corporation (IFC) was founded in 1954 to provide equity capital for private enterprise. The International Development Association (IDA) was founded in 1960 to provide low-interest loans to the poorest nations. As of June 30, 1983, the World Bank had approved outstanding loans of $69.8 billion to its 144 member nations.

In principle, any country can join the World Bank. The major donors – the United States, the United Kingdom, Japan, West Germany, and France – marshal over 40 percent of the votes and dominate the institution. In effect, they have veto power over membership. However, votes are distributed in proportion to the countries' economic power. *

World Bank Financing

Although it promotes development, the World Bank is primarily a commercial institution, not an aid agency. A profit has been earned in every year since 1948; in fiscal year 1982-83, investments and loans netted $872 million.

---

*Each of the 144 member governments subscribes a specified share of the Bank's capital that is proportional to its power in the world economy. For example, the United States subscribes 88,509 shares and holds 22.61 percent of the IBRD's total votes (its special drawing rights are 39.5 billion, about $43 billion), Brazil holds 10,706 shares and 2.51 percent, and tiny Lesotho holds 43 shares and less than 0.10 percent. About 10 percent of the subscribed capital is actually deposited; the remainder is "callable" money that is provided when and if needed. These reserves are a guarantee for the Bank's creditors and allow the Bank to borrow freely on the world's capital markets – with its (Standard and Poor's) AAA rating, at very favorable rates. Many small banks throughout the United States have invested in World Bank debentures.

BOX 6. The Inter-American Development Bank

Founded in 1959, the IDB, with the mission to mobilize private capital to accelerate the process of economic and social development, serves 27 Latin American and Caribbean member countries. Its funding is derived from a pool of 43 countries including European, Middle Eastern, and Asian nations. Its capital assets as of December 1983 totaled $30.8 billion, and its record of $91 billion in loans between 1959 and 1983 makes it the largest of four regional development banks. (The others are the Asian Development Bank, founded in 1966; the African Development Bank, founded in 1964; and the Caribbean Development Bank, founded in 1970.) The idea behind this first development bank originated in 1889 but was not given form until 1958, when Brazilian president Juscelino Kubitschek proposed its formation to the Organization of American States. It began operation in October 1960 and was given a major boost by the initiation in March 1961 of the Alliance for Progress, a U.S. effort that historians term the U.S. response to the Cuban revolution. The Alliance committed $500 million to the Bank's Social Progress Fund, to meet basic needs for housing, employment, land, health, and education through encouraging national planning and agrarian and tax reform. Into this atmosphere the IDB, with 35 percent of its capital provided by the United States, set about injecting large sums of low-cost capital to accelerate economic and social progress.

The IDB lists three main objectives:

To promote the investment of public and private capital in Latin America for development purposes

To encourage private investment in projects, enterprises, and development activities

To foster greater complementarity of the Latin American economies and growth of their foreign trade.

IDB operations fall mainly into three parts: provision of loans; provision of technical assistance, largely through the Preinvestment Fund for Latin American Integration; and provision of support for regional integration. The IDB lends about two-thirds of its funds at commercial rates and one-third at a special subsidized rate (2–4 percent). At year end 1983, 26.7 percent of the IDB's investments were in the energy sector, 22.2 percent in agriculture, 15.1 percent in industry and mining, 13.1 percent in transportation and communication, and the rest in education and urban development. Major emphasis has been on capital-intensive projects. In recent years it has begun to pay particular attention to the needs of the rural poor by devoting a greater share of resources to rural development. In 1978 it added a program of small-scale credit to groups and individual farmers, entrepreneurs, and craftsmen who fail to qualify for conventional sources of finance.

Critics have argued that the IDB's loans have largely benefited Latin American elites. An extensive case study of its lending in Costa Rica concluded that its activities were in part responsible for the country's increasing trade deficits. According to the study, the IDB promoted policies that reduced tariff protection, permitting foreign multinational investors with superior capitalization and technical advantages to erode national markets. These policies increased the trade deficit and contributed to an unmanageable debt burden. The study concluded that "IDB projects have weakened Costa Rica's economy and lessened the possibility for successful economic development" (DeWitt 1977, p. 126).

The Bank raises the money for its loans by borrowing from private lenders and by tapping the reserves pledged and secured by member governments and their central banks. Because of the size of those reserves, the Bank enjoys a high credit rating and has access to capital at discount rates.* Those savings allow the Bank to subsidize various kinds of loans to its clients.

IBRD loans carry interest rates slightly below market rates. Two factors, however, can negate any savings for the borrower. First, 95 percent of the loans are disbursed in U.S. dollars, deutsche marks, Swiss francs, and Japanese yen, and must be repaid in those currencies. Since currencies "float" in value against each other on the world's capital markets, the debtor assumes the risk of future fluctuations. Second, in 1982 the IBRD began charging variable interest rates, so that the borrower also bears the risk of higher future payments. That risk can extend for a considerable time, since the repayment schedule extends from 13 to 20 years. There is, however, a three-to-five-year grace period prior to the first repayment.

The IFC uses Bank funds, borrowed from the IBRD at floating interest rates, to promote private investment in the Third World. "It uses its own resources to assist investors to assemble the necessary financing, technology and management needed for the establishment of productive enterprises" (World Bank 1982b, p. 17). In 1982 the IFC undertook investments of $612 million, one-third of them syndicated to commercial financial institutions.

The IDA grants noncommercial "credits." These loans have a 50-year maturity, with repayment commencing 10 years after the signing of the agreement. There is no interest charge, although there is a service charge of 0.75 percent per annum and a commitment fee of ·0.50 percent on undisbursed funds.

---

*In fiscal 1982 the Bank borrowed $8.5 billion (65 percent more than in 1981) at an average interest charge of 11.19 percent, well below the prevailing market rate most countries could obtain. Moreover, since borrowing in previous years had cost less and the Bank pays no interest on members' subscribed capital, the average cost of borrowing was 8.15 percent.

Organization and Operating Methods

The World Bank's activities are organized both by project and by region. Project divisions plan for and prepare specific proposals, for example, ensuring that an urban development scheme for Gambia is technically feasible. However, each country also is within a particular regional division, so that each project has two judges. The regional or country economic unit must reconcile each project with the wider perspective of how the Bank views the borrowing nation's total needs and its financial and organizational capabilities.

The World Bank annually prepares a comprehensive survey of each client's economy. This is called a "country economic memorandum." A typical memorandum would analyze recent economic data, often by sector, in the light of pending development issues. The social situation – including public health conditions, literacy and educational levels, and employment – would be contrasted with government policy and commitments, and the solvency of public finances. The nation's current balance-of-payments status would accompany projections of future exports and imports and the government's planned investment program. Often the report will also focus on specific issues or problems that concern the Bank, such as "price distortions." These detailed memoranda provide the background information for Bank decisions on financial and project assistance.

The idea for a specific project may originate with the government or be proposed by a World Bank staff member. Once a specific project seems to fit in with "needs," the emphasis shifts to technical considerations. If, for example, the Bank's data support the government of Indonesia's request for assistance in developing coal mines as a valid priority, the Bank may recommend that consulting engineers be hired through international competitive bidding to prepare detailed project plans. When these plans are complete, the IBRD will send a "mission" (several staff members or consultants) to appraise the project and recommend its acceptance or propose modifications. When agreement between representatives of the Bank and the government is reached on all project specifications, a formal loan agreement is negotiated and then presented to the Bank's board of executive directors for approval.

If the project is approved, Indonesia would then invite international bids for the necessary equipment and design and construction services. Goods and services may be obtained only from countries that are Bank members (although Switzerland is also eligible). In principle, money is released only after receipt of verified project-related expenditures.

THE EVOLUTION OF WORLD BANK POLICY: 1946-80

The history of the World Bank can be divided into four stages. The first, from 1946 to 1955, primarily financed the postwar construction of Europe and Japan. From 1955 to 1968 the Bank continued to emphasize the construction of infrastructure but shifted its lending to developing countries. Then, in 1968, Robert McNamara became president of the Bank when there was a growing need to develop Third World markets to absorb the excess production capacity of the advanced industrial nations. During McNamara's tenure the World Bank expanded and became more bureaucratized. Lending shifted into high gear and new kinds of "social investment" programs were funded. In 1981 McNamara left the Bank and a reappraisal of his policies ensued. Financial discipline and better coordination with the private sector to finance projects assumed greater importance, and Tom Clausen (former president of Bank of America) was selected by President Carter to lead the transition toward a renewed neoconservativism.

In effect, the governing philosophy of the Bank's first two decades equated development with growth. Investments concentrated on building tangible economic infrastructure – such as dams, power plants, roads, ports, and communications networks – rather than people-oriented projects – such as literacy campaigns, vocational schools to upgrade labor skills, and programs to eradicate malaria. Between 1961 and 1965, 76.8 percent of all Bank lending was for electric power and transportation, while only 6 percent supported agricultural development and only 1 percent was allocated for social programs. Until 1958 lending stayed between about $300 and $400 million annually; in the next decade it increased to between $700 and $800 million per year. Credit policy stayed cautious: creditworthiness was measured strictly by the ratio of debt service to exports. In part the caution was due to the reluctance of private lenders and member governments to underwrite social investments (Mason and Asher 1973; Ayers 1983).

The change in World Bank policy that began in the early 1970s under Robert McNamara grew out of three coinciding forces. First, stagflation softened consumer demand in the industrial world and threatened new investment and growth there. Second, burgeoning OPEC surpluses had to be recirculated if the level of industrial production was not to be further depressed. And third, Robert McNamara was a forceful leader who knew how to expand and mold a bureaucracy. One consequence was that annual World Bank lending increased twelvefold, from $935.5 million in fiscal 1968 to $12.4 billion in fiscal 1981 (see Figure 4.1). By the end of 1981, cumulative Bank and IDA lending totaled $92.2 billion, all but $13 billion committed during McNamara's presidency. Meanwhile, staffing had grown by two-thirds, and the Bank had become the world's largest lender of development resources. The sheer volume of loans and the amount processed per capita by project staff ballooned. An assembly-line mentality governed project preparation, and cranking out the greatest possible number of loans in a fiscal year became the norm.

A shift in resource allocation accompanied this expansion. A series of policy papers prepared in the early 1970s indicated that the Bank's "trickle-down" strategy of development was working unevenly. The impressive growth rates

FIGURE 4.1. World Bank Lending, 1973-82 (billions of dollars)

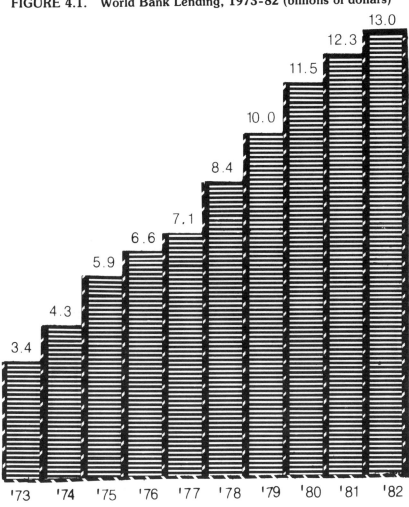

Source: Compiled by author.

in Third World economies were not being translated into improved living standards for the poorest 40 percent of their populations. Subsequently the Bank began to focus on new kinds of projects. This strategy emphasized the rural and urban poor and social sector lending, including education, basic health, family planning, and low-cost housing projects. Agricultural and rural development became priorities, and loans to these sectors in 1981 were four times greater than the total for all fiscal years between 1947 and 1968 (Ayers 1983).

TABLE 4.1.   Sectoral Distribution of IBRD/IDA Commitments (percentages, by fiscal years)

	Through 1963	1964-68	1969-73	1974-78	1981-83
Agricultural and rural development	6	11	20	31	27
Communications	1	3	5	2	2
Education	–	3	5	4	5
Industry*	13	12	14	19	15
Nonproject	17	8	6	5	9
Population and health	–	–	1	1	1
Energy	31	29	18	13	20
Tourism	–	–	1	1	–
Transportation	32	32	26	17	12
Urban development	–	–	–	3	4
Water supply	–	2	4	4	5
Total	100	100	100	100	100

*Includes industrial projects and industrial development financing through development finance companies and other intermediaries.

Source: World Bank.

McNamara's retirement has produced another reappraisal of Bank goals and methods. Shortly after assuming the presidency, Tom Clausen said the Bank "is not the Robin Hood of the international financial set, not a giant global welfare agency." Three major trends are emerging. First, the Bank is striving for credibility among donor countries and is particularly seeking the goodwill of the Reagan administration, which had called for a reorientation of its philosophy. Second, the Bank's rapid and massive expansion during the 1970s led to heavy borrowing to meet new loan commitments. Third, with the mounting Third World debt crisis, several new approaches to cofinancing have been introduced.

Cofinancing

As the burden of Third World debt grows heavier, the probability increases that eventually one or more borrowing governments will default on loan payments rather than impose domestic austerity programs that are too harsh and stir up civil unrest. Consequently, the commercial financial community seeks greater involvement with the World Bank and IMF to secure loans. The World Bank defines cofinancing as

. . . any arrangement whereby funds from the World Bank are associated with funds provided by other sources outside the borrowing country in the financing of a particular project. Funds from other sources may support parts of an overall program of the entity or agency in the sector with which the World Bank project is concerned. These funds are regarded as co-financing if the World Bank has played an active role in promoting or inducing their contribution.

Three main types of partners have been found for cofinancing. First, there are official sources, primarily governments and their agencies, and the multi-lateral financial institutions. A second source has been found in export-credit institutions, usually governmental agencies that finance the procurement of goods and services for export from a particular country. Finally, private financial institutions – primarily commercial banks but also insurance companies, pension funds, and other private sources – have played a role.

Cofinancing by the World Bank and these other institutional partners rose from $496 million in 1973 to over $7.4 billion in 1982, representing 28 percent of 1982 financing. The percentage is expected to increase substantially in future years.

In fact, the World Bank not only has been trying to link new sources of capital for loans but also has searched for internal solutions in domestic economies to ensure that resources are used efficiently. However, the Bank's efforts in the 1970s to redirect resources toward the poor increasingly seemed to run parallel to, rather than converge with, the policies of Third World governments. Some Bank analysts thought that the statist, nonmarket approaches being adopted by governments to redistribute income and protect the poor were fiscally unsound and were undermining many developing economies.

Traditionally, the World Bank has had two levers to shape and promote internal compliance. First, the sheer size of its lending confers authority. In the late 1970s, for example, the IDA financed 13 percent of Bangladesh's domestic investment. When a country is dependent, it is likely at least to listen politely, if not attentively. Of course, the projects that are negotiated with the Bank require more than listening. Clauses stipulate how the project is to be implemented. Although project lending may increase the Bank's power in a specific arena, it seldom translates into influence on broader policy issues.

Structural Adjustment Lending

Starting in 1979, the Bank initiated a policy reform of structural adjustment loans (SAL) to help countries cope with balance-of-payments problems. The loans support a wide variety of activities and were designed to be "quick disbursing," in contrast with project loans, which typically take between one and three years of preparation and negotiation prior to initial disbursement.

Similar in form to IMF stand-by agreements, the SAL provides leverage over a wide range of domestic policies (see Table 4.2). Prior to implementation there is a series of economic policy negotiations between the Bank and the government. Areas in which the Bank seeks to influence a government usually include the following:

1. Pricing policies, including tariff reductions and subsidies to consumers and producers

2. Import liberalization, opening of markets, reduction of tariff barriers, and provision of export incentives and elimination of subsidies to importers

3. Public investment priorities in response to reduced public financial resources and changes in international prices, such as energy prices

4. Budgetary and debt management, including changes in fiscal policy, such as increased user charges for public utilities like water and electricity

5. Balance-of-payments management, including reduction of import controls and tax reductions to promote direct foreign investment.

As of June 1982, 13 of the Bank's 75 active borrowers had concluded SALs. The loans totaled $2.1 billion, and nonproject lending accounted for 9.9 percent of 1983 lending. Providing "a unique opportunity to achieve a more comprehensive and timely approach to policy reforms," the Bank considers the SALs to be "complementary and mutually reinforcing" of IMF standby agreements. A more skeptical observer might wonder if the scale of such intervention is appropriate to promoting "development."

And, more to the point, it is not certain that such "long-term" structural reforms will either work or work in time. In 1983, responding to "crisis conditions," the Bank was forced to complement SALs with a special action program to assist a number of countries that had agreed to take out project loans but could not proceed because they could not raise the necessary domestic counterpart funds. The Bank made quick-disbursing loans for projects that varied from importing fertilizer in Pakistan to funding an export development fund to finance imports of spare parts, packaging materials, and other goods needed by Jamaican exporters to maintain production.

FUNDING THE BOTTOM LINE

In practice, the World Bank is a strange hybrid: both something more and something less than a commercial bank. It makes long-term loans at or near market rates of interest for a wide variety of infrastructural projects, yet it also provides interest-free credits through IDA and pursues a wide range of development-related activities far beyond the scope of a private lender. The

Bank prepares sector policies and research papers that establish an agenda for research in development. Through in-country dialogues it promotes its version of development to the Third World and tries to actively influence national economic policy. The Economic Development Institute and project activities provide technical assistance and the means to train technocrats in developing countries. For example, a World Bank loan helped catapult the Jordan Electricity Authority from a small entity with no project implementation capacity to a sophisticated public utility that could plan and administer a host of new power projects (Ayers 1983).

Since the Bank pursues such a complex and extensive scope of activities in more than 100 countries, it is difficult to determine its effectiveness in promoting development. Moreover, as this chapter has already suggested, "effectiveness" and "development" are slippery terms: at different times the World Bank has focused on building roads, dams, and other infrastructure to raise national output or on building housing, revitalizing agriculture, and providing jobs to improve the quality of life of the urban and rural poor. In addition, it is easy to imagine Bank projects seeming to work at cross-purposes: promoting equitable growth in one country and maintaining a backward and exploitative oligarchy in another. Both possibilities, in fact, can be reconciled with the Bank's overarching goal of modernizing the international economy to preserve its capitalist variant over the long term.

Basically, three main schools of thought have emerged to judge the effectiveness of the Bank. Conservatives, often associated with institutions such as the Heritage Foundation, have charged that its operations have undermined capitalist alternatives in developing countries. The director of the Office of Management and Budget in the Reagan administration has criticized the Bank for supporting state planning in some countries and not being "vigorous in using the leverage inherent in its large lending program to press recipients to redirect their economies toward a market orientation" (David Stockman, quoted in Ayers 1983, p. 12).

Radicals have focused their fire on the Bank's "imperialist" tendencies. These critics believe that the institution reflects the prevailing structure of North-South relations between the developed and developing nations, and is unduly responsive to the dominant forces in the international economy. According to this view, private banks, MNCs, and the U.S. government manipulate the Bank, which, in turn, works hand in hand with governing elites in Third World countries to set a development agenda that ignores the poor (Payer 1973; Hayter 1971). These critics point to IBRD projects, such as industrial export zones, that give the AICs access to the cheap labor and resources of the Third World. Moreover, the Bank's international procurement system for projects favors enterprises from industrial countries. These sales contracts for equipment and construction services not only are lucrative but also enhance Third World market penetration by the MNCs.

TABLE 4.2. Key Components of Structural Adjustment Operations: February 1, 1980–June 30, 1981

	Senegal	Turkey[1]	Guyana	Kenya	Bolivia	Philippines	Mauritius	Malawi
Trade policy								
Exchange rate policy		x			x			
Tariff reform and import liberalization	x	x						
Export incentives	x	x		x		x	x	x
Improved institutional support for exporters (export insurance and financing, export promotion institutions)		x	x	x		x	x	x
Specific programs for major export or import saving sectors	x		x	x	x	x	x	x
Sector policies								
Energy:								
Pricing policy		x	x		x		x	x
Conservation measures		x	x					
Development of indigenous sources		x	x				x	x
Agriculture:								
Pricing policy	x	x	x		x			
Improved institutional support (marketing, etc.)	x	x					x	x

72

Industry:

Incentive system		X	X			X
Institutional improvements and subsector programs		X	X			X

Public investment program

Revision and review of sectoral priorities	X	X	X	X	X	X
Strengthening of institutional capacity to formulate and implement public investment program	X		X			X

Public sector enterprises

Financial performance	X	X	X	X		X
Institutional efficiency	X	X		X		X

Resource mobilization

Budget policy	X	X	X	X		X
Interest rate policy	X	X	X			X

Debt management

Strengthening of institutional capacity to manage external borrowing		X	X	X	X	X

[1] Includes two structural adjustment loans to Turkey.
Source: World Bank.

Finally, there is a conciliatory viewpoint that supports the general thrust of Bank activities. (Probably most of the staff at the Bank would subscribe to this position.) It argues that the institution has resources that can be used, and are used, to encourage governments to promote socioeconomic development that is equitable. If land reform, rural development, and judicious technical specifications do not always achieve their desired effects, that is because the World Bank is not omnipotent and must work within prescribed limits. Governments can, and do, ignore the Bank's representations.

Clearly, each of these three positions contains elements of truth. We shall seek to expand and review some of the main pros and cons.

Redefining the Market

Although some development projects may be vital, they do not fit the criteria that would make them candidates for private financing. For example, a bauxite-mining/hydroelectric complex was proposed in West Africa but seemed impractical because of the high incidence of malaria. Feeling that malaria control is a "public good," private investors refused to underwrite a disease-prevention program because benefits would extend to payers and non-payers alike – and beneficiaries should be willing to personally pay the costs. The World Bank saw the long-term rather than the short-term gains, and financed the project.

Similarly, private businesses or investors are often unwilling to undertake infrastructure projects, such as building rural roads, electric systems, or public schools, because the start-up costs are high and the rate of return is low. On the other hand, the long-term social and economic benefits of such investments can be enormous.

The World Bank is able to tolerate the divergences between the social benefits and private costs that are due to external economies, understanding that improvement in infrastructure can lead to the formation/expansion of new private investment opportunities by increasing the size of markets and thereby allowing domestic producers to take advantage of latent economies of scale (U.S. Treasury 1982).

Promoting the Free Market

The World Bank also tries to correct internal market imperfections in borrowing countries. For example, managerial advice is given to borrowing countries to foster more efficient resource mobilization. The World Bank encourages countries to adopt open trading policies that promote export industries while reducing import barriers that foster uncompetitive import substitution.

Sometimes the advocacy of free markets has an ideological dimension. Since the mid 1970s, the World Bank has invested heavily in agricultural development. In addition to reaching and improving the lives of larger numbers of the poor more directly, these programs have been justified as a way to extend, develop, and promote free markets. Technical assistance not only helps small farmers produce and sell cash crops, but also creates a climate that encourages peasants to align themselves "with the private market-oriented forces which exist elsewhere in the economy."

Sometimes the Bank's penchant for using private-sector remedies and prices to resolve the ills of the poor can be counterproductive. Critics have argued that the Bank has an ideological and institutional blind spot that ignores the effectiveness of public ownership in delivering services such as electricity and health services. A U.S. Treasury report shows that 67 percent of IBRD/IDA lending in 1980 was "to support private sector activities which would be in the public sector in the United States," while "only 8 percent of lending supported public sector activities which would clearly have been undertaken by the private sector in the U.S." (U.S. Treasury 1982, pp. 161–62). The U.S. Treasury report further points out that a study of World Bank country reports undertaken by the House Committee on Appropriations found that the Bank's analysis and recommendations generally follow "neoclassical economic lines . . . [emphasizing] the need for open international trading systems, and the use of world market prices to reflect real opportunity costs" (1982, p. 162).

Providing Access to Capital Markets

The World Bank also provides services that reduce the risks to private lenders of Third World borrowing and thus increase the inflow of capital from private financial markets.

Collecting information or intelligence about the numerous countries that are members of the Bank is costly. No private bank could afford such an enterprise, and in the absence of vital data, few lenders would finance industrial development, much less the building of infrastructure. The World Bank coordinates with the IMF to gather and disseminate information, often granting a stamp of approval that can catalyze private investment. That certification can extend to cofinancing arrangements that permit private banks to control their risk, providing World Bank experts for project appraisal and administration free of charge and virtually guaranteeing loan repayment. A default against the World Bank would be regarded as default against the nations that are the Bank's shareholders, including most of the major economic powers.

Countercyclical Financing

The World Bank and other multilateral financial agencies also can cushion the downside of cyclical lending by private banks. During the 1970s, when prices for Third World commodity exports soared, loans from private banks were easily negotiated and borrowing rose rapidly. As prices deteriorated and balance-of-payments needs rose in 1982, new bank lending contracted from

$10.4 billion in the third quarter of 1981 to $8.0 billion in the third quarter of 1982 (*New York Times* 1982). The effect could be devastating, causing steep declines in GNP and aggravating social pressures. Development banks can stem the panic by becoming the effective international lenders of last resort. Of course, this depends on access to sufficient resources. (This will be discussed further, but for now it should be noted that the World Bank gearing ratio of loans to current total assets is only 1:1, and sharply limits lending capacity.)

Influence on Policy Management of Borrowing Nations

The World Bank has several ways to influence internal policy reforms in a borrowing nation that can extend the long-term benefits of a loan beyond the immediate project being funded. These instruments are policy dialogue, the economic reports and memoranda that are distributed to private lenders and the ongoing series of project reviews to ensure compliance with loan agreements, the size and composition of the project approved, and the formation of interagency and intergovernmental consultative groups to increase the pressure. The policy dialogue typically begins with informal discussions during a Bank mission to a country that has expressed interest in taking out a loan. The conversations may include government technocrats, elected representatives, academics, and leaders of the political opposition. The Bank representative points out possible policy impediments, which are frequently related to high tariff barriers or other economic distortions. The Bank's position is then formalized in written reports that are forwarded to the borrowing government. If those views are accepted, they become the basis for policy. If they are not, financing for the project or the composition of the proposed total lending package – especially if it includes a nonproject SAL – may be reduced. Alternatively, the Bank may seek to bring in other donors or creditors to back its views through a solid front of interagency or intergovernmental representatives. *

---

* "The Bank's relations with Brazil, its third largest borrower as of June 30, 1971, have been very warm, very cold, and tepid. Until 1952 Brazil was considered a thoroughly promising candidate for Bank lending. Then certain policies followed by the Brazilian government were considered by the Bank to jeopardize Brazil's creditworthiness. The Bank tried to use the leverage of its proposed loans to modify those policies, but this led to an estrangement with the Brazilian government. Lending declined in 1953 and 1954, and was nil in 1955-57. It was substantial, however, in 1958. From 1959 to 1965 inflation was rampant in Brazil, and between June 1959 and February 1965 the Bank made no loans.

The fall of the nonaligned Goulart government in March 1964, [and its replacement by a pro-U.S. military government] however, marked the beginning of another change in policy. With inflation gradually being brought under control and the Bank becoming more confident of Brazil's ability to manage its balance of payments, the period since February 1965 has seen a rising trend in Bank lending and a considerable increase in the influence of the Bank on Brazilian development policy, particularly in the power, transport, and agricultural sectors. (Mason and Asher 1971)

Economic Efficiency of World Bank Loans

If the Bank is going to champion internal policy reforms by borrowers, its own track record has to withstand scrutiny. The method used by the Bank in auditing its own performance is based upon the internal rate of return (IRR). This is a measure of the estimated impact of a project on the economy. The IRR is the discount (interest) rate that equalizes the present value of costs and benefits over the life of a project. In general, the higher the IRR, the more profitable the project. A study of 121 World Bank projects that were approved between 1970 and 1974 indicated that their initial IRR of 20 percent had remained unchanged following the calculation of actual costs and benefits after project completion (U.S. Treasury 1982, p. 20). This is considered to be a respectable return on invested capital.

The World Bank and the Poor

There is, however, another way to look at "efficiency." Dudley Seers once suggested that to measure the effectiveness of development programs, one has to ask how the incidence of poverty, the levels of employment, and income distribution have changed. In the mid-1970s Brazil became a focal point in a debate about the effect of World Bank lending on the poor. Several studies found that income concentration was worsening in the Third World and that the standard of living of the poor was declining despite an increase in per capita incomes (Girling 1973). For example, in Brazil the share of total income received by the upper 5 percent of the population increased from 29 percent in 1960 to 38 percent in 1970 (Fishlow 1972). Realizing that poverty was not retreating, the World Bank formulated a new strategy for "growth with equity." This, in turn, led to a shift in resources away from transportation, industry, and tourism, and toward rural development. The U.S. House Committee on Appropriations in 1978 tried to evaluate the effectiveness of the Bank's new efforts to assist the poor (U.S. Library of Congress 1978). Its report concluded that by 1977, 23 percent of Bank lending was for projects directed at the poor, compared with 4 percent in 1972. Nevertheless, hard data did not exist to demonstrate whether the poor benefited. Skeptics continued to ask why only 23 percent of all project lending was poverty-oriented. However, the evidence suggested that the Bank was redesigning and redirecting its projects to the poor. (See Box 7.)

BOX 7. Banking on Poverty

In late 1982 the Bank prepared a summary of its efforts to reduce poverty (World Bank 1982c). The report attributed the success of reaching 120 million poor people to a shift to rural development lending:

The Bank's lending for agriculture and rural development projects has increased dramatically, from $2.2 billion (19 per cent) in FY70–73 to more than $13.2 billion or 31 per cent of total Bank/IDA lending in FY78-81. A rising share of this total supported the poorest countries, and there has been greater emphasis on crops most likely to be grown or eaten by the poor.

OED audits also found that average rates of return in poverty-oriented rural development projects – i.e., those expected to provide at least half their benefits to the rural poor – were at least as good as those on other agricultural projects. Small farmers appear to obtain higher returns on investment, and to show a smaller ratio of defaults to loans. Bank projects are also effective in reaching large numbers of small farmers. For instance, small farmer projects audited in 1979 were found to have reached 660 farmers for every $1 million loaned (at a cost of $1,500 per farmer), compared with 47 farmers per $1 million (at $21,000 per farmer) in other agricultural projects. While these data cover a wide range of individual results, the emphasis on small farmers has seldom conflicted with economic and financial efficiency. . . .

Overall, the Bank's poverty strategy in the 1970s produced efficient projects that have reached the poor both directly and through some local replication; the nature of the policy dialogue has shifted in some countries; and experience gained through learning by doing has resulted in improvements in development programs. Despite political and other country-specific constraints, the Bank has often succeeded in introducing improved management methods into the solution of difficult economic and social problems. Bank projects have pioneered new approaches and institutions through which millions of poor people have been reached. In some countries the incidence of poverty fell sharply in the 1970s, and poverty alleviation policies, including the Bank's, can take some of the credit.

But massive poverty persists. Further improvements in our approach based on the lessons of the past are needed, especially because the difficult circumstances of the 1980s present the poor with greater problems and increased risks. (World Bank 1982c)

The report concludes on a cautionary note, suggesting that the difficulties of reaching the poor within the context of the present international economic order will remain difficult, if not elusive.

It has proved extremely difficult to benefit the very poorest groups who lack productive assets. These include most of the developing countries' rural landless, urban jobless, adult illiterates, and female-headed households. In addition to continued support for rural development, education, population and health programs, the Bank should intensify its efforts to understand how the productivity and employment of such people can be increased, including further experiments in designing projects that benefit the poorest families.

Better analysis of the social environment of a project, assessment of its likely social impact, and well-designed technical assistance are important to lasting and successful development activities. Projects are more likely to benefit the poor to the extent that they improve administration and management, and build a strong institutional base that will endure after the project is completed.

Source: World Bank.

In 1984, less than half a decade later, it is possible to wonder how long that trend can continue. Although world poverty shows no signs of diminishing and may even be growing, the lending programs of the 1970s come due in the 1980s. Even heavily subsidized loans may be difficult to repay, since many Third World economies are already sagging under the weight of the debt they have accumulated to finance their balance-of-payments deficits. Moreover, Third World critics maintain that doubts about the Bank's ability to achieve its self-defined goals need to be placed in a broader perspective to be understood.

Does the World Bank Accommodate Alternative Economic Models?

Some critics argue that the Bank attempts to prevent the emergence of radical regimes or helps subvert them financially so that they may be overthrown (Hayter 1971). As evidence they cite the halt in Bank lending to Brazil (1959-64), to Chile (1979-83), and to Indochina (1975-77) (U.S. Treasury 1982; Mason and Asher 1973). In each a social democratic or socialist government was in power when lending dried up.

The Bank's defenders retort that the cessation of new loans to those countries occurred because their governments pursued recklessly inflationary economic policies, not because of a clash over political ideologies. The articles of agreement that govern the IBRD prohibit the Bank from using ideology to deny loans to a country if its finances are sound. In fact, the Bank has several times been in the uncomfortable position of having to reduce its lending to newly democratic governments because of their unsound fiscal, monetary, or foreign-exchange policies while raising its financing to military regimes that could enforce national austerity programs (Mason and Asher 1971, p. 478).

Moreover, during the 1970s and early 1980s several socialist countries joined the World Bank. The institution's staff is exposed more frequently to socialist methods of economic management. Although the Bank continues to advise and encourage these countries to use market solutions to problems, a more diverse membership may broaden the debate within the organization about what development paths are permissible and about what actually works (see Knight 1983).

U.S. Influence over World Bank Policy

Instead of being soothed by official reassurances of Bank impartiality, Third World critics point out that the institution has been particularly subject to U.S. pressures on lending policy. At least one U.S. congressman proudly agrees, calling the World Bank and its affiliates "the major multilateral vehicle for expression of American interest in the Third World" (Lewis 1981). Of course, others express concern about the Bank's adherence to policies for ideological reasons. The Committee on Banking, Finance, and Urban Affairs of the U.S. House of Representatives cautioned:

> It is potentially counterproductive for the United States Government to publicly urge the MDBs [multilateral development banks] to press countries to adopt particular economic policies, especially if such policies are seen as being strongly ideological. If the MDBs are viewed as politically biased and as merely an extension of U.S. foreign policy, their effectiveness will be diminished. (1982, p. 30)

The perceptions of opportunity and danger in influencing Bank policies rest on the incontestable reality that U.S. contributions account for a large part of the Bank's financial base. The Reagan administration's reluctance to provide the additional funding the Carter administration had pledged underscores the U.S. willingness to apply pressure. Following the change in U.S. and World Bank administrations, Mahbub ul-Haq resigned as the Bank's vice-president for policy planning. The press reported that he was "convinced that he [could] do nothing in Clausen's new World Bank, subservient as it is to the hardliners in the U.S. administration. The impact of right-wing economics is . . . destroying all that the Bank achieved in the McNamara years" (quoted in Ayers 1983, p. 230).

There is also evidence of U.S. pressure that seems unimpeachable. In order to gauge the degree of U.S. influence, the Treasury subjected recent policy decisions to an empirical investigation. Seventy issues were identified over the previous ten years as cases in which "the United States had pursued a specific objective by seeking to change MDB policy, practice, or procedure" (U.S. Treasury 1982, p. 60). The most significant of these issues were then selected and classified as successes, partial successes, or failures. In about 85 percent of the cases, the United States was successful or partially successful because it used its financial leverage. The few examples of failure or partial success – such as promoting human rights – were largely blamed on the poorly defined and vacillating manner of employing available resources: the United States simultaneously continued bilateral aid while opposing MDB loans, creating the impression that its policy lacked coherence. Among the "successes" were halting lending to Chile, blocking PLO observers from IBRD and IMF annual meetings (1979–81), halting the World Bank energy affiliate, and resuming concessional lending to Indonesia, Thailand, and the Philippines.

Does the World Bank Promote Unnecessary Projects?

If the World Bank has sometimes caved in to U.S. foreign policy priorities and withheld financing, those exceptions stand out because the general tide sweeps in the other direction. Banks are in business to lend money. Their earnings are related to the volume of loans placed and the "spread" between the banks' costs of obtaining funds and the interest rates they charge clients. The IBRD is also in business to earn money. Although its profits are not distributed to shareholders, they are used to pay salaries and overhead and to fund the IDA. Moreover, the IBRD's role and prestige are enhanced by the size of its lending, and that is true for each department within the Bank. Consequently there is great pressure to expand lending and to measure job performance by rapid loan processing.

Informal documentation indicates that country quotas are targeted. For example, the lending goal for Brazil during fiscal 1983 may be set at $2 billion. The IBRD derives its quota by estimating a client's balance-of-payments shortfall, then subtracting likely private investments and private-sector loans. The difference between financing needs and "likely" resource availabilities is then parceled out among the World Bank, the IMF, and the IDB. The U.S. Treasury report notes: "The close correspondence between actual and proposed IBRD levels in recent years tends to corroborate the anecdotal evidence cited in *Forbes* and elsewhere that the World Bank has, as a matter of policy, emphasized achievement of specific lending targets" (1982, p. 172).

This quantitative approach, which was promoted by Robert McNamara, can place enormous pressure on loan officers, who become desperate to find projects toward the end of the fiscal year. During the late 1970s the number of poor-quality loans – those "with moderate problems" of implementation – increased (U.S. Treasury 1982, p. 172). Critics say that, at best, this demonstrates inadequate and hasty evaluation by loan officers or, at worst, indicates a willingness to "hard sell" projects to unenthusiastic borrowers. It certainly supports the view that the Bank lends beyond the absorptive capacity of nations.

A 1983 study of MDB project implementation in the Caribbean supports that conclusion and extends it to other lenders. Sixty percent of IBRD projects were experiencing problems severe enough to threaten project completion. In the Dominican Republic alone, only 10 percent of World Bank projects – which totaled some $235 million – were problem-free. The major stumbling blocks were slow disbursement of loan money and a lack of management capacity. These problems were closely related: the Dominican government was heavily overcommitted and could not spend the money made available to it by the World Bank and other lending agencies. The 15 key projects (of a list of 80) were an average of nearly two years behind schedule. Thus, more money was being pushed into the country than it could possibly handle, which led to poor project selection. One stark indication of borrowed resources being wasted was a $125 million dam that was financed by the IDB; it was built on a river that was dry much of the year.

Is the World Bank Predisposed Against the New International Economic Order?

Many responsible advocates in the Third World hope that the program of the New International Economic Order (NIEO) can resolve the chronic problems of poverty, unemployment, and production (see chapter 11 for a detailed discussion). The topic of the NIEO, despite widespread discussion in much of the literature on economic development and the fact that it was the focus of the influential Brandt (North-South) Report, meets stony silence at the Bank. In fact, a comprehensive (though by no means exhaustive) reading of World Bank literature revealed only one substantive reference to the NIEO (in a July 1981 working paper, *The Political Structure of the New Protectionism,* prepared by a consultant). Although one should not expect the Bank to be amenable to proposals that undermine its raison d'être, it is disturbing to find an unawareness of the NIEO as a legitimate attempt by the Third World to articulate the development agenda.

REDIRECTING WORLD BANK POLICY

No one doubts that the problems of developing countries – indeed, of the present international economy – are severe, and often intractable. Those difficulties transcend present policies, and a willful blindness or deafness to new approaches will not make them go away. The World Bank can play its part in the dialogue that is emerging between the advanced industrial and the developing nations by exploring new alternatives.

First and foremost, the Bank should be more disinterestedly analytical rather than reciting a litany of blanket prescriptions for economic development by rote. For instance, the Bank's "free-trade theology" – a term coined by cynical Bank staff members – should be replaced by a more objective and diverse appraisal of economic prospects and by recommendations that improve trade but respect the need of Third World governments to protect fledgling domestic industries. Economic difficulties stem not only from poor government policies but also from inequities – including trade barriers to Third World goods in the advanced industrial countries – in international markets (see chapters 7 and 8). The Bank might even advocate reforms similar to the EEC's in its Lomé Convention, which gives preference to Third World exports. Trade liberalization could then be weighed not as a cornerstone of development but as a policy appropriate in some circumstances and inappropriate in others. Other development strategies, including import substitution, targeted industrial protection, and countertrade, would be analyzed for comparative advantage. That would also mean reassigning research funds to study and test proposals of particular importance to developing countries – such as the design of efficient but fair commodity stabilization schemes. A World Bank primarily motivated by the development issues facing its members could weigh funding needs more impartially. Loans to countries would not depend on noneconomic ideological grounds. In fact, the Bank might test new theories by providing extra technical assistance to countries exploring new approaches to development.

Second, the question of who bears the costs of development needs to be addressed. The Bank at present badgers governments to use free-market solutions to correct economic distortions. Tax reform should be an equal priority. Currently the rich in many developing countries largely escape taxation and even contribute to low domestic savings rates by depositing their liquid wealth in private overseas banks. Consequently potential government resources are drained, and that contributes to the need to borrow foreign capital. If more of this hidden pool of wealth could be tapped, Bank policies – particularly under SALs – that emphasize raising the prices of government services, cutting back on public services, and abandoning price controls on essential consumer goods (such as food and housing) might not be necessary. At least the burden of austerity borne by the poor could be lightened.

In fact, the supply-side economics advocated by the Bank may be entirely inappropriate for some nations facing complex problems that have their own unique histories. Thus, the Subcommittee on International Development Institutions of the U.S. House of Representatives affirmed:

> The Subcommittee recognizes the inability of the free market to perform certain functions, and believes that the United States should be willing to examine solutions to development problems which may combine public and private sector ownership and decisionmaking. Ideological underpinnings should not prejudice MDB appraisal of policies in borrowing countries. (U.S. House of Representatives, Committee on Banking, Finance and Urban Affairs 1982)

Third, the World Bank must realize that many of its projects are too large, and should be scaled down to appropriate levels. With its emphasis on meeting lending quotas, the Bank has overlooked implementational capacity. In some cases the Bank requires countries to assume administrative functions that the Bank is incapable of meeting (for example, the demand for nations to establish effective project-monitoring systems that the Bank itself lacks). The Bank claims that working on a smaller scale is uneconomical because such projects require a heavy expenditure of expensive staff time.

In any event, the Bank should provide more technical assistance for project management. There is a clear lack of managerial expertise in the Third World, and projects that must pay for themselves quickly rarely have the capital to invest in refinements that promise long-term payoffs. These are the kinds of investments the Bank is in an advantageous position to make. Its 1983 *World Development Report* made a start at addressing this issue. While there is still a rather excessive emphasis on price distortion and "getting prices right" as the sine qua non of development policy, the new-found attention to management – not only of projects but also of state-owned enterprises – is laudable.

Finally, debt relief should not be considered a pariah. Since the Bank is one of the principal creditors and is dependent upon private banks for its own capital, it is reluctant to examine the issue objectively. The Bank is also, however, an intermediary institution, ideally placed to analyze potential solutions and offer valuable recommendations to the world community. Unfortunately, up to now its record is spotty. First, the Bank claimed there was no problem; then it began looking at the debt burden from the point of view of its wealthiest donors. The Brandt Commission has strongly recommended that the developing nations receive a greater voice and more power within the Bank. That may be a precondition for any objective examination of various schemes of debt moratorium or any other proposed reform.

BOX 8.   SAL Case Study: Jamaica

A proposed structural adjustment loan with Jamaica that was negotiated in 1982 indicates the degree of detailed action to which the government of Jamaica had to agree to prior to approval of bank lending.

The Jamaican SAL covers a number of areas and issues. A principal weakness identified by the Bank centered on savings and investment. The Bank believed it was structurally desirable to increase current savings of major public enterprises and proposed price hikes for public services, such as water and electricity. Prior to the release of any SAL funds, eight specified public enterprises would have to present detailed programs for increasing their prices. A second concern was management of the balance-of-payments deficits that resulted from inefficiencies in allocating foreign exchange. The government was asked to eliminate the licensing system that had been instituted under the previous Social Democratic government to ensure that incoming foreign exchange was used for development. The SAL program also reemphasized private capital. The government was asked to set up a new national investment promotion corporation and establish bilateral business coordinating groups, a condition set forth in an IMF extended-fund-facility (EFF) loan to the Jamaican government. Furthermore, a free trade zone had to be created to stimulate exports and quantitative restrictions on imports had to be eliminated prior to Bank lending for industrial credit. In all, a 15-point program with detailed annotations was laid down as a precondition for obtaining the SAL.

BOX 9. Indonesia vs The World Bank

A major controversy arose between the Bank and the conservative government of Indonesia in 1981 over a 600-page economic report on the Indonesian economy. The report called for reduced controls over economic activity and for reform of government procedures that favored businesses in bidding for contracts with state-managed enterprises. Such protectionism runs against the developmental philosophy of the Bank's principal donors (although the AICs often discriminate against imports from each other and, particularly, the Third World). The document suggested that Indonesia should establish a "deregulation commission . . . to disentangle" current licensing and investment procedures and shift toward a more "outward looking trade policy." Finally, the Bank demanded that prices determined by the market should replace administrative measures to allocate financial resources even if prior interventions were intended to promote social equity.

The Indonesian government viewed the document as a "capitalist diatribe" against its economic system that profoundly disregarded social and political realities. One minister remarked, "It is based on a misconceived proposition. If all you are interested in is growth, then okay. But we are interested in social development, too. . . . We do not like their attitude or their analysis." For a while stalemate ensued. The Bank continued to insist that economic efficiency and the attainment of Indonesia's comparative trading advantage demanded elimination of controls that were common in the countries of the Organization for Economic Cooperation and Development (OECD). The Indonesians were equally persistent in defending those controls as essential for balanced growth and thriving domestic enterprises.

Apparently the Bank's arguments were persuasive. In its 1982 *Annual Report*, it reported the following: "To encourage exports, measures were . . . initiated that will have the effect of strengthening export capacity in the long term and promoting structural adjustments." Indonesia was listed as the Bank's second largest customer, with loans of $926 million.

A World Bank-financed project in India employs large numbers of skilled and unskilled workers to line the Rajasthan irrigation canal. This project, financed with an $83 million credit from IDA, was to develop 200,000 hectares of irrigated land.

Source: Ray Witlin for World Bank, Reproduced with permission.

5

THE INTERNATIONAL MONETARY FUND: A THIRD WORLD CRITIQUE

The IMF is the principal institution for promotion of international cooperation on issues of money and finance. One of its major tasks is to provide short-term, low-cost loans from a managed pool of the world's currencies to nations that are experiencing balance-of-payments deficits. During the 1970s and early 1980s, an increasing number of Third World nations, affected by the slowdown in the world economy, failed to earn enough foreign exchange from their exports to pay for their imports, and the IMF was pushed out of the wings and onto center stage.

Nevertheless, the IMF is not popular, particularly among the developing nations. When loans exceed a limited initial level, the IMF often requires a "stabilization program" that details precisely how the borrowing nation should manage its economy. This is known as "conditionality." An IMF stabilization program usually involves trade liberalization and deflation of the domestic economy. Workers and the poor are hardest hit by austerity, and when the economic and social costs are severe enough, they can undermine the government. These sacrifices can seem bitterly ironic, since several studies have demonstrated that stabilization programs offer no certain success and can even aggravate the debt. Meanwhile, critics from the Third World are convinced that the IMF, which is largely controlled by the United States and the Western European nations, is unfair. These observers argue that the IMF may act to protect and safeguard the world economy, but it uses methods that favor the private international banks and the ACCs. Those charges are not without foundation, since they have obvious historical roots.

After all, the IMF was formed by the United States and the major European nations through the Bretton Woods Agreement, signed near the close of World War II, to accomplish a specific mission. The institution was created to forestall a destructive spiral of competitive devaluations and trade restrictions like the one that had deepened and prolonged the Great Depression among the industrialized capitalist economies. Article I of the Constitutional Agreement, which established the IMF, stated that its broad objectives were the following:

> To facilitate the expansion and balanced growth of international trade, and to contribute thereby to the promotion and maintenance of high levels of employment and real income and to the development of the productive resources of all members as primary objectives of economic policy.
>
> To give confidence to members by making the general resources of the Fund temporarily available to them under adequate safeguards, thus providing them with the opportunity to correct maladjustments in their balance of payments without resorting to measures destructive of national or international prosperity.

Some 30 nations joined the fund in 1944 and pledged to support those objectives. By the beginning of 1983, the IMF had 146 members; Hungary was the most recent and Poland's application was pending. The growth in membership and the inclusion of socialist economies mirrors the profound transformations that have occurred in the international economy. The IMF has remained – sometimes passively, other times actively – at the center of efforts to ensure that the world monetary system keeps pace with those changes. Although the institution has not yet buckled, it is faced with mounting pressure.

> At the opening of the 1980s, the U.S. Treasury referred to the IMF as: ". . . the principal source of official balance of payment financing; . . . its resources are available to help member countries implement adjustment programs that will enable the borrower to bring its payments position into line with sustainable capital flows." (National Advisory Council 1981, p. 27)

This description seems bland until it is placed in the context of the avalanche of debt sweeping the developing countries. The IMF has become the often unwilling leader of efforts to uncover the rubble, the lender of last resort to Third World governments. As a "financial taskmaster," the IMF demands policy changes in exchange for its loans. Those agreements are a "seal of approval" that Third World governments can then use to reassure private banks. The IMF has even been known to twist the arms of private banks reluctant to continue lending to debt-ridden Third World governments.

Although the IMF has averted default by the major debtors, its policies thus far are a holding action. The long-term consequences of temporary measures are still unclear. In order to understand the actual as well as potential effects upon the Third World, the institution, its methods, and its policies need closer analysis. This chapter will begin with a description of the institution and move on to a critical evaluation of its performance.

IMF STRUCTURE AND OPERATION

Structure and Objectives

In order to foster economic growth and prevent a recurrence of the Great Depression, the IMF was set up to administer a mutual payments system to facilitate the international transfer of funds and promote trade. Perhaps the best-known activity of the fund is its role in cushioning the impact of both temporary and chronic balance-of-payments deficits. The Fund seeks to prevent nations with trade imbalances from imposing tariffs that could set off an international trade war. In effect, the IMF buys time for member countries to sort out their imbalances by providing low-cost, short-term loans from a common pool of currencies. The Fund uses its resources to try to reduce and smooth out both the duration and the magnitude of imbalances in payments between nations, since large and enduring payments imbalances can provoke painful and abrupt adjustments – such as drastic reductions in imports or expensive financing – that could undermine the world trading system.

The Fund has several tools to accomplish its mission. It provides each member nation with a "credit tranche," a specified quota of capital that can be borrowed at nominal cost to correct any international payments imbalances. (Currently members may draw on their quotas at a cost of under 1 percent.) The Fund also provides a forum where member nations can consult and collaborate to develop international monetary policy. The IMF consults routinely with each country about its national economic policies. It also acts as a financial broker, buying currencies from industrialized creditors and then reselling them to the treasuries and central banks of debtor member countries.

The IMF makes its loans from its Common Fund. Each member country deposits a quota of its currency into the Common Fund when it joins. In effect, debtor members pledge all or part of this quota when they borrow from the IMF's reserve of stronger currencies. Normally the repayment schedule is one to five years, but a welter of criticism from the Third World resulted in the new EFF and stretched credit maturities under exceptional circumstances to as much as ten years. In 1981–82 "drawings," the term for these loans, were normally available at interest rates that ranged between 1 and 7 percent, depending on the amount borrowed. (The Fund charges users 0.50 percent for use of the reserve tranche, 0.25 percent for a commitment fee on undrawn amounts of standby and extended borrowings, and 6.25 percent for debt above the ceiling defined by the quota of the member country's currency on deposit.) The IMF controls a pool of gold, currencies, and (as of January 31, 1981) credit worth $171.1 billion. Outstanding loans in 1982 totaled $15 billion.

The IMF and its advocates contend that the institution has been a vital buffer. Otherwise, countries would be forced to rely solely upon bilateral negotiations with their creditor nations and upon the private banking system for this type of finance. As prewar history amply demonstrates, such an ad hoc system is inadequate for providing the level of financing required. Furthermore, the IMF's services provide a carrot (or a stick, when the IMF refuses to assist) to entice debtors away from trade restrictions and currency-exchange controls. Of course, that is under normal conditions. The recent magnitude of debt makes trade restrictions and controls more appealing to beleaguered Third World economies, since those strategies are often more direct and effective. Those governments are also becoming more suspicious of IMF motives. One writer has described the Fund as "a mechanism for rich nations to organize coopera- tive action in their dealings with less developed countries" in a world no longer structured by colonial relations (Gisselquist 1981).

How the IMF Lends: The Case of Jamaica

In August 1972 Jamaica was experiencing balance-of-payments difficulties. Imports exceeded exports by $197 million, and this was the ninth successive annual trade deficit. Moreover, inflows of capital for investment, which had peaked in 1970 during installation of aluminum processing facilities, declined by one-third. Consequently, the reserves of foreign exchange that Jamaica had set aside from years when there was a balance surplus and had used to finance new imports, declined by one-third even though the overall volume of trade was growing. Jamaica turned to the IMF and borrowed $16 million from its reserve tranche. This borrowing was automatic and unconditional, requiring a simple assertion of need that was supported by an obvious deficit in the balance of payments. That is, Jamaica did not have to devalue its currency or undertake any specific adjustment in economic policy. The government merely had to tell the IMF that it would take corrective measures. Although the cur- rency was devalued in January 1973, Jamaica's leaders used the loans to main- tain the new exchange rate until April 1977, thereby holding down the prices of imported food and other staples to prevent undue hardship for the poor.

By the end of 1976, following the OPEC oil price increase and continued deficits in the balance-of-payments current account, Jamaica's foreign reserves and its access to commercial bank credit were virtually exhausted. The balance- of-payments crisis was exacerbated by multinational aluminum companies, which were trying to restrict Jamaica's bauxite and alumina exports to pressure the country to stop its promotion of an International Bauxite Association to set higher prices for these commodities. This crisis was also due to the high pro- pensity to import spare parts and other supplies that was built into Jamaica's industrialization strategy. With little room to maneuver, Jamaica approached the IMF for a loan of $75 million. Since this amount exceeded the country's reserve tranche allotment, Jamaica had to agree to a "high conditionality" stand- by credit that was accompanied by a specific set of measures that the govern- ment would undertake in order to reduce the deficit.

Jamaica agreed to restrict its deficit bank financing, to repay its arrears to foreign creditors, and to restrain wages. A year later, with no economic improvement (in part due to inadequate funding in 1977), Jamaica returned to the Fund for additional financing. The IMF then agreed to make a loan of SDR200 million (about U.S.$220 million) available through the EFF. In return, Jamaica had to implement a 30 percent currency devaluation; income and price policies to reduce wages and increase profits; a shift in resources from the public to the private sector; a policy change from administered controls of foreign-exchange allocation to market forces; the removal of import controls, trade restrictions, and multiple exchange rates; and repayment of arrears on amortization of private sector debt (Sharpley 1981).

Types of IMF Lending

The IMF offers several kinds of financing, depending on the borrower, its needs, and its circumstances. Unconditional lending is available from the reserve portion of the country's gold and foreign currency deposits with the IMF. Low conditionality funds are available from the Compensatory Financing Facility (a fund introduced in 1963 for countries facing temporary export shortfalls or price rises for specific imports – primarily cereals – and the Buffer Stock Financing Facility (which makes loans to finance contributions of products to an international buffer stock). High conditionality lending typifies amounts beyond a country's first credit tranche. Such loans generally take the form of a standby agreement, such as was negotiated with Jamaica in 1977. Loans are disbursed in several installments, usually over a period of one to three years, and must be repaid in a maximum of five years. Countries can tap all or part of each installment if specified performance criteria have been met. If the criteria are not met, the IMF board of directors can withhold future installments or new loans.

The EFF, introduced in 1974, provides longer-term loans for structural economic adjustments that cannot occur in a single year. The Supplemental Financing Facility (1979) and the Enlarged Access Policy (1981) provide additional lending up to 45 percent beyond a country's quota limit, at higher interest rates than the standard IMF lending rate (Williamson 1982). In order to gain access to the high conditionality funds, borrowers submit a letter of intent, a set of promises to attain the specified performance targets.

The IMF also issues special drawing rights (SDRs). These are currency units containing 40 U.S. cents and fractions of 15 other currencies. (As of February 1, 1983, the value of the SDR was U.S.$1.09.) SDRs are a form of "paper gold," created by the IMF and distributed among member countries to provide the international liquidity needed to finance world trade. SDRs have been distributed on several occasions to countries with weak balances of payments to purchase goods from nations with strong payments positions.

IMF SURVEILLANCE AND CONSULTATION

The IMF conducts surveillance by gathering information about the condition of a country's economy and evaluating the appropriateness of government policies. Consultation then occurs through a series of meetings between IMF economists and the economic managers of the country to discuss those policies. Consultation is mandatory when outstanding loans are greater than 125 percent of a nation's quota, and the surveillance is used to monitor how well the country has adhered to the conditions of its borrowing agreement.

The IMF describes the consultation process as one of its most significant functions:

> The regular consultations between the Fund and its 100 member countries are one means by which the Fund keeps itself informed of economic developments and policies in member countries, obtains the basic materials for the exercise of surveillance over exchange rate policies, and fulfills certain other jurisdictional responsibilities. Each consultation constitutes one of the most significant activities of the Executive Board, the Fund's management and the staff. Their great achievement has been to build up, on the basis of a close relationship between member countries and the Fund, a process for the exchange of confidential information and a framework for effective cooperation among them. This achievement has proved particularly important in recent years when shifts in international payments have been unprecedentedly abrupt and large, and adjustment has often required the Fund to act quickly and to help coordinate domestic and external policies of more than one member country. (Brau 1981, p. 13)

Initially, consultations were held with only a few countries, to discuss restrictions on international payments and transfers, but over time the scope of discussions has broadened extensively. By 1981 consultations were held with all member countries and covered a wide range of issues pertaining to domestic and external policies. Usually the IMF is represented by a team of four economists and a secretary. The staff collects all available factual information about the major sectors of the local economy in order to prepare a written report about recent developments. The mission generally stays in the country for two to three weeks and meets with a wide range of government officials as well as representatives of trade unions, private business, and financial institutions.

The work of the mission usually comprises two phases. An initial period of fact-finding is followed by policy-oriented discussions with government officials about economic problems and how to solve them. Considerable attention is focused on the country's balance-of-payments situation, exchange-rate policies, and adjustment needs. The mission then prepares a preliminary assessment of the economic and financial situation within the member country, the policy stance of government authorities, and, sometimes, recommendations.

That report is presented to the Executive Board of the IMF for policy decisions and to determine when and how loans will be made. What is unique about the Fund's consultation is that

> While other organizations, such as the Organization for Economic Cooperation and Development and the European Economic Community, meet regularly with their members on economic and financial matters, *only the Fund approaches near-universality with regard to the number of member countries, the stage of development of their economies and the diversity of economic philosophies governing the management of these economies.* (Brau 1981, p. 13; emphasis added)

Together, surveillance and consultation provide the IMF with a forum to prod and persuade the countries that compose the international economy to integrate their efforts. When the country being consulted has borrowed or wants to borrow funds, discussions take a different tone and focus on specific conditions.

"Conditionality in the Fund refers to the policies that members are expected to follow when using Fund resources in order to be able to cope with their balance of payments problems" (Brau 1981, p. 16). Typical conditions that will be specified in an IMF program for balance-of-payments stabilization will include the following measures: liberalization or abolition of foreign-exchange and import controls; devaluation of the country's currency; a domestic anti-inflationary program that will control bank credits and the government deficit by curbs on government spending, increased taxation, and the abolition of consumer subsidies on basic food stuffs; and a program of greater hospitality to foreign investment (Hooke 1981).

The priorities outlined in the IMF's definition of "conditionality" reveal a distinct orthodoxy. Following conventional economic wisdom, the Fund maintains that devaluation of an overvalued currency will raise the price of imports and reduce their domestic consumption while lowering the price of exports and making them more competitive on international markets. The net result should be a closing of the balance-of-payments gap and a shift in domestic resources away from consumption and toward production. Similarly, the IMF's anti-inflationary programs are designed to increase domestic savings for investment by business rather than subsidizing consumer purchases, even for basic necessities. This reflects the Fund's view that development occurs through integration into the international manufacture and exchange system, with each developing country specializing in its own "technically feasible" range of export products while importing needed raw materials, components for assembly, spare parts, and machinery.

For instance, in its 1978 loan to Jamaica, the IMF mandated a 30 percent devaluation of the Jamaican dollar, a balanced budget, relaxation of government price controls on essential consumer items, wage restraints, and an increase in personal taxes to boost government revenue. The 15 percent ceiling on annual wage increases combined with reduced price controls to redistribute income from labor toward the business sector. (Details of that program during its entire history are outlined in Girvan et al. 1980; Kincaid 1981; Sharpley 1981.)

AN APPRAISAL OF THE IMF

> The men in the IMF . . . were the fellows who decided, for example, that if Italy needed a break, they would revalue the Lira so some Fiats could be sold in France or England; and Oscar Delgado was one of their top men for tropical LDCs ("Lesser Developed Countries"). . . .
>
> For two days Oscar and his colleague pored over figures in . . . almost total ignorance of the real conditions which were producing these figures. . . . (Henzell 1982, pp. 281–82)

Beginning in the 1970s, the IMF became a lightening rod for Third World criticism of structural inequalities in the international economy. Third World awareness of IMF policy grew out of necessity. Huge rises in petroleum prices boosted the cost of vital energy imports. They also set off inflation in the industrial economies that raised the costs of a wide range of other imports – from manufactured goods to foods – and countries as different as Jamaica, Peru, and Zaire soon encountered balance-of-payments problems. From 1966 to 1970 the nonoil-producing developing countries tapped IMF resources 143 times, compared with 205 times between 1976 and 1980. The amounts drawn jumped by 342 percent, from 2.6 billion to 11.5 billion SDRs, while world trade grew by 480 percent. Simultaneously the number of times that industrial countries had recourse to the IMF doubled, from 16 to 33, while the total amount rose by 78 percent, from 10.6 billion to 18.9 billion SDRs (IMF 1982).

As finance ministers from the Third World had growing contact with the IMF, they began to feel that a caste system was at work. Tanzania's finance minister, Amir Jamal, expressed the sentiments and frustrations of many others when the World Bank and the IMF held a joint meeting at Toronto in September 1982:

> The IMF and World Bank were primarily established to safeguard the economies of the already industrialized societies. . . . On achieving political independence almost all developing countries have acceded to membership of the two institutions from the very inception of their political independence. . . . As empirical evidence so amply illustrates, [they] had little choice but to accept the scheme of things which history had pre-empted for them.
> The IMF and World Bank are monumentally pervasive. In varying

degrees by omission and commission, their global impact is not only that of consolidating the historically inherited asymmetry in the community of nations, but also of creating despair and despondency when the need is that of giving hope and confidence. (*Multinational Monitor* 1982, pp. 20-21)

INEQUITABLE TREATMENT OF THE THIRD WORLD

What was the basis of Jamal's criticism? First, the IMF maintains a double standard on loan policy that favors the industrial, capitalist, G-10 countries.* Sydney Dell, project director at the U.N. Commission on Trade and Development (UNCTAD) and the U.N. Development Program (UNDP), points to the preferential loan conditionality that Great Britain received for its sizable drawings (11.1 billion SDRs) between 1965 and 1970. Comparing them with the detailed economic policy prescriptions for such junior members as Peru in 1976 and Egypt in 1977 is like comparing a facelift with heart surgery. This was neither an exception nor an oversight, since Dell states that "Information placed before the Executive Board [of the IMF] showed that the number of performance criteria in stand-by agreements for members in Latin America and Asia had on average been much greater than for members in Europe" (1981, p. 12).

The effects of this double standard also stand in stark contrast. The Institute for Food and Development Policy found that IMF conditions on Third World loans adversely affected living standards and provoked violent reactions:

> The imposition of IMF policy guidelines, resulting in dramatic price rises for basic necessities without corresponding wage increases, has set off riots in Peru, Turkey and Egypt. When Egypt was forced to end food subsidies and reduce food and clothing subsidies to meet IMF stipulations in 1977, people unable to afford these necessities rioted; 78 people were killed.** (Lappé et al. 1980, p. 126)

In a later paper Dell examined conditionality from another angle, contending that the IMF places the burden of adjustment on the debtor country. He argues that the Fund fails to consider the source of the deficit and thereby ". . . appears to shrug off its responsibility for ensuring that the burden of adjustment is distributed equitably and efficiently among countries" (1982, p. 600). Even the Council of Economic Advisors recognized the problem that deficit

---

*The G-10 countries are the United States, Great Britain, Germany, France, Japan, Canada, Italy, the Netherlands, Belgium, and Switzerland.

**An added irony is that while the IMF staff members seem to have little difficulty recommending the end of food subsidies for Egyptian workers, whose average annual income is less than $400, they enjoy heavily subsidized lunches (a first-class meal, served by a waiter in the superb IMF dining room, costs only $5 to $7) despite annual salaries of $50,000 to $100,000.

countries could not restore balance-of-payments equilibrium unless other nations tried to reduce their net surpluses (1973, pp. 124–25). Nonetheless, the IMF concentrates its attention on the debtor economies. Admittedly the Fund has little direct leverage over the policies pursued by the AICs, but it has shown no interest in digging to the root of the debt problem.

When the Fund imposes conditions on loans to developing countries, a host of adjustment policies open up the debtor countries economies to outside competition. Supposedly, exchange-rate adjustment and the lifting of trade and payments barriers that restrict imported goods will encourage the affected economy to produce and sell more exports to work itself out of debt. However, these policies cover only half the equation. The industrial, creditor nations are not subjected to conditionality, and often continue to maintain obstacles to imports from debtor countries. Perhaps it is a question of whose ox is being gored. The United States complains that trade restrictions exacerbate its adverse trade balance with Japan, without acknowledging that similar barriers close off the U.S. market to imports from the Third World. Thus, one-sided IMF policies can perversely reinforce inequity and indebtedness by forcing borrowing countries to compete with imports in their domestic economies while providing no reciprocal openness for markets in the developed world.

The inequality of IMF policies reflects the institution's structure. In accordance with the Bretton Woods Agreement, votes are distributed in rough proportion to each country's economic power as measured by its GNP. The revival of Germany and Japan has produced some redistribution of power, although within the same narrow circle. As of January 1983, the G-10 countries together held 51 percent of the votes, with the U.S. share at 20 percent. Since most decisions require an 85 percent vote, the U.S. has effective veto power over any significant decision.

The Brandt Commission treated the subject of power sharing in its report:

> The Bretton Woods International Monetary system reflected the economic and political relations of the time. Since then much has changed – and the new system should reflect the changing political and economic circumstances of nations. The new international monetary system should have a pluralistic base in which no single political entity or small group of entities plays a predominant role. (Brandt et al. 1980, p. 218)

The report then recommended the development of a broader-based leadership governed by fair and explicit rules that would not be enforced selectively, depending on the borrower's shareholding. Moreover, it called for greater diversity in the staffing of the IMF, which is primarily white and male, and which by convention always has a European managing director and a U.S.-appointed deputy director.

The futility felt by the developing countries was clearly expressed in the communiqué issued by the Inter-governmental Group of Twenty-four of International Monetary Affairs following a Washington meeting in February 1983. That session coincided with an IMF policy meeting to consider the desperate need for a substantial increase in IMF quotas, a move the United States had blocked for two years. The Group of Twenty-four had called for an immediate doubling of quotas, while the United States opposed any increase greater than 50 percent. The developing-country ministers also expressed regret that the IMF had decided not to increase the supply of SDRs to stimulate the world economy, and "reiterated the call for the establishment of a link between SDR allocation and development finance" (Group of Twenty-four 1983, p. 4). Moreover, they "cautioned against the current tendency for the Fund to shift from three-year to one-year [lending] programs. . . . " and emphasized that adjustment programs also should be framed in the context of growth-oriented policies. Finally, they "stressed the importance of expanding the Compensatory Financing Facility, both in terms of access and conditionality" (Group of Twenty-four 1983, p. 4). The ministers were aware that none of their proposals could be passed without U.S. approval, and the United States, as expected, ignored their plea.

INEFFECTIVENESS OF IMF POLICY PRESCRIPTIONS

There were sound empirical data to support the call for a quota increase. At the Bretton Woods Conference, John Maynard Keynes had insisted that, to avoid monetary difficulties, the minimum IMF resource base had to equal 16 percent of world trade. By the early 1980s IMF quotas equaled only 3 percent of world trade, and even that figure was deceptive.

While the nominal value of quotas totaled about $67 billion, only $20 billion was lendable, and the share of SDRs in overall world reserves had been falling since 1972 – $12 billion SDRs would have to be allocated in 1983 just to catch up. The resources of the IMF were plainly inadequate to meet the borrowing needs of the Third World.

That shortfall and the IMF's rigid monetarism partially explain why Third World countries turned to private bankers for capital during the 1970s. Large-scale debtors like Mexico and Brazil sought more expensive private bank loans rather than the cheaper resources of the IMF in an attempt to safeguard their sovereignty from Fund conditionality. By turning a deaf ear to borrowers' needs and refusing to negotiate terms reciprocally, the IMF exacerbated rather than ameliorated the approaching debt crisis of the 1980s.

And there were warning signs. Ever since the early 1970s, a number of analysts had begun to question the effectiveness of IMF stabilization programs. In 1974 Cheryl Payer wrote *The Debt Trap*, a "book about the efforts of poor nations to gain some control over their own economies, and the role of the

IMF in frustrating these efforts" (1974, p. x). Payer viewed the IMF as an obstacle to autonomous national development and used a series of eight case studies to contrast the development process in six countries "forced to accept" IMF advice with what occurred in "break-away" countries. (See Box 10.)

BOX 10. The Philippines and the IMF

The Philippines is a classic example of the type of economy that the IMF and its sister institution, the World Bank, attempt to forge throughout the Third World. Throughout the 1970s the Philippines was under one kind of stabilization program or another, making it by mid-1980 the Third World country most indebted to the IMF.

Working closely with the World Bank, the Fund used its tremendous power to restructure Philippine production along the lines of an "export-oriented" development strategy. This consisted of a concerted effort to push productive capital away from production for the internal market – by destroying the mechanisms sheltering Philippine firms from multinational competition – to a one-sided emphasis on producing labor-intensive manufactured exports. Attracting investment to export production also meant a policy of low wages and constant currency depreciation to ensure the competitiveness of Philippine products in export markets.

This growth strategy, however, could succeed only if the international economy continued to expand and Western and Japanese markets remained open to Philippine exports. Both these conditions began to vanish in the mid-1970s. First, the international prices for sugar and coconut products, the Philippines' chief export crops, plunged. Then, in 1980, demand collapsed further with the onset of the international recession. In reaction to the economic downspin, the United States, Japan, and Western Europe began erecting protectionist barriers against labor-intensive manufactured imports from the Philippines and the rest of the Third World. In a confidential internal report the Fund admitted that its strategy of export-led growth in the Philippines had failed: "The staff shares the view . . . that export promotion has become more difficult in the present climate of uncertainty of the international economy as well as the trade restrictions faced by Philippine exports."

This confession was, of course, no help to the Philippines, whose current-account deficit widened sharply with the combination of weak exports and inexorably rising imports (which included raw materials and machinery for the ailing export industries). By mid-1983 the deficit had risen to almost $3 billion, up from $2 billion in 1980. To bridge the gap, the country borrowed heavily from the Fund and the big banks.

In a more balanced economy the decline of the export sector can be balanced by the expansion of internal demand to ensure continued growth.

But in the Philippines, years of following the IMF-World Bank strategy of depressing wages to gain "export competitiveness" had so gutted the internal market that deep recession became the only possible outcome. In 1982 the Philippines' GNP growth rate was down to 2.4 percent, the lowest in Southeast Asia. The Fund, then, has helped saddle Filipinos with the worst of all possible worlds: an economy racked by deep recession and weighed down by an impossible external debt burden.

Source: Bello and Kinley 1983, p. 13. Reprinted by permission of *Multinational Monitor* © 1983.

The linchpin of all IMF stabilization programs for the Third World is the liberalization of exchange and import controls. Usually trade liberalization is supplemented by a host of domestic anti-inflationary measures: currency devaluation, the removal of government subsidies, and limits on foreign financing to counteract the larger balance-of-payments deficits that often initially accompany an austerity program. Payer found that in each case study, the IMF stabilization program resulted in a takeover of domestic business. The prescribed devaluation would inflict heavy losses on domestic producers by raising the costs of essential imports and interest on past debts while trade liberalization robbed them of protected markets. Meanwhile, foreign-owned affiliates used their preferential access to credit and imports through their parent companies to take advantage of currency devaluation. Increased profits could be used to buy out local firms. Payer also noted that devaluation frequently encouraged a shift in food production from domestic to export markets, depressing the living standards of the poor.

Supporters of the IMF point to Indonesia, which received substantial credit following the overthrow of the leftist Sukarno government, as an example of a successful adjustment program. However, Payer questioned the efficacy of the IMF program, since $4 billion in new debt was added between 1966 and 1974. Much of this new borrowing financed balance-of-payments shortfalls that could largely be attributed to the profit transfers of multinational corporations and the increased imports of consumer goods that followed trade liberalization. In addition, over 9,500 Indonesian firms collapsed during this period; even the country's famed textile industry was depressed while imported, finished textiles were flourishing. Payer concluded that the success of IMF stabilization rang hollow:

"The success is that of the great multinational corporations, who have through the IMF cadged their governments into financing the balance of payments deficits which their profits have caused; and of Japan, who has secured through IMF policies the assurance that Indonesia will continue to export its petroleum and timber to serve the needs of the Japanese economy rather than its own. (Payer 1975, p. 90)

Similarly, Brazil, despite the phenomenal growth rate recorded in the early 1970s, was no success story for IMF prescriptions:

> The only period [in] which [Brazil] followed [IMF] instructions very faithfully, 1964 to 1967, was also the period of the worst business depression and a rash of take-overs by foreign companies. The stabilization program worsened income distribution, but could not restore production or put the balance of payments on a stable footing. (Payer 1975, p. 165)

That experience provides the context for exploring why Brazil preferred private bank loans and studiously refused to negotiate another standby agreement with the IMF during the late 1970s and early 1980s, even when its economy had started to unravel from its onerous debt burden. Only in January 1983, when private loans vanished, did Brazil seek assistance from the IMF. One measure of the desperation that governs both sides in the present debt crisis was revealed. The IMF seemed more concerned with bailing out the private banks from immediate default than with "reforming" the Brazilian economy. In fact, the sense of past inequality is so extreme that irresponsibility may be encouraged. In early 1984 the *New York Times* reported that Brazil was routinely ignoring IMF-imposed conditions (*New York Times* 1984).

The problem, as Payer sees it, is that the IMF sponsors the wrong form of adjustment in its stabilization programs. The IMF is correct, she says, "when it tells governments that financial discipline and occasional painful adjustments in the structure of production are necessary for the health of the balance of payments," yet "its use of foreign aid as a bribe deliberately frustrates the very type of financial discipline and production adjustments which are most badly needed" (Payer 1975, p. 210). Too often the emphasis on trade liberalization, high technology, and exports "is built on servicing the needs of the rich countries, or more precisely the corporations of the rich countries . . . [and] will bring in the latest technological gadgets . . ." but will not produce development. Instead, what is needed is a policy that ensures that everybody has enough food to eat and builds on this to provide more amenities as it becomes possible to produce them (Payer 1975, p. 213).

Carlos Díaz-Alejandro (1981) also has been unimpressed with IMF stabilization efforts in Latin America. Arguing that the economic deflation and retrenchment reached extreme levels, he labeled the Fund's activities as "overkill." Sydney Dell takes up that theme and extends it to the Fund's activities throughout the Third World. "Overkill" has become pervasive and "could well be used . . . to describe the [IMF's] national and international programs of adjustment adopted in the 1970s and early 1980s" (1982, p. 597).

According to Dell, the Fund has strayed far from its purpose, "the promotion and maintenance of a high level of unemployment and real income and . . . the development of the productive resources of the members'. . . ." Instead, its prescriptions have commonly, "in a situation of increasingly inadequate effective demand, growing underutilization of productive capacity and soaring unemployment, [exerted] pressure . . . for even greater reductions of demand, which are likely to increase the volume of idle capacity and unemployment still further" (Dell 1982, p. 598).

One reason that IMF programs are ineffective is the political naiveté that underlies the technical solutions. (See Box 11.)

BOX 11. Do IMF Prescriptions Make Sense?

A rational and consistent strategy for resolving the LDC debt crisis must answer to three somewhat contradictory requirements: sustaining a balanced, noninflationary process of world economic recovery; protecting an increasingly fragile global financial structure; and allowing the many nations currently engaged in the transition to democracy to achieve this goal without violent internal disruption. In this context serious doubts can be entertained as to whether the IMF's single-minded devotion to export expansion and internal austerity are conducive to meeting these needs.

Simultaneous export growth in the many newly industrializing countries runs up against several obstacles. Historians of the 1930s have pointed to the role played in that economic disaster by the absence of an importer of last resort. Who will buy the flood of exported manufactured goods that the IMF expects will be forthcoming as LDCs compress domestic demand and reallocate resources to the external sector in order to generate the foreign exchange necessary to service debt? Given the nature of recent economic cycles in the developed countries, it is not at all certain that growth in import demand can be rapid enough to satisfy LDC needs for positive trade balances without stimulating either a return of inflation (that would choke off recovery) or a surge of protectionist pressure (that Western governments would have great difficulty controlling).

At the same time, IMF prescriptions for fiscal and monetary austerity threaten the delicate transition to more democratic forms of government currently occurring in several major countries in Latin America. Newly emerging moderate forces will find it almost impossible to cope with more radical tendencies if austerity programs have removed all ability to cushion inevitably painful adjustments by means of welfare support measures, subsidies for basic necessities, land and labor reform and the like.

Success in this process of political liberalization requires a gradualist approach that would give the LDCs more time to make the internal structural adjustments their economies so badly need. If, however, a longer time horizon of this type is called for from the perspective of the debtors, a way will have to be found to guarantee the stability of advanced country financial institutions that are likely to suffer delays in debt-service payments and large potential losses.

Ultimately, the most serious danger in the present situation is that the institutions with the power to manage the process of change – Western governments, private commercial banks and the IMF – will be unable to agree on a concerted plan of action, as each looks only to its own narrow interests. As a first step, IMF programs should be sensitive to the political pressures within LDCs by moderating the pressure on internal demand. This will allow LDCs to import more from one another, rather than relying exclusively on markets in the industrial countries. Moreover, IMF programs, perhaps in conjunction with the World Bank and Western aid agencies, should address themselves not only to short-term macroeconomic adjustments but also to structural and socio-economic changes that could ultimately create a more-balanced and less-externally dependent process of economic development.

Source: Coleman 1983, pp. 156, 162.
Reprinted with permission of *Institutional Investor*, September 1983.

The IMF blames the balance-of-payments deficit on cost-induced inflation and prescribes demand deflation through wage rollbacks, wage restraint, and reduced government services as a cure. Unfortunately, the cure can be as fatal as, and even more painful than, the disease. In Peru a 1976 IMF austerity program cut workers' buying power in half. Subsequently the price of bread jumped 1,000 percent and infant mortality climbed 30 percent (Carrizo 1979). Social conflict increased and led to riots. Meeting the requirement implicit in the IMF's demand-reduction policies is like trying to build a skyscraper on a fault line. Long-term development requires social consensus and a sharing of the social burden to maintain or increase levels of worker productivity. Since IMF conditionality tends to undermine social cohesion and political stability, it rarely achieves lasting gains. It rearranges the rubble and calls it "home."

What happens when a Fund stabilization program actually produces the intended results? The Chilean economy from 1974 to 1982 provides one test case for IMF policies. Chile did all the "right" things, closely adhering to the Fund's recommendations. A reestablished free-market economy was opened wide to foreign trade, the currency was devalued, a model code to attract foreign investment was introduced, and the government adopted monetary policies combining restrictions on the money supply with public austerity. These policies promoted a boom in financial services and imports, and a renewed influx of private investment ($5.4 billion in additional investment were scheduled to occur from 1974 to 1981). Yet U.S. businessmen, who control 80 percent of Chile's foreign capital, found that by 1980 the IMF model was sputtering. The low tariffs made imports so cheap that few domestic investments could compete. Consequently, only 11 percent of the authorized foreign investments were actually made. And, beginning in 1982, foreign investors, led by Exxon, started backing out (Diehl 1982). By early 1983 Chile's economy lay in shambles.

A study by René Villareal (1980) on the effectiveness of IMF policies in Latin America found that recommended devaluations did not generate or reallocate resources to improve the balance of payments. Rather, IMF policies generally depressed gross domestic product (GDP), wages, and profits. Following Chile's adoption of IMF policies in 1974, "The Chilean economy suffered a great contraction. GDP was lowered by almost 15 percent, industrial production was down 23 percent and gross investment was out by 31 percent. At the same time, unemployment increased markedly. . ." (Economic Commission on Latin America 1976, p. 165). Villareal concluded that as soon as the economies began to grow again, external factors, which remained unaffected by the IMF program, reemerged and pressures soon mounted for a further devaluation. The relief provided by IMF-imposed "adjustment" was temporary.

Some of the most far-reaching studies of the effectiveness of IMF programs tend to confirm these results. Connors (1979) and Killick and Chapman (1982) conducted systematic studies of the balance of payments, national output, and inflation before and after stabilization programs in developing countries. The findings of both studies reveal that despite their being targeted by Fund stabilization programs, there was no marked or consistent improvement on these key variables.

Feinberg (1983) points out that IMF standby agreements in Latin America and the Caribbean may be malign rather than benign. Not only does the Fund frequently misjudge the structure of the local economy, but the policy measures that are proposed to control inflation are frequently inflationary themselves.

The IMF commonly defends its failures by maintaining that countries typically delay their approach to the Fund until their economies are barely breathing and beyond the reach of reasonable efforts at resuscitation. G. Russell Kincaid, an IMF economist assigned to Jamaica during the late 1970s, wrote that Jamaica's bitter experience with the IMF between 1977 and 1979 did not teach the lesson that the Fund needed to be more adaptive or flexible in its future operations. Rather, it "demonstrates the desirability of approaching the fund at a timely stage. However, unfortunately, this was not the path pursued by Jamaica" (Kincaid 1981, p. 21).

A more objective appraisal would not overlook how the IMF-imposed devaluation and trade liberalization contributed to the havoc. Policies designed to cut real wages (and thereby production costs) to make Jamaica's exports more competitive worsened instead of improved the country's balance of payments, simply because most of Jamaica's exports were price-inelastic in relation to demand. Lower dollar prices for Jamaican sugar and bauxite did not increase sales. What devaluation really meant was that the country would receive less foreign currency for its exports while paying more Jamaican dollars for imports. Consequently, internal inflation soared, class conflicts boiled, and capital flight increased. There was no improvement in either the balance of payments or national income.

The effects of IMF programs are especially severe when imports are vital to domestic production. Katseli outlined what commonly happens:

> Suppose that we consider a less developed country that imports intermediate goods to be used in domestic production under fixed coefficients and exports agricultural goods or raw materials whose supply is inelastic in the short run. This simplification might be pertinent for a country like Madagascar, the Sudan or even Kenya, all of which have negotiated stand-by agreements with the IMF. . . . A devaluation will not affect the terms of trade and the effect on the balance of trade will depend on the initial trade balance. Given a large trade balance (this is common in most countries which undertake a stand-by agreement) the exchange rate adjustment [of the Fund] will magnify it. The quantity exported might even be reduced if intermediate imports are used in the export sector [which is common] leading to even more perverse effects. . . . Thus in the presence of intermediate imports, the argument that devaluation is a useful tool for promoting competitiveness becomes at best uncertain. (1981, p. 361)

IMF POLITICAL FAVORITISM

Some skeptics have wondered if the IMF's policy toward Jamaica (and, by implication, similar Third World nations) was more deliberate than blind. That is, did the United States and its European allies use the IMF to curb or even undermine Jamaica's outspoken social-democratic government? Girvan and Bernal underscore the political ramifications within Jamaica of the IMF austerity program:

> In political terms, however, the IMF diagnosis implied that the root of [Jamaica's economic] problem was the shift in the balance of advantage in favor of labor at the expense of capital, and in favor of the public sector at the expense of the private sector. . . . Thus, behind the concern for "sound economic management" there lay an . . . opposition to the class and ideological content of the [social-democratic] PNP government's policies. In order to gain access to IMF resources and secure the "Good Housekeeping Seal of Approval," the government would have to agree to a program of adjustment whose main elements would be drastic cuts in real wages, severe compres-

sion of demand, and retrenchment in the public sector. Such policies would alienate precisely those social and economic groups on which the PNP government based its support, while trying to appease those groups which were diametrically opposed to everything the PNP stood for, and which had sworn to derail the process of democratic socialist change. (1982, p. 41)

Subsequent events enacted that scenario. Realizing that the Fund's conditions would mean sacking 10,000 government workers, Jamaica broke off negotiations in 1980 after a bitter public debate. The IMF became an issue in the ensuing national elections. The PNP government was soundly defeated, largely as a result of the previous economic difficulties. The new conservative government immediately sought and received a standby loan from the IMF and massive inflows of foreign capital from the United States. Nevertheless, a good part of the inflows merely financed a carnival of consumerism. The economy continued to deteriorate, the trade deficit widened enormously, and the foreign debt grew at an annual rate of 25 percent. In 1983 Jamaica flunked the economic performance criteria for continued IMF lending. In contrast with its treatment of the Manley government, the IMF quietly waived the economic performance test.

The list of countries judged by a political double standard is extensive. For instance, when Argentina's right-wing military regime drew $194 million in upper credit tranche during 1977, the Jamaican precedent should have implied high conditionality. Although Argentina's inflation rate exceeded 150 percent annually, the IMF imposed conditions much less severe than those being demanded of Jamaica, where the inflation rate was only 35 percent. In Chile the IMF lent the socialist Allende government $95.3 million but imposed severe conditions on a further $191 million. That endangered the government's economic program. Following the right-wing military coup in 1974, $373 million was quickly disbursed to the Pinochet junta, which was implicated in thousands of deaths, including those of many former government officials (Gisselquist 1981). Perhaps the Alice in Wonderland logic reached its height in Nicaragua. Just nine weeks before the overthrow of Somoza, the IMF deposited $22.3 million in the country's central bank. The standby agreement signed a few days before the final insurrection depended on mirrors for its justification. Its success required restoration of business confidence, a reversal of capital flight, and an increase in government revenues at the very moment a prolonged, and ultimately successful, general strike commenced. Wealthy Nicaraguans were following their capital to Miami. Even had Somoza won the latest round of battles, the private sector had abandoned him. Yet the Fund maintained that its program was "technically sound." One can only surmise the pressures and convoluted reasoning behind such an appraisal (Feinberg 1983).

It should be noted that despite apparent hostility to nonmarket socialism within the Third World, the IMF views Eastern European members differently.

Several factors may account for this seeming discrepancy. First, the Western industrial democracies have tried to use trade as a lever to increase the independence of the Eastern European countries from the Soviet Union. Second, these countries provided a large new market for Western European manufacturers during the era of détente. This trade was often financed by the large European and American private banks. Thus, recent IMF policy toward these countries may have more to do with protecting an overextended international banking network from collapse than with new-found admiration for Eastern European socialism.

THE IMF AS PROTECTOR OF PRIVATE INTERNATIONAL BANKS

This view has been most cogently expressed in the writings of conservative, "supply-side" economists. Jude Wanninski (U.S. Treasury 1982) argues that the IMF is operated in the interest of the international commercial banks, with the aim of averting an international collapse and their confluent bankruptcies. The role of the IMF, according to this view, is to squeeze the taxpayers in the Third World to ensure that they do indeed service their international obligations.

The IMF uses both carrot and stick to accomplish this end. The carrot is the promise of more loans and the arrangement of additional lending from the private banks and government sources. This procedure was evident in the 1982 Mexican and 1983 Brazilian rescue packages orchestrated by the IMF. Loan approval by the IMF is the first step to "free up" additional private resources to meet past commercial obligations. In February 1982 the IMF pushed through a $4.9 billion loan to Brazil, equivalent to 30 percent of Brazil's debts to U.S. banks: "The agreement . . . will be greeted with relief in financial circles" (*Washington Post* 1983).

However, each time the IMF puts together a loan package to prevent a debtor country from going into default, the strain becomes more evident. Present IMF policy leaps from stone to stone, and each leap is further from shore. The austerity programs tied to Fund loans make those stones smaller. If or when the final splash comes, there is no assurance that the private banks won't fail. Already members of the House Banking Committee have drafted legislation tied to a U.S. increase in IMF funding that is designed to force banks to take costly write-offs of loans, reportedly so that the banks will not be able to pass on their losses to the U.S. taxpayers.

The only long-term solution is to make the Third World economies viable, and the other actors in the international economy will have to absorb their share of the investment costs. For the IMF to play a part in solving the debt problem, greater imagination and more flexible methods have to be adopted. Most important, the problem needs to be defined more clearly, and that will probably require internal reform of the Fund by providing more representation of Third World interests.

PART II

THE POLITICAL ECONOMY OF TRADE

6

TRADE THEORIES AND ECONOMIC DEVELOPMENT

Trade among nations follows channels that are carved by political as well as economic forces. In turn, international commerce can spur or retard national economic development and powerfully influence domestic political institutions. It is impossible to understand the patterns of growth within the Third World without appreciating the evolution of international trade. From the first voyages of Portuguese traders around the Horn of Africa to the later entry of British merchants into India, the flag of empire accompanied the search for new sources of wealth. The discovery of the New World powerfully affected Western nations' trade with non-Europeans.

The New World was seen as a vast, underutilized resource, open to conquest and exploitation. The flow of wealth, particularly from Spanish America, initially was one-sided; better characterized as plunder than as exchange. As European national rivalries spilled overseas, maritime trading powers raced to establish colonies that would guarantee future access to raw materials and commodities. With the industrial revolution the international trading system expanded and diversified. Colonies that supplied foodstuffs and raw materials became markets for manufactured goods. Thus, for instance, textile mills in Manchester, England, transformed Egyptian cotton into cloth that was sold in India. Trading relationships underscored political relationships: British naval and merchant fleets linked the far-flung corners of an empire upon which the sun never set. Two world wars, however, dimmed that luster. Since the late 1940s the colonial empires have nearly vanished, and the new nations of the Third World have sprung up in their place.

Nominal political independence has not altered, and in many ways is sharply limited by, the relative economic dependence of the former colonies. National economies have continued to become more integrated into a world economy, and the breakup of colonial empires has complemented the general relaxation of tariff barriers to open up and rationalize markets for all industrial powers. The AICs still sit at the heart of international trade, importing raw materials and exporting manufactured goods.

In the 1970s the balance of economic power showed signs of shifting. OPEC was the first Third World commodity cartel to successfully set a price structure. Other Third World countries tried to import new technologies and use their large pool of cheap labor to make the international trading system into a lever for developing and diversifying their economies. That early optimism dimmed during the 1980s as a worldwide recession, triggered by recurrent rises in energy costs, led to ballooning debt burdens in the nonoil-producing countries of the Third World. The recession also dampened the demand for oil, and hairline cracks in the OPEC alliance threatened to become fissures. Earlier chapters have examined how the world's financial system has contributed to the present crisis. This chapter will begin to explore the role of trade.

TRADE AND THE INTERNATIONAL ECONOMY

In simple terms, each domestic economy exists within the greater international economy. That is, from the vantage point of any particular country, goods are imported from and exported to the international economy.

Move to a series of alternative vantage points, and the perspective becomes more complex. The international economy comprises and interrelates over 150 national economies. The statistical combinations of possible trading partners is enormous. Figure 6.1 helps to make those strands intelligible by diagramming the web of trade flows between blocs of countries. The numbers represent the value of imports and exports in billions of dollars. The trading blocs are the European Free Trade Association (EFTA), the EEC, OPEC, and the centrally planned economies and nonoil developing countries. The United States, Japan, and Canada are included as individual "blocs." This provides a somewhat more complex picture of commerce. For example, it shows that Japan exported $17.3 billion of products to the EEC while importing $6.4 billion. Likewise, $31.9 billion in goods was exported to, and $20.8 billion was imported from, the United States. Japan's $56.8 billion of oil imports from OPEC was offset by exports valued at $18.5 billion.

The fact that the numbers do not always even out suggests that something is missing. In addition to the exchange of goods, there is a worldwide flow of capital. International capital flows among private and public institutions occur for a variety of reasons:

1. Borrowing and credit to finance commercial transactions (usually through short-term private loans)

2. Direct foreign investment

FIGURE 6.1. Regional Breakdown of International Trade in 1980 (billions of dollars)

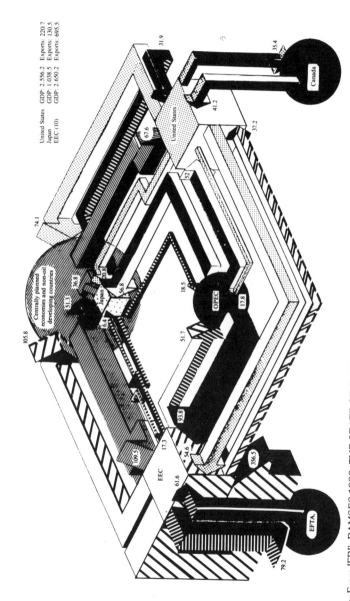

United States	GDP: 2.556.2	Exports: 220.7
Japan	GDP: 1.038.5	Exports: 130.5
EEC (10)	GDP: 2.650.2	Exports: 695.5

Source: From IFRI's RAMSES 1982: THE STATE OF THE WORLD ECONOMY, Copyright 1982, Institut Francais des Relations Internationales. Reprinted with permission from the Ballinger Publishing Company.

3. Capital transfers to earn investment income

4. Long-term public and private loans to corporations or governments building infrastructure, financing productive projects, or covering budget deficits

5. Interest payments on long- and short-term loans

6. Repayments of principal on private and public loans

7. Public and private grants (such as gifts from UNICEF to purchase disaster relief supplies).

Each category represents movement of financial resources into and out of a particular country. Some money goes as risk capital to establish a direct claim on future production through the construction of a new factory or the purchase of shares in an existing factory. Alternatively, loan capital may finance infrastructural projects, such as roads or a hydroelectric dam. The lender, in turn, receives interest. Trade loans finance imports of machinery, equipment, and consumer goods. Some loans (or grants) are made by "official" lenders and multilateral banks, and through bilateral aid. Other flows are private transfers between individuals – for instance, when a worker living in New York sends his mother in the Dominican Republic a monthly check to help pay for educating his brothers and sisters.

The Third World earned most of its foreign exchange – more than 70 percent between 1960 and 1980 – by exporting commodities such as sugar, coffee, copper, tin, and oil. In 1980 these earnings for low- and middle-income oil-importing countries totaled $238 billion, and official bilateral aid and loans added another $26 billion (World Bank 1982). Nevertheless, the Third World (excluding OPEC) ran a trade deficit – total exports less imports – of $71 billion, nearly three times the sum of development assistance. Some of that massive shortfall ($26 billion) was covered by private bank loans. Private foreign investment accounted for another $8 billion. The rest came from drawing down foreign-exchange reserves that had taken years to accumulate.

In the international economy, trade and finance are mates. Deficits in annual trade flows – when more goods are imported than exported – must be offset by foreign borrowing or foreign investment. During the 1970s the Third World countries, as a group, rapidly expanded their exports but faced rising deficits in their trade balances. Why? Part of the answer may be systemic, but it also seems likely that faulty investment decisions were made because of an inadequate understanding of how international trade works.

WHY NATIONS TRADE

Why do countries trade with each other? One answer is self-evident: it can be profitable. But what makes it profitable? Rules of common sense apply. The trading nation usually owns or produces a product that someone else wants.

A trade occurs when people or countries possess surpluses (more than can be consumed internally) or when an urgent need arises and a buyer is willing to sacrifice internal consumption or to mortgage future consumption to obtain the "essential" product. For example, Canada produces more wheat than it can eat, but not a single banana. Bananas are abundant on the Caribbean island of St. Lucia, but St. Lucia grows no wheat. A trade is struck: Canada exports wheat to supply St. Lucia's bakeries while importing bananas to stock its supermarkets.

Theories of international trade seek to reveal the underlying causes of trade between nations. An explanation of the trade between Canada and St. Lucia is the difference in international costs of production. Countries purchase goods abroad to avoid paying a higher price for domestic production.

But why do costs differ? International trade theory suggests, and common sense concurs, that the differences are attributable in part to the relative abundance of the factors used in production or to advantageous production conditions. These in turn may be influenced by the pattern of demand. For example, France exports wine. Its land and climate are particularly suited for growing grapes. The French wine industry is centuries old, and the country has a pool of skilled agricultural laborers and vintners. And wine is a staple of the national diet. The large domestic demand provides the foundation for a large-scale industry with a decreasing marginal cost structure, meaning that each additional bottle costs less to produce than the previous one. Fixed production costs can be spread out over a larger number of bottles, and that reduces unit cost and the final selling price.

Trade, then, follows what economists refer to as the principle of comparative advantage. That is, each country is comparably better suited climatically and geographically than most other countries to produce a particular export. St. Lucia could grow wheat, but on its steep hillsides and with its tropical climate, the selling price would vastly exceed Canada's, which in 1981 was $200 per ton. Likewise, Canada could grow bananas in hothouses, but constructing and heating those buildings would raise production costs well beyond the 16 cents per pound Canada pays to import bananas from St. Lucia.

Most countries of the Third World export unprocessed commodities – bananas, raw sugar, cotton, bauxite – and import manufactured goods. Why? According to trade theory, the answer is because of international differences in prices and costs. However, trade also may occur because of differences in economic specialization. Or, as Paul Samuelson once put it: "Comparative advantage means that the fat men do the fishing, the lean men the hunting, while the smart men make the medicine." For example, in 1977 Cuba imported tractors from the USSR; in exchange the USSR purchased frozen fish from Cuba. The Soviet Union has one of the world's largest fishing fleets. Why would it import fish from Cuba? There are several possible explanations. Perhaps it costs the USSR less to produce more tractors and trade them to Cuba for fish. Since the Cuban fishing fleet does not have to travel far to secure its catch, its production and maintenance costs, and therefore its selling prices, may be lower. Or perhaps Cuba offers a different variety of fish. In fact, the country's lobster catch is strictly reserved for export to earn foreign exchange for the purchase of tractors and agricultural implements. Similarly, Cuba, along with many Third World countries, must import electric power generators. Those complex and costly machines are manufactured in few countries. At present neither Cuba nor most Third World countries have the combination of technology and market demand to make the generators.

In summary, nations trade for a variety of reasons, and the benefits often transcend mere differences in relative costs. Additional benefits include the following:

a. Trade provides consumers with access to products that are not otherwise available. For example, Marco Polo brought tea from China, adding a major new item to the European diet. International trade allows Brazil's national airline, Varig, to purchase high-speed Boeing 727 jets; without trade, Varig would have to fly domestically produced, 15-seat Variante propeller planes.

b. Trade provides new markets, making it possible to harvest idle resources. Plantation and large-scale agriculture, common throughout the Third World, intensifies the use of land and labor in producing sugar, coffee, and other export crops.

c. Where production involves large fixed costs, trade can "vent" surplus production and reduce domestic production costs. For example, the economic viability of the U.S. nuclear power equipment industry is entirely dependent upon exports in order to share overhead and to reduce domestic unit costs.

d. Finally, nations may use trade to stimulate rapid economic growth. Brazil, Mexico, and Taiwan used trade during the 1960s and 1970s to increase national income. (This approach, formalized into the concept of an "export-led" growth model, will be examined later in more detail.)

THE FAILURE OF TRADE THEORY

If trade is to spur rather than retard balanced economic development, certain conditions must be met. The traditional or neoclassical theory of international trade rests upon a set of assumptions, some of which are both highly restrictive and unrealistic. Among the most important assumptions are the following (Todaro 1981, pp. 348ff.):

a. Productive resources may vary in quantity but are of equivalent quality and are fully employed in all nations – that is, the quality of labor in Haiti and the United States, for example, is the same.

b. Factors of production (land, labor, and capital) do not move between nations – that is, there is no movement of capital and no significant labor migration.

c. The technology of production is freely and readily available to all nations – that is, all nations can, for example, freely acquire U.S. aerospace technology.

d. Consumer preferences are not influenced by producers – that is, advertising does not affect consumers' tastes or the quantity of their purchases.

e. International prices are determined strictly by the forces of supply and demand – that is, there is no manipulation nor price setting by multinational corporations or commodity cartels.

f. National economies may adjust freely to changes in international prices by increasing or decreasing their production of goods without chaotic social or economic dislocation – that is, if the United States were, for example, to close its automobile industry because the Japanese manufactured cheaper cars, there would be no unemployment in Detroit.

Some of these assumptions seem to have been coined by Lewis Carroll. The 1980s are not Wonderland, however, and it should surprise no one that many Third World economists view traditional trade theory with some skepticism. What is surprising is that these theories are used as definitive guides by the World Bank, the IMF, and GATT in recommending how Third World nations can use foreign trade to develop their economies.

This does not mean that trade-centered development models cannot work. A matrix of theories links trade, industrialization, and economic development. The key theorem holds that specialization in a particular set of export-oriented products will create the nucleus of a trained labor force, improved manufacturing techniques, and higher worker productivity. Increased profits from trade can be reinvested to import new technologies, which further contribute to economic development.

BOX 12. Free Trade and Export Promotion

A survey of the Third World's experience with the international trading system suggests that a new approach is needed to bolster its economic performance in the 1990s. Yet there are conflicting views on how to proceed. Perhaps the most popular view is that liberalization of the market and pursuit of export promotion is the way forward. This means that underdeveloped nations should eschew preferential trading arrangements, protectionism, and import substitution in favor of open markets and low tariff barriers in order to spur domestic manufacturing without the adverse price distortions that tend to produce high cost-price structures in nations that protect domestic manufacturers. A strong advocate of this policy is Ann Krueger, vice-president for research of the World

Bank. Summarizing a decade of her research in finance and development, she wrote:

> One of the problems of attempting to associate alternative trade strategies with growth rates is that the trade strategy itself is but one influence on the effectiveness with which other factors of production are employed. . . . An increase in the rate of growth of export earnings of one percentage point annually was associated with an increase in the rate of growth of GDP of about 0.1 percentage points. Even if this does not imply causation, the results indicate a strong relationship between export growth and the overall growth rate. (1983, pp. 6–8; see also Krueger 1978)

Although there is a wide gulf between the empirical findings and policy prescriptions, there is even more disagreement about how to stimulate a nation's exports. While some evidence indicates that export promotion may be a productive avenue, other evidence suggests that the nations that have become the world's foremost traders – Japan and South Korea – reached this point only after a period of extensive protectionism.

Korea's experience in particular has been the subject of much dispute. Two recent studies suggest that the source of its success is far more complex than the mere pursuit of "export-oriented" policies and "virtual free trade conditions for exporters," as suggested by Little (1981). M. K. Datta-Chaudhuri, an Indian economist, writes:

> In the field of economic development, two mutually exclusive sets of associated ideas are often juxtaposed against each other: one set consists of capitalism, free trade and export promotion and the other, socialism, State intervention and import substitution. In our view these collective representations have done considerable damage to our understanding of the Korean phenomenon. The Republic of Korea is a highly interventionist State promoting capitalist development through selective intervention in both export promotion and import substitution. (1981, p. 76)

Y. C. Park likewise points to the Korean government's leading role in carrying out the outward-looking strategy. The lesson of South Korea that he finds is that:

> Developing countries should perhaps pay more attention to an integrated industrialization, as opposed either to import-substitution or export promotion, a strategy that focuses on building a network of interrelated industries producing consumer goods as well as capital and intermediate goods with the primary purpose of satisfying internal needs rather than world market demand. (1981, p. 117)

The experience of the advanced industrial nations suggests that trade liberalization is a policy honored more in the breach than in the observance. Speaking at the IDB's Conference on Economic Integration, William Gaillard, representative of the EEC delegation in Washington, stated, "Experience shows that simplistic trade liberalization, particularly in agricultural economies, is dangerous. This is so because while demand grows slowly, supply fluctuates and can easily rupture an agricultural economy." Consequently, the EEC protects its industries under an umbrella of tariffs and agricultural subsidies.

This model attempts to make the lack of development into an asset. Although most Third World countries lack an industrial base, the latest and most efficient technologies can be imported, thereby skipping intermediate developmental stages. For example, plastic shoes, which are produced by an advanced injection molding technology and are cheap to make, have largely replaced leather shoes in many parts of the Third World. In order to manufacture these shoes, the equipment and materials – in this case polyvinyl chloride – must be imported. Once that investment is made, the production of plastic shoes creates a new item for domestic sale, perhaps reducing imported shoes. The new product also can be exported, which in turn generates new opportunities for employment and further income. The confluence of growing demand and growing production expands savings for reinvestment, provided enough skilled workers and managers are available.

Gustav Ranis, one of the foremost proponents of export-led industrialization, calls this process "diversifying manufactured exports by way of trade promotion, or export substitution." This strategy has been successfully used by Hong Kong, Singapore, Malaysia, Taiwan, and South Korea, all of which registered impressive economic growth during the 1970s.

Nevertheless, as the world economy began slipping into depression in 1980, underlying problems surfaced. First, export substitution is a double-edged sword. When the world economy enters a recession, trade shrinks, and so does domestic production for export. Consequently, there are steep declines in domestic income and employment. The multiplier effect goes into reverse.

With the trade depression of the 1980s, this strategy was increasingly criticized. Markets began to contract, prices of Third World exports plummeted, and debts mounted. Economists in the Third World began to feel that the international trading system was not structured to favor long-term Third World development. Some began calling for revisions in that system. Some of the key issues and concerns are discussed in the following chapter.

7

TRADE CONFLICTS
OF THE 1980s

Thus far, the 1980s, with its good news/bad news punchline about world trade, seems like an exercise in black comedy. First, the good news. During the 1970s, according to the IMF, the international economy was a hotbed of activity: world exports soared from $283 billion in 1970 to $1,845 billion in 1980. The world economy seemed ever more productive and integrated. East-West trade was stimulated by the opening of China, the initiation of massive joint ventures such as the trans-Siberia pipeline, and a boom in grain sales. In just three years, 1977–79, U.S. exports of agricultural products to the Soviet Union doubled to more than $2 billion. Meanwhile, the Western European economies, which stood at the center of East-West commerce, enjoyed a booming trade with Soviet bloc countries. In 1980 alone, West German trade with the USSR grew by over 20 percent (Bressard 1982).

The bad news was implied by events in the Third World. Although trade was also booming there, was it a sign of life or of impending instability? The answer is not immediately clear. On the one hand, Third World manufacturing exports grew and much of that trade was South-South, suggesting that regional integration of markets was occurring and that whole groups of Third World economies were reaching the takeoff point in self-sustained development. On the other hand, most Third World nations were running massive and chronic trade deficits, and foreign MNCs were actually spearheading and dominating the growth sectors of various national economies.

So, which way was up? The growth of manufacturing exports and South-South trade seemed to indicate that the Third World's desires for increased industrialization, a reduction in dependence upon primary commodity exports, and increased regional interdependence were being realized. Between 1970 and 1980 Third World exports of manufactured goods grew from $24 billion to $60 billion in constant prices (UNCTAD 1981). Meanwhile, intraregional and interregional South-South trade rose from $3 billion to $30 billion (Bressard 1982, p. 99). However, the growing trade deficits and the dominance of MNCs implied that growing Third World trade was not resolving structural contradictions and generating self-sustaining growth. Much of the growth in Third World trade seemed precariously nonindigenous, the result of MNCs shifting their foreign investment focus from production of commodities to production of manufactures. A prime example was the global shift in electronics production from the United States and Western Europe to the Far East – Taiwan, Singapore, and Hong Kong.

The internationalization of capital is not new; it dates to the nineteenth century. Since the early 1960s, however, a new feature has appeared – what one writer has called the "globally integrated manufacturing system" (Moxon 1974). Offshore production, in which plants are established in many countries by U.S. corporations for export back to the United States, is now very common. This process has raised a host of issues that bear on trade relations, the rise of protectionism, and the performance of the international economy (see NACLA 1976). "Up," then, seems to point north, to the advanced industrial economies.

In many respects this new dance step – two steps forward, one step back – symbolizes contradictions in the world economy:

a. The fragile basis of the international trade that sustained postwar growth is becoming evident. The resurrection of the Japanese and Western European economies brings those countries increasingly into conflict with the United States. Emerging trade and investment wars will set the tone for the 1980s.

b. The political role of trade has been heightened by confrontations provoked by the U.S. government in 1982 over West-East technology transfers.

c. Third World economic insecurities stemming from deteriorating trade balances are heightening political insecurities and may push the underdeveloped nations into greater economic cooperation.

THIRD WORLD-FIRST WORLD TRADE CONFLICTS

In times of economic boom and rapid growth, expanding trade benefits the rich and the poor. In times of economic weakness and decline, the bottom drops out of trade, and conflicts arise as countries seek to shore up domestic industries and employment. Both positive and negative effects are magnified in the Third World. Since the Third World economies are hinged to the advanced capitalist economies, their economic fortunes march in lockstep with the advanced capitalist world. According to World Bank estimates, the growth elasticity of trade is about 1.5. That means that a 3 percent growth rate of GDP in the industrialized capitalist countries generates a 4.5 percent growth rate in the Third World. As the rate falls off by 2 percentage points in the advanced capitalist countries, it falls more steeply – by 3 percentage points in the Third World (UNCTAD 1981).

The worldwide recession/depression of the early 1980s has increased tensions between the First and Third Worlds on economic policy. Three issues stand out as areas of particular conflict: commodity prices and the deteriorating terms of trade between the advanced capitalist countries and the Third World; hidden trade barriers that discriminate against Third World exports; and export enclaves that result in unequal exchange, a process by which the Third World's earnings from trade are limited to producers connected with the enclave. Each of these issues is complex and needs closer examination.

COMMODITY PRICE STABILIZATION

The economies of most Third World nations are heavily dependent upon export income. Commodity sales account for the bulk of that revenue, but the price structure for staples such as coffee and tin is volatile. Unstable export earnings for a few key products can reverse the gears of the entire economy. When export income falls, purchases in other sectors decline, resulting in sharp reductions in investment, employment, and government revenue. It is particularly difficult to plan investments because fluctuations in revenues frequently produce discontinuities in long-term capital improvement project and development programs. That uncertainty results in higher risk premiums on borrowed funds and higher costs of fixed capital formation.

Although this snowball theory is logically coherent, it is not universally accepted. One neoclassical critique (MacBean 1966) attempts to demonstrate that wide swings in profit and loss margins are only marginally attributable to price fluctuation, and that the impact on other economic sectors has not been as damaging as had been supposed. A later study by Knudsen and Parnes (1975) corroborated these results on methodological and statistical grounds. Meanwhile, a further study by Gkzakos (1973) tested the effects of export price instability by using cross-national data to measure the rate of growth of export income and then of the growth of real per capita income. The study concluded that export instability clearly inhibits economic development.

Despite the continuing theoretical controversy and the evidence, M. J. Lord of the IDB concluded that "On the basis of the evidence . . . it appears that export instability has been a justifiable preoccupation for several Latin American countries" (Lord 1980, p. 223). He found that the economies of countries dependent upon exports of sugar, copper, and beef were especially vulnerable, then went on to conclude that "Important potential gains may consequently be derived by a number of countries in Latin America from international agreements because of the disruptive effects that could otherwise hinder their economic development progress. . . . There is little doubt that export instability can produce serious disruptions in the growth of an economy" (Lord 1980, p. 235).

What kinds of commodity price stabilization agreements have been proposed, and why are they important? Most proposals concentrate on a few key commodities (the UNCTAD proposals deal with ten "core commodities": sugar, cocoa, sisal, copper, cotton, coffee, rubber, tea, tin, and jute). These measures have the dual objectives of maintaining price fluctuations within a band of plus or minus 15 percent of the average price for the past five years, while limiting the deterioration in the comparative values of primary commodities and industrial goods. Some proposals reach further, to propose measues to raise commodity prices over time.

To accomplish these objectives, price stabilization proposals focus on one or more of the following six steps. First, buffer stocks of various commodities would be set aside. Second, a "common fund" for financing international commodity stockpiling would be set up (UNCTAD 1976). Third, wider access to compensatory financing has to be provided to Third World countries experiencing balance-of-payments deficits from export shortfalls. Fourth, trade barriers in the AICs that restrict imports of primary products and processed commodities from the Third World need to be lowered. Fifth, Third World countries need to diversify their activities into the processing, distribution, and marketing of commodities, where the lion's share of profits is made. Finally, additional research and development that will improve the marketing and competitiveness of primary commodities vis-à-vis substitutes (for instance, cotton vs. synthetics) must be subsidized (Behrman 1979).

In order to understand why commodity price stabilization is important, one has only to chart the recent history of price movements. According to UNCTAD:

> Commodity prices (excluding petroleum) in real terms declined steadily throughout the period 1950-1972. After a short recovery in 1973-1974, they fluctuated sharply during the remainder of the 1970s, drifting generally downwards toward a level even below the nadir of the early 1970s. By the end of 1980, commodity prices in real terms had reached the lowest level for the past 30 years. (1981, p. 66)

The commodity trade of the Third World is acutely sensitive to world ecoomic conditions. Sniffles can rapidly become pneumonia. Instability, measured by the deviation from trend purchasing power, during the 1970s was from two to four times greater than in the 1960s. Moreover, the shortfalls in earnings grew systematically from 2.5 percent in 1970-71 to 14 percent in 1974-75 and 18 percent in 1979-80. The increased earnings during 1972-73 and 1976-78 did not offset the bad years. Meanwhile, neither import prices nor volumes declined sufficiently to compensate for unstable export receipts. Therefore, the drop in export earnings in poor years was due to deteriorating terms of trade as well as to poor export volumes.

An example of the extreme volatility of prices appears in Figure 7.1. For example, the price of sugar rose from 8.1 cents per pound in 1970 to 65.4 cents in 1974, only to fall to 17.2 cents in 1978. At the moment of writing (June 1984) sugar stands at a fraction over 6 cents per pound.

Such extreme fluctuations make meaningful planning of output or marketing hazardous not only for policy makers in the developing countries, but also for the farms and enterprises that produce and market the commodities, and for eventual processors and refiners. For example, in August 1982 Exxon canceled a $1 billion project in Chile after a nose dive in copper prices, and many workers were laid off. The Dominican Republic saw substantial profits from its sugar exports in 1980 evaporate into a disastrous $200 million loss in 1982. Swings of this magnitude place extreme strain on governments, reducing public revenues while increasing the need for public services. If the swings are too violent, governments – like strings – can break.

The side effects extend beyond national boundaries. Price fluctuations of imported raw materials generate inflationary pressures in consuming nations,

FIGURE 7.1. Commodity Price Instability, 1973-82

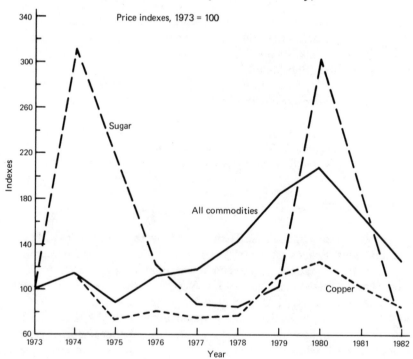

Source: IMF.

as was seen throughout the 1970s. Import prices that rise even temporarily to extreme levels cause ripples throughout domestic economies (Cline 1979). There also tends to be a ratchet effect; higher retail prices for manufactured goods rarely fall back to their previous levels. In this way the extreme movements in commodity prices exert a magnified effect upon the international price level and further reduce the Third World's terms of trade.

Several factors contribute to the wild swings in commodity prices of Third World primary exporters:

1. Crops such as cotton and coffee are vulnerable to changing weather, which can sharply reduce harvests, thereby driving prices up. (For example, the Brazilian crop failure in 1974–75 pushed coffee up by over 200 percent.) On the other hand, unexpectedly "perfect" weather can lead to record yields and falling prices.

2. The demand schedules for primary products are relatively inelastic. Small variations in supply can lead to large swings in prices and earnings.

3. A few MNCs often control the marketing of raw materials. For example, through collusion and use of their market power, the major oil companies (known as "The Seven Sisters") were able to maintain low crude oil prices until 1973. Then they joined forces with OPEC and switched tactics, boosting oil prices to their present level (Schneider 1975).

4. Econometric studies covering the 1950s and 1960s indicate that variations in production and the commodity concentration of producing countries, rather than price swings are the dominant causes of income fluctuations in the Third World (MacBean 1966). However, the problem with these analyses is that production varies with prices: producers reduce output when prices are low. The time lag involved in matching supply with demand so as to increase profits can be considerable, however. If reserves of commodities are inadequate, producers can go bankrupt. This of course is the logic behind U.S. and EEC farm price supports, which make agriculture in the United States and Europe profitable.

5. Access to markets in advanced countries is often restricted. For example, a series of quotas and tariffs provides U.S. sugar growers with preferential treatment in the United States and Europe. Ironically, the Third World is prevented from competing in its area of greatest comparative advantage, thereby substantially reducing incomes and employment, while meager sums of foreign aid and loans are given to fund development.

Earnings from commodity exports represent 55 percent of the Third World's nonpetroleum exports. The massive swings in earnings have contributed to recurrent balance-of-trade deficits and rising indebtedness. Estimates by Jere Behrman for the Overseas Development Council project that price stabilization could increase the annual incomes of producer countries from $500 million to $5.1 billion, depending upon the number of commodities involved. Estimated savings for industrial countries – even after subtracting the costs of operating the stabilization schemes – would net $4.6 billion annually due to the macroeconomic benefits from lower inflation (Cline 1979).

An accurate appraisal of costs and benefits depends on understanding how a buffer stock scheme – the central measure for commodity price stabilization – would operate. The classic case among primary commodities involved the combination of a relatively inelastic supply schedule and an inelastic demand schedule. In any given year the world supply of sugar will vary with the acreage planted, prevailing weather conditions, and yield per acre. Meanwhile, the demand for sugar remains relatively unresponsive to price changes; traditionally, consumers have not substantially reduced or increased their consumption of sugar, even when prices skyrocketed or fell precipitously. (With some variation this basic situation prevails for all of UNCTAD's ten core commodities.) Appendix A provides a more detailed analysis of what happens in this kind of supply-and-demand relationship, and the impact a buffer stock arrangement would have.

Between 1963 and 1972 developing countries would have realized potential gains of $5.4 billion if a buffer scheme including eight commodities ($24 billion for 13 commodities) had been in operation (Behrman 1979, p. 96). Consumers would have received indirect savings from reduced inflationary pressures. Subtracting the costs of operating the buffer stocks from the net gains in revenue (but not the benefits derived from reduced inflation) would have produced gross revenues of $2.2 billion for eight commodities and $28.8 billion for 13 commodities (Behrman 1979, p. 97). An initial fund of between $6 and $10 billion to purchase and store commodities would have been required to finance such a scheme (UNCTAD 1976; Behrman 1979). (Behrman maintains that the consumers and producers of copper and tin would be net losers under a commodity price stabilization scheme and would bear a substantial part of overall costs in maintaining such a system.) While there would have been winners and losers during any period, the winners and losers would change from one period to another. However, the main advantage is that the collective world welfare could be enhanced by such a scheme.

Commodity price stabilization promises much larger incomes for producer nations, but those benefits may be the tip of the iceberg. Oligopolistic industries dominated by MNCs often utilize fluctuating commodity prices as "cost justifications" for their own price increases. "Cost savings" when commodity prices fall are seldom fully passed on to the consumer. For example, retail sugar prices in the United States soared in 1975 when bad weather damaged the crop in several cane-growing countries. The price of refined sugar has subsequently remained well above trend even though record crops have been produced. Distributors simply chose to widen their profit margins. Behrman suggests that reduced inflation in the U.S. economy alone might save $15 billion in a decade. There would be similar but smaller benefits to European and Third World economies.

The net gains from reduced inflation far outweigh the operating costs of a price stabilization system. A World Bank team has concluded that systemic benefits will extend to all commodity crops – that is, total gains from stabilization are positive and gainers can compensate losers, leaving everyone better off (Brook et al. 1978). Its empirical analysis found that Third World countries would earn greater export revenues for cocoa, coffee, wool, and jute, and the price stabilization of wheat would lower import expenditures. The data for sugar and cotton are statistically inconclusive but indicate higher profits.

To conclude, the stabilization of commodity prices can greatly reduce the volatility of investment income, unemployment, and government revenues in the Third World. The most thorough current assessment suggests that the Third World would earn $5.4 billion over a decade if eight key commodities were controlled. In addition, producer governments and businesses could improve their planning for investment and qualify for lower-risk premiums on loans. Such "secondary" savings will probably exceed, and will certainly magnify, the effective use of larger commodity profits. Meanwhile, there seem to be rather limited prospects for increasing the future trend of export prices via commodity price stabilization (any such consequence would be anathema to the advanced capitalist world). Paradoxically, the advanced countries may gain most from commodity price stabilization through reduced worldwide inflationary pressures. Such systemic savings would benefit everyone: the Third World, the ACCs, even the socialist world.

HIDDEN BARRIERS TO TRADE

In October 1982 the French government decreed that all imported videotape recorders (mainly Japanese) must clear customs at Poitiers, a small city in the interior of France, rather than Le Havre, the main port of Paris. The delay in entry and processing of the machines will raise their costs (Lohr 1982). When U.S. baseball bats arrive in Japan, each must be unwrapped, inspected, and rewrapped. Indian exports of shirts and blouses to the United States are restricted by quota, and an internal consumption tax is levied by the EEC on coffee imported from the Philippines (Anjaria et al. 1982). These are examples of hidden, nontariff barriers that restrict international trade flows.

Nontariff barriers are multiform. They range from import licensing requirements that may be applied in a discriminatory fashion, to import quotas for sugar, to a variety of surveillance practices, quarantines, and arbitrary requirements and standards, to outright prohibitions against the exports of a particular nation – for instance, Cuban exports to the U.S. market. The U.S. government has initiated antidumping investigations, and will impose counterselling duties if it finds that foreign steel producers are being subsidized by their governments to undercut U.S. producers in the U.S. market. Other governments require that certain kinds of imports, such as TVs or autos, must contain a minimum number of domestically produced components. In general, any practice that restrains exports from one country to another or impedes the entry of one class of products constitutes a nontariff trade barrier.

A five-part list of nontariff trade barriers appears in Table 7.1.

The first group singles out methods of government participation in trade that either restrict imports from or subsidize exports to Third World countries. They may take the form of grants, tax credits, "buy-national" purchasing, or state trading. A second group involves customs and administrative entry procedures – such as the levy of antidumping duties, arbitrary methods of customs clearance, and requirements for certificates of origin – that discriminate against foreign products.

A third group applies nonmarket quality or "safety" standards as a "cover" for inhibiting imports. For example, arbitrary testing of a product may increase the wholesale cost and thereby make it less competitive with domestically produced goods. A fourth group concerns specific limitations on trade, which include numerical quotas for imports from a particular country or for a certain product, "voluntary" export restraints, and licensing requirements. It also includes minimum pricing devices, such as the now defunct American Selling Price (ASP), which levied a duty not on the invoiced cost but on the comparable American manufacturer's list price. The final category, charges on imports, covers a variety of items from prior deposits to cover the costs of customs services, to discriminatory taxes on specific products or the application of special duties – for example, the special tax on imported liquors.

Additionally, the GATT listing conspicuously omits restrictive business practices. These methods allow large firms to squeeze small firms out of a market. The practices may be overt, such as lobbying for export restrictions for specified domestic markets, or covert, such as selling below cost in a market to drive a competitor out of business (see United Nations 1969, 1978).

Recently the UNCTAD secretariat has begun to monitor the use of nontariff barriers by the major trading nations. The data show that the barriers are concentrated against agricultural exports, predominantly through the use of variable levies. Other measures include discretionary licensing, global quotas, tariff quotas, and voluntary export restraints. The percentage of imports restricted by nontariff barriers for highly protected sectors – plant products, foods and beverages, leather products, and footwear – ranges from less than 5 percent to over 90 percent.

TRADE DEVELOPMENT AND
THE INTERNATIONALIZATION OF CAPITAL

Intel Corporation is located in the heart of California's "Silicon Valley," the rapidly developing center of the U.S. electronics industry. More than 3,000 Intel workers produce a variety of components for use in computers, calcu-

TABLE 7.1. GATT Illustrative List of Nontariff Barriers

Group	Barriers
1	Government participation in trade Trade-diverting aid Export subsidies Countervailing duties Government procurement State trading in market-economy countries Other restrictive practices
2	Customs and administrative entry procedures Valuation Antidumping duties Customs classification Consular and customs formalities, fees, and documentation Samples requirements
3	Standards Standards Packaging, labeling, and marking regulations
4	Specific limitations on trade Quantitative restrictions Discriminatory bilateral agreements Export restraints Minimum price regulations Licensing Motion picture restrictions
5	Charges on imports Prior deposits Credit restrictions for importers Variable levies Fiscal adjustments at the border or elsewhere Restrictions on foreign wines and spirits Discriminatory taxes on automobiles Statistical and administrative duties Special duties on imports

Source: Adapted from Golt 1974, p. 31.

lators and other devices that require memory systems. When Intel's engineers develop a design for a new electronic circuit or process, technicians in the Santa Clara Valley, California plant will build, test and redesign the product. When the new item is ready for production, however, it is air freighted to Intel's plant in Penang, Malaysia, There, Intel's Malaysian workers, almost all young women, assemble the components, tediously hand soldering the fiber-thin wire leads. Once assembled, the components are flown back to California for final testing and/or integration into a larger end product. And, finally, they're off to market, either in the United States, Europe, or back across the Pacific to Japan (NACLA 1976).

Third World export platforms have become increasingly common. Large corporations searching for cheap labor and resources have increasingly moved their production facilities to Asia, Latin America, the Caribbean, and Africa. This is part of a process termed "the internationalization of capital." Although it dates back to the late nineteenth century, when British banks commonly purchased shares in foreign companies, the 1960s began a new phase. MNCs chiefly based in the United States began to establish overseas subsidiaries for assembly and export. In 1961 the first Mexican facility to assemble electronic components was started. In 1964 General Instruments set up the first U.S. electronics factory in Taiwan, in 1968 National Semiconductor moved into Singapore, and Intersil opened a semiconductor operation in India in 1974 (NACLA 1976, p. 13).

Several factors contributed to this expansion. Beginning in 1963, section 807 was added to the U.S. Tariff Schedule. This provision reduced duties on any product whose parts originate in the United States and are sent abroad for assembly. Duty is paid only on the value added abroad. Section 806.30, which applies the same provision to any metal product, has been in effect since 1930. Articles that are imported into the United States under this section include semiconductors, aircraft parts, iron and steel products, and electronic components. Items covered by section 807 include apparel, electronic parts, sewing machines, and office machines. By 1975 over 70 percent of all U.S. electronics imports entered under sections 806.30 and 807 (NACLA 1976).

The new internationalization of capital also has been stimulated by the export processing zones (EPZs) that have sprung up in many Third World countries. EPZs are usually set up along international borders or around ports, and include tax and foreign ownership exemptions that make them attractive to investment by foreign corporations.

Although the boom that occurred throughout the 1960s and 1970s from EPZ-related activities was designed to spur domestic economies, actual development was more limited. When corporations produced their goods in several countries or vertically integrated their production on a world scale – for example, producing semiconductor crystals in the United States, assembling them in Barbados, and marketing them in Europe – it reflected a growing international division of labor. In effect, technology remained concentrated in the developed countries while the Third World provided cheap labor for the less-skilled assembly-related tasks.

While production by these subsidiaries for export nominally enhances the host countries' trade balances, the transactions are largely fictitious, in the sense that they represent internal transferring within the MNC. Thus, a section 807 textile plant in downtown Kingston, Jamaica, imports ready-cut cloth to be sewn into training brassieres for export to the United States. The only local content is the labor of the 60 women who in 1982 were paid a subsistence wage of $30 a week. The textiles are supplied ready-cut by J. C. Penney, the U.S. distribution chain, for reexport to J. C. Penney. Consequently, there is little likelihood that the Kingston assembly operation will diversify or spark related growth in the Jamaican economy. This is development inside hermetically sealed test tubes.

Such operations, however, do raise important issues. If the export processing factory was not located in Jamaica, wouldn't local workers have fewer jobs, and wouldn't the Jamaican economy earn less foreign exchange? The answers to these questions are not obvious. First, we must recall that plants locate in a Third World country to take advantage of lower wage scales. Wage rates typically start very low; if labor costs pass a threshold of relative advantage, a firm will move to another location. Jamaican workers may be learning job skills and making money today, but tomorrow their jobs may be exported. One electronics executive explained that once wages reach "about 60¢ per hour [in electronics] it is uneconomical to use offshore facilities because of other costs involved. Offshore facilities have only a three-to-five-year useful labor advantage" (NACLA 1976, p. 16).

Even where employment is transient, it has been argued that MNC subsidiaries broaden and diversify a country's labor pool by employing large numbers of women workers. On the one hand, this is positive because it often brings women into jobs from which they may have been excluded, and provides them with income and on-the-job training. On the other hand, the motives for such "equal-employment" policies are not always egalitarian. In Singapore plans to hire 75,000 female factory workers were developed in order to avoid local minimum wage laws, which did not apply to women.

Finally, multinational subsidiaries are vulnerable to a variety of trade-related pressures, both internal and external. The activity of the EPZ may be curtailed via a "voluntary" export restaint or the imposition of some other form of non-tariff barrier. Or a domestic credit squeeze may restrict needed imports for processing and lead to layoffs and reduced exports. This occurred in Mexico's border EPZ industries in late 1982.

The two main export industries – electronics and textiles – experienced high instability during the 1970s. Between 1969 and 1971 a recession caused a 15 percent drop in sales. The textile industry responded by laying off 400,000 workers around the world. In Mexico's border EPZ, where garment production is common, 37 factories closed while 53 new ones opened. There is little job security, and the industry makes a limited contribution to regional development. A 1979 study of Mexico's border EPZ concluded: "The Border Industrialization Program (BIP) has neither solved the employment problem nor made any contribution to integrated development in the region. The BIP is a stop-gap measure of a government confronted with crisis-level unemployment, yet unable and unwilling to undertake the necessary structural changes" (Baird and McCaughan 1979, p. 139).

Similarly, a World Bank study of Colombian textile exports tracked the roller-coaster ups and downs of that industry. Clothing exports rose from less than $1 million before 1970 to over $50 million in 1974. Then they plummeted to $30 million in 1975 and have remained at about that level. Fluctuating prices and exchange rates, and the lack of internal economic transportation crippled the industry before it could take off (Morawetz 1980).

More recently, evidence has been accumulating that even the foreign-exchange earnings from the EPZs appear to be evanescent. A study of economic development in the Far East found that exporting sectors had to borrow increasingly to meet their import requirements – especially agricultural imports – because production for export interfered with domestic production. As countries such as Brazil, Mexico, and South Korea have belatedly discovered, export-led growth requires extensive imports of components, raw materials and state subsidies. Agricultural labor is drawn off the land to work in higher-paid industrial sectors – far more workers than the limited number of new jobs – raising the cost of food production and often increasing relieve on imported foodstuffs. When world markets are favorable, these added costs are easily managed, but when export markets grow slowly or even decline, the country has to borrow increasingly to pay for industrial and agricultural imports (Frank 1982).

APPENDIX A
COST AND BENEFITS OF COMMODITY PRICE STABILIZATION

In Figure 7.2, P and Q represent the trend sugar prices and quantity, respectively, which are determined by the normal supply schedule S. If, however, there is a bad sugar crop, supply is reduced to S^* and the price rises to P_2. If there is a particularly good crop due to extraordinarily good weather or the planting and harvesting of more acreage following a period of prevailing high prices, then supply increases to S^{**} and the price falls to $P_1 Q_1$. What is significant is that relatively small fluctuations in supply produce pronounced swings in price.

A buffer stock facility would help stabilize prices by stockpiling surplus production in good years to sell during a bad year when supplies are scarce. Consumers would benefit by paying P_0 instead of the higher price P_2 in low-output years, while producers would gain by receiving P_0, instead of the lower price P_1, in high-production years. Behrman's (1979) analysis demonstrates that under most conditions the sum of benefits is positive, although in some cases

FIGURE 7.2. Commodity Price Stabilization

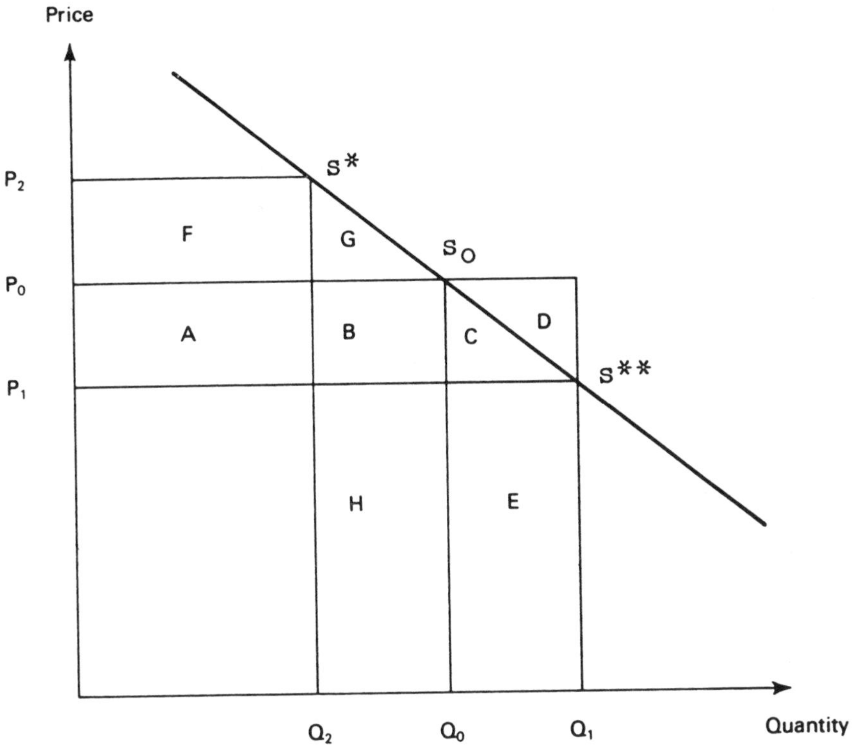

Source: Compiled by author.

(depending upon the slopes of the demand and supply curves) only producers benefit.

In surplus years, when production exceeds the trend, consumers pay $A + B + C$, while the benefit to producers from selling their production, Q, at a higher price is $A + B + C + D$. The buffer stock scheme must bear the cost $C + D + E$. The excess of costs over benefits in a good, high-output year (excluding storage costs) is $C + E$.

When a poor crop yields shortfall, the supply curve shifts to S^*, stocks accumulated during the high-output year are sold at price P_0, preventing the price from rising to P_2. Consumers save the amount $F + G$, while producers lose F in excess profits. The buffer stock scheme earns $B + H$, and the net benefit to all parties is $B + G + H$.

Summing up, over a period of years in which surpluses and shortfalls are equally likely, the net profit for producers is $A + B + C + D - F$ — that is, incomes will rise. Consumers will realize a net loss of $F + G - A - B - C$ through higher prices. For all parties the net result is positive: $B + G + H - C - E$. In reality, the actual configuration of net beneficiaries will vary with the exact slope of supply and demand schedules. It is possible that with altered assumptions, consumers might end up ahead.

Operation of a buffer stock incurs overhead costs. In order to maintain prices within a narrow range, commodities will have to be stockpiled for various periods of time and buffer stock managers will need sufficient financial as well as commodity resources. The overall cost of buffer stock operation is composed of four elements: the present discounted storage costs; present discounted value of the losses on sales of commodity holdings; stock deterioration costs; and transaction costs.

8

THE GATT AND
THE THIRD WORLD

The General Agreement on Tariffs and Trade (GATT), established in 1947, is the principal institution for uprooting obstacles to the free flow of trade. Member nations account for over 20 percent of the world's exchange in manufactured goods, raw materials, and foodstuffs. For over 25 years GATT has influenced international trade policy through a series of multilateral negotiations to gradually reduce tariff and nontariff barriers. In addition, GATT has provided a forum for resolving trade disputes between countries.

GATT fulfills several significant functions in the panoply of institutions concerned with multinational trade. First, it has been the medium for developing a set of rules and procedures to govern trade. Second, GATT's organizational structure is supplemented by a secretariat of skilled experts whose research and documentation assist the disciplined negotiation of trade agreements. Finally, beginning in 1964, and after 20 years of indifference to the special problems of the Third World, GATT recognized the urgent need of the Third World nations for better access to the markets of the AICs. (Perhaps the tardiness should not be surprising; as late as 1960 only 13 Third World nations were members of GATT.)

Although GATT succeeded in breaking down many barriers to free trade, the beginning of the 1970s brought greater discord. The early postwar consensus unraveled with the recovery of Europe and Japan, the rise of the Third World, and the emergence of détente and the attendant conflicts surrounding East-West trade. GATT has found it increasingly difficult to weave together the increasingly divergent interests among its varied membership. Indeed, the failed Geneva summit of November 1982 has raised doubts about GATT's ability to maintain its past gains, much less its ability to respond to new demands.

This chapter will begin by reviewing the history of GATT and the principles and methods that GATT employs to structure trade policy. This will be followed by an analysis of the effects of GATT negotiations on the liberalization of trade (with special attention on the Kennedy and Tokyo rounds of multilateral trade negotiations). Next, the organization's current difficulties in building upon those successes and in counteracting the revival of "protectionism" will be explored. The concluding section evaluates GATT's impact on the Third World.

HISTORY OF GATT

GATT grew out of the failure to realize a much more extensive trade organization, the ITO. The Bretton Woods Conference of 1944 proposed reorganizing the world economy around three institutional cornerstones: the IMF, the ITO, and the IRBD. The ITO was expected to negotiate reductions in tariffs, international trade quotas, and other discriminatory practices that had undermined the world's prewar economy.

The ITO was stillborn. A conference at Havana in 1947-48 wrote a charter for it. However, influential members of the U.S. Congress decided those provisions would infringe on national sovereignty. The original ITO document included measures for promoting employment and economic policy, and economic development and reconstruction. Furthermore, it was to be empowered to seek regulation of restrictive business practices and to promote intergovernmental commodity agreements. The charter was never ratified by the United States or any country, and the ITO never left the drawing board.

To replace the ITO, GATT was created in 1947. The GATT mandate was far less inclusive and concentrated on removing restrictions to international trade. Membership in GATT was voluntary, with each government having one vote. Although GATT would later record impressive accomplishments, many issues that ITO was directed to address have proved to be beyond GATT's means, particularly in the area of intergovernmental commodity agreements.

What GATT does provide is a framework of rules and standards for international trade. At root it is a forum for negotiation and conciliation. Beginning with an initial membership of 19 countries in 1948, it now includes over 80 nations. In addition to most of the advanced capitalist nations and many Third World nations, the socialist countries of Cuba, Czechoslovakia, Rumania, and Yugoslavia are members. In addition to the 80 full members, there are 24 provisional members. These two groups combined account for more than four-fifths of world trade. Since GATT countries are the world's principal traders, any concerted agreement among them is usually decisive. Together, the GATT nations can set norms to govern trade, impose guidelines to justify selective retaliation for unfair trading practices, and waive mutually agreed-upon practices in certain instances.

Through seven major bargaining sessions from 1947 through 1979, the GATT members have made major progress in reducing world tariffs. Nevertheless, little has been achieved in removing nontariff barriers, the major check on expanded world trade. Although the ACCs have partially agreed to dismantle their extensive systems of import-licensing restrictions on nonagricultural products, GATT has been unable to develop effective guidelines because numerous exceptions have been granted to countries with powerful special-interest lobbies, those with special domestic agricultural programs, and some with development policies that attempt to protect infant industries. GATT's major success – reduction of world tariffs on most manufactured goods – reflects the agenda of the ACCs; there has been much less progress in removing barriers to exports from the Third World. Thus far the Third World does not have enough bargaining chips to override the protectionist sentiments that arise in the First World when domestic vested interests are threatened, particularly in agriculture, where restrictions abound.

GATT PRINCIPLES

There are three fundamental principles of GATT. First, trade is nondiscriminatory, with all contracting parties bound by the most-favored-nations clause. Second, domestic industries can be protected only through the customs tariff and not through other commercial measures such as quotas. Third, consultation is the one way to resolve trade disputes.

Nondiscrimination

The most-favored-nations clause specifies that a country will not give one nation better treatment than it gives all contracting parties of GATT. The first article specifies in detail that each nation shall treat the products of all contracting members alike with regard to import and export duties and subsidiary charges, and the rules and formalities governing importation and exportation, internal taxes, and other internal regulations.

Theoretically, the intent of the clause is to ensure that each nation's products are treated equally. However, the means of realizing that intent – reciprocity – cannot equalize what is excluded. Reciprocity means that governments reduce tariffs mutually through negotiations. Governments make these concessions to maximize their gains from trade cooperation. However, a bargain can be struck only when all parties have something to gain. Reciprocity breaks down when countries have little to offer. Consequently, the products of special interest to smaller countries without much bargaining power, such as Grenada's nutmeg, are only infrequently brought into the process.

Concessions

A concession is a promise either to lower the duty on a commodity, and keep it at or below that level, or not to raise the duty on that item. Concessions are usually negotiated with the principal supplier and then, in accordance with the most-favored-nations principle, generalized to all suppliers. A duty limited by concession is considered "bound." Any subsequent action that upsets the exchange is deemed an injury, and the affected nation can seek compensation equivalent to the value of the concession that is unbound.

Customs Duties and Quantitative Restrictions

The second important principle of GATT limits how countries can protect their domestic industries. This principle states that except under special circumstances, only customs duties, which operate by price, are acceptable. Quantitative restrictions, which operate by number or volume, are prohibited. Customs duties are considered "honest" because they are fixed and predictable. Exporters in foreign countries consequently can anticipate the impact. Nontariff restrictions, especially quotas and exchange controls, are more arbitrary, and the exporter can never be certain how the product will be treated: if it will actually be allowed to enter a country at a reasonable price.

Quantitative restrictions on imports usually are quotas. These may be fixed either globally or by country of origin, and are usually operated through import licenses for specified goods. Quotas are especially prevalent for fresh and processed foods. Quantitative restrictions also are applied through multiple exchange rates, which regulate how much domestic currency is needed to buy enough foreign currency to pay for specified imports. If the exchange rate is much higher than normal, or if the amount of foreign currency that can be "bought" is curtailed, the effect can be the same as a quota – that is, a quantitative or volume restriction. Although foreign-exchange arrangements are partially regulated through the IMF, they are still being used to restrict the free flow of trade, particularly by governments trying to avoid or minimize balance-of-payments deficits.

Much has been written condemning the use of quotas and other quantitative restrictions. First, they impede the total volume of trade. Second, they shelter domestic prices and production against the changing requirements of the world economy, and lead to ineffective use of resources. Third, they stifle private enterprise and lead to the overregulation of domestic business. For quotas, in particular, to work, public officials rather than the marketplace allocate imports and exports among private traders. Finally, they lead to bilateral and discriminatory trade flows, cutting newly emerging suppliers off from markets and freezing trade into narrow channels.

Still, quotas and quantitative restrictions persist, even in the AICs that promote trade liberalization. Governments operate by a "no injury" philosophy. If lower tariffs or other policies lead to a bulge in imports, threatening an organized or politically powerful sector of the domestic economy, the practice is reversed and measures are taken to prevent such "disruption." For example, during the 1970s the Dominican Republic developed its clothing industry until it became the third leading exporter of brassieres to the United States. At that point U.S. clothing manufacturers pressured their government to impose quantitative restrictions on Dominican brassieres. No one asked if the domestic industry was inefficient or if its shrinking base meant that U.S. resources could be better invested in other areas.

"Voluntary" quotas or voluntary export restraints (VERs) were applied. Although the use of a "voluntary" quota or VER can have the same effect as a quantitative restriction, it does have some differences. A "voluntary" quota is imposed by exporters or an exporting nation on sales of certain commodities. Since the exporter "wishes" to limit overseas sales, such quotas are treated differently by GATT. The fact that the exporter's restrictions are imposed under the threat that otherwise compulsion will be used, is ignored. Voluntary quotas usually arise from industry-specific pressures, and typify large, politically influential but "declining" industries such as the U.S. textile, auto, and steel producers.

VERs are inherently less effective than quantitative restrictions in reducing imports. Even if the level of commitment were equal, it is easier for most countries to control imports than exports. Under a system of VERs, the governments of most countries lack the resources to adequately supervise private industries. Final destination of a cargo is difficult to determine, since the products can simply be rerouted through nonrestrained countries. Unlike quantitative restrictions, VERs are usually confined to one exporter of a product at a time. When that is coupled with the ineffectual leverage importing countries have over small producers – such countries have little to lose from sanctions – the net effect may be to encourage other exporters to compete for openings in the domestic market of the country imposing the VER. However, it may also be pointed out that even though VERs are less restrictive, they can be implemented with less risk. According to GATT, VERs are generally recognized as an "under-the-table" but legitimate device that permits countries to avoid both domestic and international trade rules.

Consultation

The third important principle of GATT is the concept of consultation between trading parties. GATT works basically as a contractual agreement and has no institutional arm to police its rules. Members have a vested interest in localizing disputes and resolving them before they escalate into trade or tariff wars that could threaten the whole structure of international trade and the postwar prosperity it has fueled. In other words, GATT must be made to work and members to comply because the alternative is unthinkable. (In this respect the formalized ground rules GATT has established resemble the arms control treaties of the postwar era.)

Importantly, the GATT treaty spells out circumstances that justify countries' temporary deviation from the rules. For example, it specifies terms under which member nations may erect trade barriers to protect their balance of payments. It also provides rules for counteracting dumped or subsidized imports. GATT handles trade disputes by providing a forum for disputants to negotiate their problems. When one member feels its terms of trade are being violated, it requests consultations with the "offender," and negotiations proceed.

If the consultations fail, GATT appoints a panel of experts to evaluate the dispute. If the panel decides that a nation's trading interests have been injured, that country is given a "release from obligation to the offender," and the door is open for retaliation. Retaliation can take many forms, including the withdrawal of "bound concessions" or the imposition of quotas on the offender's exports. Protectionism, then, is not eliminated from the international system, but controlled. Orderly procedures for handling disputes give time for tempers to cool and tend to localize responses and link them to clear causes.

MULTILATERAL GATT NEGOTIATIONS

Resolving bilateral trade disputes has been a major GATT activity, but by no means its only function or purpose. Under GATT there have been seven multilateral negotiating sessions to lay the groundwork for international trade rules and codes of conduct. The first convocation occurred at Geneva in 1947. That was followed by a second at Annecy, France, in 1949 and subsequent meetings at Torquay, England, in 1951, at Geneva in 1956, and again at Geneva in 1960-62. The best-known were the Kennedy round, held at Geneva from May 1964 until June 1967, and the Tokyo round, held at Geneva from 1973 to 1979.

At these rounds of negotiations, bargaining takes place multilaterally, with all involved countries dealing jointly on matters of trade policy. In this round robin the trick is to match the concessions countries desire with those they are willing to grant. Before the negotiations begin, each country proposes export products for which it would like to have concessions made. After the participating members exchange their lists, each country draws up counterproposals of concessions it is willing to grant and turns them over to GATT. Members then meet and bargain. When the multilateral session is over, each country presents its new tariff schedule, including all products that have received concessions.

The Kennedy Round

The Kennedy round was the sixth in the series of multilateral tariff and trade negotiating rounds held by GATT. Between 1964 and 1967, 46 nations participated, but the session was uniquely effective because the two main economic powers – the United States and the newly enlarged EEC – came to the bargaining table with unprecedented strength. The U.S. negotiators had unprecedented powers to lower tariffs as a result of the Trade Act of 1962. An earlier GATT amendment permitted the formation of regional customs unions, and since the late 1950s the EEC and the EFTA had been formed. With the success of the Marshall Plan and the particularly rapid growth of the EEC, the United States was no longer the unquestioned economic power, and it was under pressure to reduce its barriers to trade if it wished to avoid being priced out of increasingly integrated European markets.

In the Kennedy round there were four principal negotiating areas: agricultural trade, industrial tariffs, nontariff barriers to trade, and trade with the LDCs. Major progress was made only in the area of industrial tariffs.

In agricultural trade the main problems stemmed from various internal subsidies for these products. Since 1955 agricultural policies and trade had been exempted from the GATT rules. The United States initiated that proposal to protect its extensive system of farm price supports. By the time the Kennedy round of negotiations got into full swing, the United States had surplus production in certain agricultural products, especially grain, that it wanted to sell in the important markets of the EEC. However, the EEC had begun to subsidize its own agricultural sector and wished to shelter it, not only for economic but also (as in the case of France) for domestic political reasons. Most of the agricultural negotiations centered on grains, though special groups also met to deal with meat and dairy products. It was felt that if the tariffs for grains were toppled, the other agricultural dominoes would fall in a neat line.

In the end, the tariffs on grain remained upright, and the only result was a protracted debate on agricultural policy. Indeed, agreement was never reached on the basis and method of negotiation. A very limited agreement on wheat was announced but later proved ineffective. Some tariff reductions on meat, poultry, and fruit were made, but these gains were minor compared with the many remaining areas of disagreement between the EEC and the United States.

The negotiations to reduce industrial tariffs were the great success of the Kennedy round: key concessions were made for chemicals, iron and steel, textiles, and pulp and paper products. One of the main sticking points had been the ASP, a discriminatory system of customs valuation in use by the United States. The EEC contended that the U.S. practice of using the ASP imposed a trade obstacle, particularly in the benzenoid chemical industry. Under the ASP system, imported benzenoid chemicals, some rubber footwear, and certain wool knit gloves were assessed duties on the value of competing U.S. products rather than the value of the imported article. The EEC and United Kingdom insisted upon the abolition of the ASP as a condition for any concessions to U.S. chemical exports. After much debate and study the ASP was retained, but the United States granted concessions of 50 percent on all but its lowest chemical tariffs. In turn, the EEC cut its tariffs on chemicals by 20 percent. (The ASP was not retracted until the close of the Tokyo round.)

For iron and steel the major issue was the protectionism fostered by the steady expansion of Japanese exports. Both the U.S. and the European steel industries were losing sizable chunks of their markets to the relatively more efficient Japanese producers. U.S. and EEC steelmakers clamored for import controls. In 1968 the "voluntary export restraint program," under which the major non-Communist steel producers agreed to limit their steel exports to the United States, was implemented.

Progress also was limited on textiles because of strong protectionist policies that have essentially exempted many items, particularly woolens, from tariff cutting since the Smoot-Hawley Tariff Act of 1930. Imports from Japan during the 1950s were increasingly competitive with the goods of American producers. In the mid-1950s Japan agreed to voluntary export controls for 20 textile products. Instead of reducing American imports, however, the reduction in Japanese exports was taken up by other competitors, such as Hong Kong. In 1962 the first multilateral agreement that regulated textile trade was reached. By the end of the 1960s, Japan had joined Western Europe and the United States as large net importers of textiles. Soon, domestic political pressures on a threatened textile industry mounted. Consequently, there was a consensus among industrial countries to keep tariffs on textiles at a level substantially higher than the average for other manufactured products. Significantly, this was one area where some Third World countries were becoming more competitive, but that position did not translate into influence on the GATT process. In fact, the progress made on both textiles and steel and iron was not so much in freeing up trade as in structuring trade in a way that would reduce the possibility of a trade war among the leading economic powers. This does not mean that progress was not substantial. For instance, almost all major participants made significant concessions involving U.S. industrial imports – over 80 percent of the U.S. list. Moreover, preliminary discussions were undertaken on dismantling nontariff barriers, talks that would bear fruit in the Tokyo round.

The Tokyo Round

At the commencement of the Tokyo round of negotiations, the two major protagonists were still the United States and the EEC. However, a vastly increased trade volume and a dynamically expanding national economy made

Japan a very important partner in these negotiations. In 1960 the United States accounted for over one-third of the world's estimated GNP of $1,500 billion, while Japan's share was only 3 percent. By 1975 the world's GNP was roughly $5,000 billion, but the U.S. share had fallen to about 28 percent, while Japan's share had risen to nearly 10 percent.

The scale and surge of Japanese penetration, especially into U.S. markets, was starkly contrasted with the difficulty of exporting to Japan. The low levels of Japanese imports could only partly be explained by tariffs. Therefore, an important element of the negotiations was directed at dissolving nontariff road-blocks. (Nontariff barriers to trade are summarized in Table 7.1.) To assure future access to the markets of the United States and the EEC, Japan had to demonstrate its own adherence to GATT and its willingness to grant concessions of full reciprocity.

Negotiations on the nontariff barriers to trade resulted in six major agreements referred to as "codes." These agreements lay out new international rules for subsidies and countervailing measures, anti-dumping laws, government procurement, technical barriers to trade (such as product standards), customs valuation, and import licensing.

GATT defines subsidies as bounties or grants (usually provided by a government) that confer a financial benefit on the production, manufacture, or distribution of a good or service. Subsidies can effectively undermine the benefits of tariff or other trade concessions obtained through multilateral bargaining, and threaten the usefulness of the whole multilateral trade negotiations (MTN) exercise. All governments use subsidies in one form or another to achieve national economic objectives. Subsidies can be outwardly or inwardly directed: they can promote exports or prop up strategic domestic industry, such as shipbuilding. Subsidies also take on a bewildering array of forms – from direct cash grants to credits against taxes, concessionary loans, the provision of infrastructure services such as factory space, tax rebates or investment credits, R & D subsidies, tied foreign aid, utilities subsidies (such as price controls on domestically produced oil and natural gas), or loans from the Export-Import Bank.

Under the Code on Subsidies and Countervailing Measures, the country whose products have been economically injured by a foreign subsidized product can impose "countervailing" duties (CVDs). The CVD can equal the alleged net subsidy borne by an imported good. Before such compensatory charges can be levied, however, the entire industry must be found to be injured or threatened with injury, and that damage must be the direct result of subsidized imports. Industries in decline because of other factors, such as a change in the pattern of consumption within a market, would not qualify under this code. It is also important to note that this and the other five codes enacted during the Tokyo round of GATT apply to and bind only signatories of the agreements. For countries that assume obligations under the code, products that benefit from subsidies would be protected from the threat of CVDs unless injury is demonstrated. For countries that remain outside the code, no such test will apply, and CVDs can be imposed at will.

Although the "subsidies code" is an improvement over previous agreements under GATT, critics believe it provides countries with large internal markets (as in the United States) with disproportionate power to defend themselves against disturbances caused by cheaper foreign production. The "subsidies code" states that CVDs are to be imposed in an amount no greater than the net subsidy, and then only where subsidized imports cause or threaten material injury to an industry of the importing country. Prior to January 1, 1980, when this code took effect, the use of export subsidies on nonprimary manufactured products was prohibited only if the subsidy led to the sale of the export at a price that undercut comparable domestically produced items in the importing country's market. Further, the prohibition did not apply to export subsidies for primary mineral products, such as iron ore. The new code vastly expands the illegal category to include any export subsidies that displace the exports of another signatory.

For example, in early 1984 the United States imposed CVDs on Brazilian steel exports as part of an intense campaign for protection by the U.S. steel industry. The result: Brazil was forced to reduce its steel exports needed to service its debt, while U.S. steel producers charged higher prices and earned higher profits than under Brazilian competition. (See Farnsworth 1984 for a detailed discussion of disadvantages of the protective legislation to the American consumer.)

The second code negotiated during the Tokyo round seeks to restrict dumping: sellers charging lower prices in a foreign market than they do at home. When the price of an imported good undercuts manufacturing costs or sells at less than fair market value, dumping may injure or destroy domestic industry. The code further states that the fair-market-value price determinations must include the subsidizing effects of certain tax rebates or remissions in the computation of the purchase price. The code authorizes compensatory duties to offset unfair pricing by private exporters.

The third code tried to open government purchases to competition from imports and to improve policies. The agreement provided a number of detailed rules for tendering procedures to ensure openness, equity, and information. Governments must publish invitations to bid on all upcoming procurements in a timely fashion and must use the same selection criteria to evaluate the bids of foreign and domestic companies. This agreement has an enforcement provision that gives every firm the right to be told why its bid lost and why the winner was selected. Firms are also to be provided with an opportunity to appeal procurement decisions.

The Agreement on Technical Barriers to Trade (which became effective January 1, 1980) was designed to eliminate the use of standards and certification systems to impede imports. Product standards, certification systems, and procedures for testing conformity of products can be manipulated to bar imports or to deny the right of a certification mark for imported products, making them less desirable to consumers. Testing can also be conducted arbitrarily or in a way that increases product cost. The "standards code" seeks to eliminate these technical barriers by requiring signatories to publish a notice of proposed standards and to supply copies of these standards when they are requested. Major trading partners must publish a notice of their proposed standards, provide copies of these standards, and allow other nations to comment on them.

The Agreement on Customs Valuation (effective January 1, 1981) concentrated on defining the base price of goods for duties more fairly. It provides a primary measuring system and a series of adjusting methods that must be applied in sequence. The primary method uses transaction value as a yardstick. That is, duties are charged on the basis of the price paid by the importer for the goods, not on arbitrarily assigned values, such as the selling price of comparable domestically produced items. That base value is then adjusted upward to include hidden costs borne by the importer, such as selling commissions and packing costs. This effectively put an end to barriers like the ASP.

The Agreement on Import Licensing Procedures (effective January 1, 1980) seeks to simplify the procedures that importers must follow to obtain import licenses. The code requires open publication of what steps are necessary to receive a license and of other useful data about the overall system, such as the number of, the value to, and the identity of those who receive permission to import.

The agreement on these six codes was a significant accomplishment. For the first time nontariff barriers were limited through negotiation. In addition, tariffs were reduced an average of 33 percent on $125 billion – about 7 percent – of total world trade.

Among the failures of the Tokyo round was the failure to meet the specialized needs of developing countries. As the negotiations opened, a primary goal had been

> . . . to secure additional benefits for the international trade of the developing countries so as to achieve a substantial increase in their foreign exchange earnings, the diversification of their exports, the acceleration of the rate of growth of their trade . . . and a better balance between developed and developing countries in the sharing of the advantages resulting from this expansion. . . .
> (Tokyo Declaration, Sept. 12-14, 1973)

As negotiations concluded, one U.S. negotiator remarked, "Tokyo was a deal cut between Japan, the U.S. and the Europeans."

Although the average tariff cut for all industrial products was 33 percent, reductions on items of interest to the Third World – such as textiles, leather goods, and agricultural products – amounted to only 25 percent. Moreover, no measures were passed to promote Third World exports, and most discriminatory practices that industrial countries traditionally used to limit imports from the Third World remained intact. Consequently, only one Third World country, Argentina, signed the Procès-Verbal, and only 10 signed the Tariff Protocol (Kemper 1980).

The November 1982 Meeting of Ministers

In November 1982, against a backdrop of rising protectionist pressures and increasing use of VERs and orderly marketing agreements (OMAs), an 88-nation conference of economic and treasury ministers from the world's major trading nations was convened by GATT. The meeting was supposed to lay the groundwork for a new proposal to halt a resurgent protectionism by reducing import pressures in ways that would boost world trade over the long term. However, the timing was inauspicious; many of the industrial countries faced both trade deficits and domestic unemployment rates in excess of 8 percent, the highest since the Great Depression. A GATT report estimated that as a result of the deteriorating international economy, some $24 billion of exports had been placed under special restraints that violated the GATT agreements. Meanwhile, 40–48 percent of world trade in 1982 was subject to quotas and non-tariff restrictions (*Washington Post* 1982). The total value of international trade had just declined for the second successive year.

Three distinct viewpoints emerged at the conference. The Third World position was complicated. With two-thirds of the world's population, the Third World in 1982 accounted for only 15 percent of world trade. Divisions between countries further fragmented their position; their economic bargaining power was not strong. The Third World had increasingly regarded GATT as a "rich man's club," and GATT had not been particularly effective in settling trade disputes of interest to the developing countries. For example, where attempts at conciliation between members fail, a GATT member can call for the formation of a GATT arbitration panel. In 1976 a panel judged that the United States had contravened GATT by giving tax breaks to exporters through "domestic international sales corporations." The United States successfully blocked adoption of the panel's report for five years. When another panel concluded that EEC farm subsidies exerted an unfair leverage on the world sugar trade, the EEC, in effect, ignored the findings. GATT seemed to work only between equals, when the injured party could economically punish the offender. The Third World hoped for actions by GATT that would extend concessions to their exports and assist their economic plight (Guest 1982).

The Europeans viewed the Geneva meeting as a holding operation. They were being criticized by the United States and the rest of the world because of their domestic program of food subsidies that generated pressures to export food surpluses. The Third World was strongly critical of EEC safeguards.

The main American objective at Geneva was to extend GATT to trade in services, such as shipping, banking, advertising, and insurance. These sectors had grown from about 5 percent of world trade in 1947 to 30 percent in 1981, and the United States wanted the Third World and the industrialized countries to lower inhibiting barriers. For example, Argentina forbade the use of TV commercials produced outside the country, and Norway had not granted a license to a foreign insurance company since 1945. U.S. revenues from service exports were over $135 billion in 1982, and services generate two-thirds of U.S. GNP. An additional target was local content legislation, which ran counter to the American free-trade philosophy.

The Geneva meeting opened with the hope that it would avert a crisis in world trade. Even if no structural reforms were forthcoming, the conference might buy time by providing governments with an alibi to forestall protectionist pressures at home. Special-interest lobbies could be told their problems were "under study by GATT." Unfortunately, even the modest hopes looked rose-tinted. A number of "work programs," including one to study the effect of protectionism on services, were formed. However, no agreement was reached to stem protectionism, and no new round of negotiations for trade liberalization was initiated. The EEC, representing 40 percent of world trade, took exception to the final communiqué on agricultural policy.

One reason for the conference's failure was self-fulfilling. All parties came to Geneva looking for external scapegoats and solutions to internal problems. Someone, everyone else, should bear the consequences of economic mismanagement, spiraling debt, and the painful political decisions that would rationalize the world's industrial production by closing older, inefficient industries – such as steel and textiles – in the ACCs and shifting them to the Third World. Few countries could make concessions in a declining world economy without fear of substantial repercussions from increasingly politicized unions. In any event, the economic disruption was too profound for the mechanisms of GATT to have any substantial impact. Instead of GATT containing the crisis, the crisis was threatening to swallow GATT. Since there was no consensus on either the issues or the solutions, Paul Tran Van Thinh, chief of the EEC delegation in Brussels, said that the conference "should never have been held at this time" (Farnsworth, 1982). Only the airlines that transported delegates and the hotels and restaurants of Geneva could disagree.

GATT AND THE THIRD WORLD

Gaining entry to the markets of developed countries is of utmost importance to the economies of the Third World. Clearly, it is the main avenue for earning the foreign exchange that is needed to pay for vital imports and the interest and principal of outstanding debt. Without imports of oil and petrochemicals, industrial raw materials, spare parts, and other intermediate goods, as well as capital and producer goods, domestic production would screech to a halt.

A 1958 GATT report, *Trends on International Trade,* first called attention to how the policies of the AICs aggravated the problems of the underdeveloped world. GATT responded by establishing several committees to study how particular problems in trade affected development (in 1964 the United Nations established UNCTAD). The committees revealed that the policies of the rich industrial nations hindered the Third World's traditional exports as well as its more recent manufacturing production: "They found high tariffs, special internal taxes, quantitative restrictions and escalated tariffs which discriminated against LDCs' exports. Because they had few concessions to offer, developing countries had been unable to make much progress in bilateral negotiations to obtain reductions in these barriers to their trade" (MacBean and Snowden 1981, p. 76). Of the 4,400 tariff concessions made in the 1960-62 Dillon round of negotiations, only 160 were on export items of interest to the Third World (Dam 1970).

Despite the documentation and criticism, little progress was made in stopping these practices. In 1963 some 21 Third World members of GATT called for an action program to remove tariff barriers, international taxes, and all illegal quantitative restrictions on raw materials and foodstuffs, and to reduce tariffs on processed exports. Although some progress was made, divisions between Third World countries that benefited from EEC and Commonwealth preferences and those that did not prevent a concerted mobilization of already limited political and economic resources (MacBean and Snowden 1981, p. 76).

Then, in 1965, a new agreement was concluded and added to GATT. It stated: "The developed contracting parties do not expect reciprocity for commitments made by them in trade negotiations to remove tariffs and other barriers to the trade of the less developed contracting parties." The subsequent Kennedy and Tokyo negotiations seemed to reply that reciprocity was not expected when no concession was given.

Third World trade concerns about GATT are both general and specific. The general issues cluster around the crisis-ridden outlook of the world economy for the 1980s. The international recession that began in 1979 produced the first contraction in trade since 1945. While Third World exports grew by 3.4 percent between 1973 and 1980, in 1981 they stagnated and then declined by 2 percent in 1982. The decline was largely attributable to declining commodity prices and stagnating demand for manufactures from developing countries (World Bank 1983). The decline in commodity prices crippled the ability to service the massive outstanding debt. What can GATT do to forestall and reverse these trends, and what has it done?

The specific Third World concerns have been expressed by the Group of 77, a growing collection (now over 90) of the world's developing nations, at the 1979 Manila meeting of UNCTAD. The declaration published by the Group of 77 discussed how GATT generally, and the last Tokyo round specifically, failed in substance and procedure to address Third World concerns. A World Bank document summarized these concerns as follows:

1. . . . many products of export interest to them were either excluded from the negotiations or received insufficient cuts.

2. There was no liberalization on quantitative restrictions or measures having a similar detrimental effect such as VERs or OMAs, particularly in the fields of agriculture, textiles and leather goods.

3. Tropical products continue to face trade barriers in developed countries.

4. The importance of export and other subsidies for achieving the social and economic objectives of developing countries and for overcoming the structural disadvantages of their economies was not sufficiently reflected in the Subsidies Code.

5. The concept of "graduation" introduced into the negotiations by developed countries would allow them to discriminate among developing countries arbitrarily.

6. In relation to safeguards, . . . no safeguard action should be used to discriminate against exports from developing countries on grounds of low cost or prices. (Kemper 1980).

In addition to these issues, there remain the constant irritations of the protectionist Multifibre Agreement reached among industrial nations, which limits Third World textile exports, and the application of CVDs on Third World exports. A further issue between the Third World and the United States is the future of the generalized system of preferences (GSP) that is intended to provide preferential treatment for Third World exports of manufactures. (The origin and nature of GSP in GATT will be discussed later in this chapter.) The agreement is due to expire in 1985. The U.S. government has announced its intention to renew the agreement (presumably following the Europeans, who in 1981 renewed it for ten years). However, the new GSP would increase the tariff rate on goods of Third World countries that had been successful in increasing their exports, such as Brazil, India, and Singapore. Until it is renewed and its specifics are confirmed, the United States can use the GSP to implicitly pressure Third World acceptance of U.S. views in the international trading system.

In addition to these specific concerns, the entire approach of GATT is viewed as discriminatory to the Third World. First, the principle of reciprocity requires that each party make a concession in exchange for a benefit. For the poor countries of the Third World, there is little that they can offer by way of concessions or compensations that would be of interest to the industrial countries. The issue is one of economic leverage. Hindley (1980) makes this point clear in his discussion of VERs. For example, if the EEC were to request VERs on U.S. exports of electronics, the United States could respond by threatening to retaliate in kind against EEC steel or chemical exports. India, however, would be unable to respond effectively. Second, despite the reductions in tariffs achieved by GATT, outside of a handful of newly industrialized countries (NICs) like Brazil, Singapore, and South Korea, the Third World does not produce the range of industrial products necessary to significantly benefit from tariff concessions.

Third World representatives have argued that with their massive debts and growing trade deficits, it would be virtual economic suicide to slash tariffs and encourage further imports. Moreover, the AICs presently enjoy a massive balance-of-trade surplus in sales of manufactures ($168 billion in 1980) to the Third World.

Generally, the existing framework of international trade, dominated primarily by market forces and guided by structures that were established by, and in the interests of, the leading industrial powers, is not responsive to the needs of developing countries. More specifically, the Third World countries, which now constitute a majority of the membership of GATT, have questioned the value of its objectives to their developmental aspirations. The free-trade ideology that underpins GATT assumes, and tends to reproduce, the present economic balance among nations. Increasingly, Third World nations feel that the few benefits they receive from GATT are like hand-me-down shoes that no longer fit, and so are tossed their way by the countries of the First World.

Another basic operating principle of GATT that has stirred controversy is the most-favored-nations clause. Although this principle ideally rules out any preferential treatment among nations through trade policy, it works quite differently.

> In practice, however, what appears just and equitable is not necessarily anything of the sort. If the United States, for instance, has a certain tariff structure and applies it equally to all countries, it means that the country *does not discriminate between producers*, but it does not necessarily follow that the United States does not discriminate between nations. If it has a high tariff on cocoa but a low one on Scottish sweaters, it means that Britain is given better treatment than Ghana. Then what is a nondiscriminatory policy in principle becomes for all practical purposes a policy of discrimination. (Soderstein 1980, pp. 233-34)

Some Third World countries feel they should be granted unilateral tariff concessions on a nonreciprocal basis by the advanced countries. They argue that most-favored-nations status and reciprocity have mostly supported the status quo, giving the advanced countries the largest tariff cuts on manufactured goods that the LDCs cannot produce competitively. In addition, they are requesting preferential relief in areas such as licensing, standards, and bilateral quotas because Third World parties are burdened disproportionately by these nontariff barriers. Because their economies are smaller and less diversified, LDCs tend to be more dependent on exports. In response to these demands and in an attempt to restore its credibility among the NICs, GATT created GSP. In the Tokyo round it was stated that the purpose of this system was to "secure additional benefits" for the LDCs in international trade. Although GSP was originally to last only ten years, it has been made a permanent part of GATT.

GSP

The GSP is a series of schemes presented by individual countries that allows trade preferences to be granted nonreciprocally to developing countries. These concessions cover manufactured and semimanufactured goods, and certain processed and semiprocessed agricultural products. Under the GSP there are, however, major exceptions, including mainly textiles, leather goods, and petroleum or petroleum by-products. The specific provisions of all these schemes vary by country, and the United States was the last industrialized nation to fully implement its system. Monroe (1975, p. 54) states:

> During the latter half of 1971, the European Common Market, Japan and Norway implemented their generalized tariff preference systems. On January 1, 1972, the United Kingdom, Ireland, Sweden, Denmark and Austria all followed suit. Switzerland and Austria joined ranks on March 1 and April 1, respectively. Australia continued to operate a limited system of tariff preferences as it had done since 1965. Canada, the most recent participant in GSP other than the U.S., activated its scheme in July 1974.

It was not until November 24, 1975, that President Gerald Ford issued Executive Order 11888, implementing the GSP. Basically, the order divided all U.S. imports from a designated set of beneficiary developing countries (BDCs) into three categories: products not eligible for duty-free treatment from GSP; products eligible under GSP; and products generally eligible except to beneficiaries that fail to meet the "competitive need" provision. Products fall into this last category if the exporting beneficiary accounts for more than half of U.S. imports of that item or if the value of the beneficiary's exports of that item to the United States exceeded $425 million during the previous year. The dollar value of the cutoff level is adjusted annually to the growth rate of U.S. GNP. If the product was not produced in the United States by the beginning of 1975, it is exempt from the "competitive means" test and falls into the first category. Finally, to be eligible for duty-free treatment under GSP, the cost or value of the materials produced in the beneficiary country plus the direct cost of processing before import must constitute at least 35 percent of the appraised value at the time of entry through U.S. Customs.

Although the GSP seems magnanimous, the key is not always the list of products an industrialized country includes. There are also sins of omission. Many manufactured and semimanufactured goods are defined as "import-sensitive," and therefore ineligible for tariff relief. For the United States "import-sensitive" products included a wide range of textiles and apparel, electronics, steel, and glass products.

Such "safeguard provisions," or loopholes, are widespread. They protect the trade interests of the developed countries while severely reducing the trade benefits likely to accrue to the developing countries under GSP. The loopholes in GSP are embodied in various technical regulations governing this category of trade. Besides constraining potential trade, these regulations are implemented through complicated administrative procedures that frustrate suppliers who qualify for GSP. One such provision is a policy developed in February 1981 under President Reagan. According to *Business America*, the official magazine of the U.S. Department of Commerce, International Trade Division:

> Under this process the President's authority will be used to limit benefits for the more developed beneficiaries in products where they have demonstrated competitiveness and to provide increased opportunities for less developed, less competitive countries. This action is designed to promote the continued graduation of more advanced developing countries from GSP benefits in products where they have demonstrated competitiveness. In addition, over time such action will help shift the overall share of benefits from the more to the less advanced and less competitive developing countries. (1981, p. 11)

Indeed, the GSP system should encourage diversified production and act as an incentive for new investment. The preferential access provided by GSP should induce entrepreneurs, both domestic and foreign, to invest in new production facilities in beneficiary countries. The theory is being severely tested, however, by the numerous safeguard provisions – which currently exempt about 2,800 products from tariff concessions – and by "competitive need" provisions. Moreover, those criteria can be amended periodically. Considering that it is much easier for an AIC to respond to domestic pressure and expand exclusionary lists than to grant unilateral concessions, a potential entrepreneur would have to weigh the long-term viability of his investment before proceeding. If GSP was judged solely by the new investment it has sparked in the Third World, it would be a failure.

The Tokyo round has made GSP a permanent part of GATT. Individual countries can, and do, review and change their tariff preference schemes annually or every few years. GSP must also be measured by what it might accomplish. In his discussions about how to use GSP to stimulate economic growth in LDCs, Monroe suggests three measures to improve the system. First, tariff preference schemes should be guaranteed for at least several years, rather than be subject to annual reviews. Second, safeguard provisions (escape clause provisions that set arbitrary ceilings for imports) should be dropped. Finally, preference schemes should be liberalized and manufactures and agricultural products should be covered (1975, p. 56). Suggestions for achieving these three goals include changing the procedural requirements for adding new products to the GSP list and raising the absolute dollar limitations on specific imports.

GSP could give the Third World an incentive to export industrial goods and, consequently, should stimulate greater investment in the export sector. However, sluggish growth in the world economy, high unemployment in industrial countries, and a strong push to protect domestic manufacturers dim the prospects for meaningful reforms. In fact, advanced countries have responded to crises in their large, important, but relatively inefficient industries (such as autos, steel, and textiles) by adding new restrictions. Governments, particularly in democracies, find it difficult to sustain the costs of the normal adjustment process of domestic labor and capital reallocation.

So long as the world economy is stagnant, a variety of voluntary export restraints, local content bills, and other protective devices will continue to exist and even multiply in spite of GATT agreements. This harsh reality and the failure to initiate another round of trade negotiations indicate that GATT will have little to offer the Third World in the 1980s. The widening realization among the nations of the Third World of GATT's inadequacies originally gave the impetus for establishment of UNCTAD. It is likely that UNCTAD will increasingly represent Third World trade interests while GATT struggles against a rising neo-mercantilism for the remainder of an increasingly tumultuous decade.

PART III

TOWARD AN AGENDA FOR REFORM

9

TOWARD A NEW GLOBAL ECONOMY: UNCTAD AND THE NIEO

Throughout the 1970s and 1980s the international economy was mired in the worst crisis since the depression of the 1930s. Third World countries were the hardest hit. This chapter summarizes the nature of the crisis, then analyzes some of the proposals for economic reform, specifically the NIEO.

EVOLUTION OF THE TRADE-DEBT SYSTEM

Following World War II, the Bretton Woods system established a framework whereby MBDs, including the World Bank and the IMF, have acted in concert to provide the necessary liquidity to finance world trade and, in particular, U.S. exports. This structure concentrated first on the reconstruction of Europe and then shifted, during the 1960s, to build up the economic infrastructure of the Third World. From the Marshall Plan on, cycles of borrowing to finance trade have driven the motor of the world's economy. At first, everyone seemed to gain. The system encouraged the formation of private corporate empires, which could market their exports of capital, relocate factories in the Third World to better compete for the newly emerging markets, and harness new sources of raw materials and cheap labor. The AICs benefited from the stimulus provided by the sale of exports and the repatriation of MNC profits earned from foreign subsidiaries. The developing countries gained from the construction of roads, dams, and schools and from foreign investment that created new industries and new jobs.

Although everyone seemed to win, in fact growth was not equally distributed. Those interests tied to commerce, manufacturing, and banking tended to benefit greatly. Those who handled trade or could claim a share in the monopolistic profits of the supplier industries profited. Those on the margin who obtained education and jobs in the industries created by the trade-debt system were helped. But many were not so fortunate. Peasants, the under-employed (many of whom would become unemployable in an increasingly sophisticated production system), and domestic producers who could not compete with the sophisticated international enterprises lost out. In some countries, such as Brazil, the income distribution worsened appreciably.

In general, however, the system worked, and would continue to operate without a major crisis as long as the growth of debt service remained below the growth rate of exports. However, in August 1971 a disturbing series of events began. In that month, following several years of severe strain, the world's monetary system was ruptured as the United States went off the gold standard. That fact made clear what had been abstractly obvious for at least a decade: gold could no longer underpin the world's currencies. The United States' unilateral devaluation shattered financial confidence and was the first stone to fall in a subsequent rock slide, culminating in the joint action of the OPEC states to boost oil prices. Severing the dollar from gold and the OPEC action together derailed the international economy from the seemingly endless growth curve of the preceding decades.

Throughout the 1970s the oil-importing Third World borrowed heavily to cover energy costs and to finance industrialization. The need for borrowing increased because of a reduction in the relative amount of public grant assistance. Instead of encouraging Third World oil importers to restructure their economies and attempt to balance their trade, private international banks were encouraged by the AICs to recycle their OPEC deposits by developing syndicated loan packages. As the lending boom accelerated, smaller banks with no overseas experience or information joined the bandwagon to gain access to the high profits available from international finance. In this giddy atmosphere the emphasis was not on appraising loan quality but on keeping the flow of capital running so that the deflationary potential inherent in the oil price rise would not choke off exports to the Third World from the industrial economies.

By the end of the decade, the Third World could not continue to absorb enough debt to sustain the international economic system. Nonetheless, the pressure to increase indebtedness was becoming uncontrollable. With the rapid emergence of the Eurodollar market, a banking system parallel to the Bretton Woods system emerged; however, it lacked such safeguards as the reserve requirements that were enacted to control domestic financial institutions following the collapse of the 1930s. A number of analysts, including those at the World Bank, hoped that rapid industrial growth would allow Third World economies to produce and export their way out of debt. Others, like those at Morgan Guaranty Trust, realized the pitfalls of that strategy, since the AICs were actively resisting the trade deficits in their own accounts that would be required for the Third World to generate trade surpluses. On the contrary, each AIC was trying to maximize its trade and payments surpluses to maintain the value of its currency.

The MNCs also contributed to the evolving crisis. Many projects were designed to recoup investment capital in less than three years, and that money was repatriated to the home office rather than reinvested locally. Many MNCs developed systems of intrafirm trade and financial transfers, so that transactions were recorded between divisions of the same international firm. This permitted "creative accounting," and profits were often transferred to the division with the lowest tax burden. During the 1970s and into the 1980s, the activities and operations of MNCs, particularly their marketing and production strategies, became increasingly complex. There was an accelerated trend toward global marketing while production was decentralized and shifted to the country with the cheapest labor costs for each production activity. The labor-intensive, low-technology activities were located in the Third World, where there was a vast pool of unskilled workers, while technology-intensive operations were concentrated in the industrialized countries. The MNCs cooperated with the multinational banks to integrate production worldwide. Nations, particularly Third World nations, found it increasingly difficult to implement independent economic policies (such as rationing internal credit so as to favor industrial activities) to stimulate their economic development.

Meanwhile, the IMF acted to ensure that debt would be repaid. It conditioned the loans so that borrowing countries abandoned domestic measures that might build up Third World surpluses, but U.S. and Western European austerity that put the heaviest burden of economic adjustment onto the poorest sectors of the population – workers, the unemployed, women and children – was pushed (UNICEF 1983).

GATT continued to promote free trade through the reduction of tariffs. However, that had little impact on the Third World, which needed the removal of nontariff barriers to its exports in the AICs. Without such assistance the development of exports in agroindustrial products, often the key to Third World development, was closed or arbitrarily restricted. A few exceptional countries, located at the nexus of regional trade flows, experienced exceptionally rapid export growth. This was true, for instance, of Hong Kong and Singapore. However, most Third World countries experienced declining terms of trade and deteriorating trade balances and had great difficulty in sustaining profitable export prices. This trend became acute in the early 1980s.

In short, according to such respected Third World observers as Mahbub ul-Haq, a former vice-president of the World Bank, the international economic system has tended to serve the interests of the AICs. The MNIs have directed their efforts toward structuring the economies of the Third World to fit the evolving requirements of the industrial countries rather than meeting the fundamental needs of their populations (ul-Haq 1976).

Under these circumstances the export-led-industrialization and import-substitution strategies that appeared so promising no longer appear to be viable for most Third World nations. Export-led growth may work for those nations, like Singapore and Hong Kong, that are located at the core of a regional trade system or those, like South Korea and Taiwan, whose economies benefit from U.S. military and strategic expenditures. Others – such as Chile, Jamaica, and Brazil – do not fit into these categories, but may grow over the short term. However, those bursts will be followed by sharp reverses and economic dislocation as local agricultural and industrial production is replaced by cheaper imported products.

Real and long-term economic development in the Third World depends on resolving two sets of fundamental, underlying contradictions. First, the debt problem must be tackled. The burden of servicing old Third World indebtedness must be lifted, so that a high proportion of capital inflows and export earnings will actually be invested in the construction of productive resources. New debt that does not generate production and foreign exchange should be avoided. Second, restrictions on Third World trade must be torn down or leapfrogged. Alternative strategies of industrialization and production for export that do not generate offsetting streams of imports and a geometrically rising debt must be developed. Such options do exist, but they do not benefit everyone, and they sometimes run counter to the financial interests of the traders and merchants who presently dominate the Third World's economies.

It is important to realize that since the 1960s, a Third World viewpoint has been developing about the operations of the international economy. The remainder of this chapter will examine the evolution of that position through UNCTAD, culminating in the call for the NIEO. Using that context, the final two chapters will evaluate proposals for resolving the debt crisis and reforming the system of trade.

THE EMERGENCE OF UNCTAD

The ITO was proposed at Bretton Woods to be the charter institution for promoting and regulating world commerce. In early negotiations to set up the trading system, the Latin American nations wished to protect their industries during their "infancy." (The infant industries argument is discussed in U.N. Economic Commission on Latin America 1950.) These countries argued that protection was needed for a limited period of time, until industries could accumulate enough productive capacity to compete with foreign firms. After that threshold was reached, controls could be removed. The Latin Americans also argued for commodity agreements between producer and consumer nations to stabilize prices and assure minimum incomes. The Havana Charter of the ITO recognized the special needs of developing countries, included special corrective policies, and provided these nations with the opportunity to help manage the organization. However, the industrial nations, led by the United States, insisted on a free-trade ideology. The U.S. Congress refused to ratify the Havana Charter, and the ITO died stillborn.

GATT then emerged as the institution responsible for regulating trade. Intended as an interim body, it failed to address the interests of the underdeveloped nations. GATT worked best by regulating trading relationships among equals. The most-favored-nations provision, which is its centerpiece, is based on reciprocity and eliminates development-promoting preferential trading agreements. Moreover, the commodities of key concern to the Third World – agricultural and tropical products – were largely excluded from agreements removing trade restrictions. Shut out of the dialogue, most Third World countries tried to protect themselves and turned inward to pursue a policy of industrialization by import substitution (Spero 1977).

In 1961 the Third World began to actively try to change the way the international economic system was managed. President Tito of Yugoslavia proposed to the first Conference of Nonaligned Nations, meeting in Belgrade, that an international conference on trade and development should be convened. Despite initial opposition from the United States, the United Nations Economic and Social Council responded to the call from a group of 77 developing countries (later christened the Group of 77).

UNCTAD met in Geneva in 1964. Attended by 2,000 delegates from 120 countries, it sought to achieve several objectives. First, the declaration of the Geneva UNCTAD stated:

> The existing principles and patterns of world trade still mainly favour the advanced parts of the world. Instead of helping the developing countries to promote the development and diversification of their economies, the present tendencies in world trade frustrate their efforts to attain more rapid growth. These trends must be reversed. (United Nations General Assembly, 18th session, quoted in Spero 1977, p. 168)

To accomplish this, the meeting proposed several actions. It called for the progressive reduction and early elimination – without reciprocal concessions – of all barriers to Third World exports. It sought increased exports of primary products and stabilization of their prices of manufactured and semimanufactured goods, and reduced discriminatory shipping and insurance costs for these products. In addition, there was a call for better coordination of trade and aid policies, which was followed by a general demand for trade over aid.

These demands came in response to a deteriorating economic situation in developing countries. Between 1957 and 1964 the value of commodities, which comprised between 80 and 90 percent of their export income, dropped 12 percent. Rising import prices had resulted in a 26 percent decline in the terms of trade. As a result, a $20 billion gap between likely income and the capital needed to attain a minimum rate of growth was projected for 1970. Moreover, payments on loans contracted during the mid-1950s were rising at an annual rate of 19 percent.

UNCTAD was seen as an institution that would devote complete attention to trade problems in relation to economic development. It would have a one-state/one-vote arrangement, in contrast with the U.S.-dominated IMF and IBRD. It began with a powerful stimulus, the widespread belief that there was an underlying obligation to ensure that the Third World would have access to the resources needed for economic development.

UNCTAD MEETINGS: 1964-83

Since its founding in 1964, there have been five further meetings of UNCTAD. These meetings have occurred approximately every four years. The Geneva meeting was followed by UNCTAD II at New Delhi in 1968; UNCTAD III at Santiago, Chile, in 1972; UNCTAD IV at Nairobi, Kenya, in 1976; and UNCTAD V at Manila in 1979. The most recent meeting of UNCTAD was in Belgrade, Yugoslavia, in late 1983. The results of each meeting will be summarized briefly.

UNCTAD I (Geneva, 1964)

The Geneva meeting established UNCTAD. Here the main demands of the Third World were presented: the nonreciprocal elimination of barriers to exports from the underdeveloped world; commodity price stabilization; additional financing to import capital goods; and improvement in secondary features of the terms of trade, such as freight, insurance, and debt fees. As a result of this session, the industrial nations agreed that future tariff restrictions would not have to be mutual. This was the first step in recognizing that national economies are substantially unequal and that the world economy will eventually stagnate unless a helping hand is extended to develop the markets and production capacities of those on the bottom.

UNCTAD II (New Delhi, 1968)

At this session the Third World bloc was represented by the Group of 77, which now included an enlarged membership. Ths bloc lobbied for removal or paving of a long list of export tariffs. However, several AICs were having severe balance-of-payments problems, and few immediate gains were forthcoming. In 1971 GATT inaugurated the GSP to provide preferential treatment for negotiated lists of Third World exports.

UNCTAD III (Santiago, 1972)

Reform of the international monetary system was at the top of the agenda. Concern was expressed about the operations of the IMF's SDRs and about how to increase and restructure international liquidity to promote trade and development. Special emphasis was placed on increasing developmental assistance along with the supply of capital.

Other issues also arose. Efforts were launched to persuade those AICs that had not yet adopted GSPs to do so, and the rest to expand their lists of "preferred" products. There were also attempts to control the policies of MNCs in the Third World, in order to enhance the flow of advanced and appropriate technology and to establish national sovereignty over natural resources. This eventually led to the founding of the U.N. Center on Transnationals in 1974.

UNCTAD IV (Nairobi, 1976)

The Nairobi conference was the first to follow the revolutionary precedent set by OPEC for pricing raw materials. Indebtedness among the nonoil-exporting countries of the Third World was increasing along with the cost of importing petroleum-based products. Meanwhile, the AICs were trying to reduce their deficits arising from imported oil by cutting unnecessary expenditures, and development assistance was slashed.

The fact that a group of Third World nations had successfully established prices for oil, albeit at the expense of other developing nations and the industrial countries, set the tone for the session. Third World representatives demanded an NIEO that focused on the formation of new commodity cartels and sought relief from the indebtedness stemming from OPEC's success. An integrated program for commodities and a common fund to finance buffer stocks was proposed. Proposals for debt relief ranged from postponing interest payments while commercial debts were consolidated and then stretching out the repayment schedule over 25 years, to outright debt cancellation for the most severely affected countries. The AICs were also asked to increase their development assistance to 0.7 percent of GNP by 1980, with 90 percent of the aid coming from untied grants and interest-free loans. There was a renewed call for better access to industrial markets and for a legally binding code to regulate technology transfers and other MNC activities.

The representatives of the industrial nations rejected the concept of the NIEO. Instead of a common fund for commodities, the United States counterproposed an International Resource Bank to finance private-sector exploration and investment in the Third World that would be supplemented by compensatory assistance administered through the IMF and the World Bank. Generalized debt rescheduling was rejected because it would erode the "creditworthiness" of the borrowers. Voluntary guidelines were proposed for MNCs.

Out of this impasse there was a small movement. Negotiations for establishment of an Integrated Programme for Commodities and a Common Fund began. After nearly 1,000 meetings the Common Fund was scheduled to start in 1982. However, only a quarter of the necessary start-up capital was ever raised, and as of the UNCTAD VI meeting in 1983, the buffer stock fund was still in mothballs.

UNCTAD V (Manila, 1979)

The international economy was still plagued by simultaneous recession and inflation. The industrial countries were becoming more protectionist, and the Third World debt was burgeoning. The Group of 77 not only proposed elimination of the restrictions on Third World exports but also suggested a general review of trade patterns to explore the feasibility of transferring whole industries (such as textiles) to the Third World. If such a plan worked, it might increase the efficiency of those industries, sidestep tariffs in the industrial countries, and encourage the AICs to shift their domestic investment capital to the growth sectors of their economies and away from industries with shrinking markets.

The developing countries also sought more immediate relief. There was a call to transform official government-to-government debts of the poorest nations into grants (Britain later responded by canceling nearly $2 billion of Third World debt). The pivotal role of the IMF was closely scrutinized. The Group of 77 asked the IMF to formally link SDR allocations to development needs, subsidize interest costs on loans, and reduce the conditionality imposed on domestic economic policy as a precondition for financial aid.

Once again, the adverse economic climate and the fundamental opposition of interests produced stalemate. The call for global trade negotiations within the UNCTAD framework was opposed by the AICs, which feared that the talks would undermine GATT. The AICs, led by the United States, adopted a strategy on substantive issues that was calculated to divide the Third World into interest groups. By the Manila meeting, cynicism began to emerge that UNCTAD was only a forum for allowing the Third World to periodically and ritually "blow off steam."

UNCTAD VI (Belgrade, 1983)

The world economic outlook worsened. In 1982 the first postwar decline in international trade was recorded; the crushing debt burden had caused 30 countries to default between 1981 and 1983. Protectionist pressures were mounting in the United States and Europe. For example, shipments of steel from debt-strapped Brazil to the United States were priced out of the market because of a special supplementary tariff.

By the time UNCTAD VI met, a series of high-level conferences (including GATT, the Commonwealth ministers' session in New Delhi, the Williamsburg summit of the five major AICs, and a meeting of Third World debtors in Buenos Aires) had already occurred during 1983. These earlier meetings both dramatized the nature of and polarized the conflicts that sprang from the depth of the global depression.

In Belgrade the Group of 77 proposed a three-pronged reform. First, it wished to restructure the IMF, the World Bank, and all regional development banks to increase net capital flows and reduce external debt. Second, the Common Fund should be ratified, so that it could begin operating in 1984; the Nairobi Integrated Programme on Commodities should be implemented to stabilize commodity markets; and conferences to negotiate how to deal specifically with copper, cotton, and hard-fiber prices should be convened. Finally, there was a renewed effort to roll back protectionism and refine the GSPs introduced in 1971. By offering a concrete plan, the developing countries turned down their rhetoric, tried to work within the international economic system, and moved toward accommodation with the AICs.

That spirit of compromise was based on the growing interdependence of the world economy. By 1983 approximately 40 percent of the exports from the Western industrial powers were consumed in the Third World. Logically, renewed real growth in the AICs seemed to depend on greater purchasing power in the developing countries, which required more concessional aid, commodity-price stabilization, a reduction in nontariff barriers to trade, and a revamped monetary system. Short-term sacrifice, spread more equitably to include the AICs, promised long-term dividends. Nonetheless, the AICs, led by the United States, continued to advocate austerity programs that placed the strains of the whole world economy on its weakest link. Third World prosperity would depend on countries "pulling themselves up by the bootstraps," overlooking the fact that there were too few bootstraps – and most of those were frayed.

Because of the continued gulf between the advanced and underdeveloped worlds, Belgrade was a failure. So disappointing was the meeting that UNCTAD's senior economic adviser referred to the session as the "Belgrade debacle." The clear lesson seemed to be that UNCTAD could not bring accord when positions were so polarized and the division of economic power so skewed. It seemed doubtful that "the sheep could coexist peacefully with the wolves" (Clairmonte, 1983).

THE NIEO: PROS AND CONS

The clamor for an NIEO, which was voiced in the United Nations beginning in the mid-1970s, grew out of mounting Third World frustrations. From 1946 to 1971, many of these countries experienced growth that seemed to lay the groundwork for real development. Health conditions improved, educational levels rose, and GNP expanded. The 1970s, however, brought harsh reappraisal.

Many of the hopes entertained in the Third World were punctured by several disturbing trends. First, the terms of trade between the developing nations and the AICs were clearly deteriorating. Second, the income disparity between rich and poor countries, as well as within many Third World countries, deepened. Meanwhile, with a few notable exceptions, the gap between the Third World's actual and potential technological levels widened. Unemployment rates had reached astounding levels and were still climbing. All of this was not new information; it was generally well known and documented (Bonilla and Girling 1973).

What was new was a shift in focus from more capital imports toward analysis of international structures and mechanisms to determine whether they were the source of the Third World's disadvantage. That analysis suggested the direction the NIEO should follow. For instance, the distribution of international financial reserves has been exceedingly imbalanced. The poor nations, with over two-thirds of the world's population, received less than 4 percent of international reserves between 1970 and 1974. Why? Because the rich nations controlled the creation and distribution of international reserves through expansion of their own currencies and through their dominance of the IMF.

Other research showed that the distribution of earnings from commodities is heavily weighted in favor of the AICs. According to one estimate, the final consumers pay over $200 billion for goods manufactured from the major primary product exports (excluding oil) of the Third World. In their final, packaged and processed form, these goods bring the AICs some $170 billion. The share of gross revenue received by Third World nations is only $30 billion. The explanation for the disparity is simple: the AICs control product processing and distribution, which are the high value-added components (ul-Haq 1976).

Finally, tariff walls erected by the AICs prevented the Third World from earning a fair share of the world's wealth. The AICs protect their agriculture through more than $20 billion in annual farm subsidies and by nontariff barriers against textile and leather imports. Underlining all of this is the fact that the Third World has only pro forma participation in the decisions taken by the paramount financial agencies: the World Bank, the IMF, and GATT.

The NIEO is, in its simplest form, a demand for economic justice and equity. To accomplish that goal, four central sets of proposals are offered. The first set concentrates on revamping the present international financial system and creating mechanisms that guarantee resource transfers from rich to poor nations. The second level of proposals would restructure the international trading system, including measures that would enforce a new code of ethics on MNC operations in the Third World. The third group of proposals would create a new pattern of industrial development, based upon national control of natural resources and a more open transfer of technology. The final measures establish the principles of political independence and of nonintervention by the AICs in the Third World. Corollary measures would promote and encourage political and economic cooperation among nations of the Third World. The NIEO's agenda is summarized in Table 9.1.

TABLE 9.1.   The New International Economic Order: Principal Issues

I.   Financial reform
1.   Linkage of development assistance to the creation of SDRs
2.   Reform of structures and procedures followed by the World Bank, IDA, and IMF to facilitate a more favorable transfer of financial resources for development
3.   Renegotiation of Third World debts on conditions that are more favorable to the Third World
4.   Transfer of a portion of armament funds for economic development and introduction of automatic resource transfer by linking those funds to a form of international taxation, royalty, or creation of reserves

II.   Trade reform
1.   Lowering of tariffs and nontariff barriers to Third World imports
2.   Measures to make natural resources more competitive with synthetics
3.   Creation of buffer stocks through the formation of producers' associations
4.   Promotion of Third World participation in "invisible" world trade, such as shipping
5.   Development of an integrated program of price supports for Third World commodity exports
6.   Indexation of Third World commodity prices to the prices of AIC exports of manufactured and capital goods
7.   Regulation of the activities of MNCs in the Third World, including adoption of a code of conduct and elimination of restrictive business practices adversely affecting Third World participation in international trade

III.   Industrial development
1.   Negotiation of redeployment of special industries from industrial nations to Third World nations
2.   Establishment of mechanisms other than direct private investment to transfer technology
3.   Guarantees for Third World participation in exploitation of seabed resources
4.   Development of special measures for meeting development needs of island economies and landlocked nations
5.   Guarantee of the rights of nations to permanent sovereignty over natural resources

IV.   Political independence
1.   Guarantees of the right of nations to choose their economic, social, and political system without foreign intervention
2.   Recognition of the right of nations to nationalize foreign property in accordance with domestic laws
3.   Recognition of the right of primary producer associations to operate without interference from the industrial powers

(continued)

TABLE 9.1. (*continued*)

4. Measures to strengthen Third World regional, intraregional, and inter-regional cooperation
5. Restructuring of U.N. organizations to give the Third World greater operational powers for economic decision making and a significant increase in voting strength in the World Bank and IMF

Source: Compiled by author.

In summary, the NIEO tries to substitute moral principles for military and economic power in shaping international relations. The underlying principles are the sovereign equality of states; the use of cooperation rather than force among nation-states; the full and effective participation of all countries in solving international economic problems; the right of each state to choose its own socioeconomic system, to exercise sovereignty over its natural resources, and to regulate internal economic activities; the maintenance of fair prices for raw materials, primary commodities, and semimanufactured exports; and mutual cooperation in trade, technology, and finance among the world's nations.

That is, the NIEO offers a utopian blueprint for transcending an increasingly self-defeating international competition. Its proponents see it as the initial step in negotiating a new environment for economic commerce that would reduce present inequities by reconciling the interests of nation-states, international institutions, and MNCs with their diverse ideological, social, and political clienteles. Despite its insistent tone, NIEO is mainly a defensive action to keep the world from succumbing to the economic conflict that arises from growing national insecurity (Brandt et al. 1980).

AIC CRITICS OF THE NIEO

AIC critics regard the NIEO as, at best, an unrealistic wish list or, at worst, a dangerous set of proposals that would upset whatever international stability remains. There is particular concern about giving more control over international reserves to the Third World. Does a responsible farmer let the fox run the chicken coop? On the bilateral level, proposals for transferring additional resources to the Third World have been met with continued reduction in the proportion of AIC aid, especially by the United States. The United States has directly opposed any code of conduct for MNCs, although several European countries – notably France and Sweden – have favored such regulation. A number of the proposals, such as the attempt to index or link commodity prices to those for manufactured goods and the proposals for international taxation, have been dismissed as unrealistic and unworkable.

In general, the position of AIC governments has been to oppose the broad-based overhaul mandated by the NIEO and to work on reforming the present economic order. Understandably, they are reluctant to relinquish present privileges or to make costly adjustments in policy. Counterproposals, such as the U.S. call for establishment of a private international resource bank, are designed to maintain the status quo. Such measures must be judged not only by the self-interest of their advocates but also by the unlikelihood that bandages can stanch the present hemorrhage of the international economy.

THIRD WORLD CRITICS OF THE NIEO

Not all within the Third World are enthusiastic about the NIEO. One of the most forceful critics is the Egyptian economist Samir Amin. He argues that the NIEO would not provide the economic basis for real independence in the Third World or even promote the self-sustaining economic growth needed for real development. Instead, Amin argues, the NIEO would produce a new division of labor that is every bit as unequal as the present one and is equally dependent upon prosperity within the AICs. The NIEO might lead to better prices and increased exports. However, there is nothing within the plan to reorient domestic economies toward meeting national needs. That would require industries in the Third World to turn away from exports and develop the internal market.

Harry Magdoff, an American economist, argues:

In the absence of a strategy aimed to burst asunder the traditional mold imposed by the long history of capitalism, the peripheral (Third World) nations remain, willy-nilly, cogs in the imperialist machine. And regardless of how aware they are of the constraints imposed by the imperialist ties, they are confined to bargaining for concessions, no matter how dim the prospects of success. (1978, p. 4)

Viewed through this prism, the NIEO skirts the main issues. Stabilizing the prices of agricultural commodity exports may increase export earnings, but it will not raise the low productivity of Third World agriculture or overcome internal social obstacles to expanding food supplies. Removing trade barriers will make it easier for Third World nations to compete internationally, but in order to compete with industries in the advanced countries, wages will have to be kept down, thereby blocking the development of internal markets. And while other proposals would increase the availability of technology, there is nothing that would develop an independent technological base. Finally, the proposal for debt reform is likely to be a mere palliative, doing little to alter the fundamental causes and processes by which Third World nations become indebted: the heavy import dependence, outflows of interest and profits, and payments for shipping as well as other fees and service charges. The aspirin might bring the fever down, but it is likely to rise again.

Finally, these critics question whether any significant changes could occur through diplomatic negotiation. Magdoff concludes that "Solutions for such problems can only arise from internal changes in class power leading to a revolutionary alteration of social priorities which elevate the interests of the masses to the paramount position" (1978, p. 11).

10
STRATEGIES FOR MANAGING THIRD WORLD DEBT

Third World debt rose from $109 billion in 1973 to $810 billion in 1984. Between 1979 and 1984 it increased by 135 percent. This increase, even adjusting for world inflation, far outpaced the real economic growth of debtor nations. Debt service payments exploded from $20 billion to over $96 billion between 1973 and 1984. Between 1978 and 1984 interest payments alone increased by over 30 percent.

This situation produced an urgent search for a long-term solution, beginning in late 1983.[*] This occurred because of the increasingly uncertain outlook for three of the major debtors: Brazil, Argentina, and Mexico. There was growing fear that one of these nations – most likely Argentina, which was least dependent upon imports – would abandon its obligations and private banks would founder, triggering a worldwide financial collapse. The proposals for debt remedy had to address several key trade-offs.

First, there is a clear need for additional resources. Vijay Joshi (1981), a World Bank consultant, recognizes that IMF financing has been inadequate to meet the needs of the Third World oil-importing nations. In 1978 and 1979 its net contribution was actually negative: Third World countries repaid more in old loans than they received in new ones. Future needs seem even more urgent; developing countries are expected to accumulate deficits of $250 billion between 1980 and 1985.

Second, relief from the massive overhang of deficits inherited from the 1970s has become a major issue. Debt renegotiations accelerated during the 1980s (see Table 10.1). Outstanding debt will have to be restructured and, at

---

[*]In the last months of 1983, the World Bank began an urgent appraisal of the debt problem, finally reassessing its faith that world recovery would relieve the debt problem. For the first time it acknowledged that the problem would not disappear substantially.

TABLE 10.1. Multilateral Debt Renegotiations, 1974-83

	1974	1975	1976	1977	1978	1979	1980	1981	1982	1983[1]
Argentina			C							©
Bolivia							C	C		©
Brazil										©
Central Afr. Rep.								P		©
Chile	P	P								©
Costa Rica		P								P,©
Cuba										©
Ecuador										C
Gabon					P					
Ghana	P									
Guyana						C			C	
India	A	A	A	A		C				
Jamaica						C				
Liberia							P	C	C	
Madagascar								P	P	©
Malawi								P	C	
Mexico							C		P,C	
Nicaragua							C		C	©

In millions of U.S. dollars

Pakistan			A						
Peru	C				C			A	
Poland							A	C	©
Romania							P	P,C	P
Senegal					P		P	P,C	©
Sierra Leone			P						
Sudan				P			C	P	P
Togo				P			P	P	P,©
Turkey	P,C	A	A,C		A		A		
Uganda							P	C	
Yugoslavia							P	P	
Zaïre	P		P	P	C		P		©
Zambia	P		P				P		P
Total amount:[2]	1,530	375	1,800	240	1,800	6,200	3,750	2,540	10,000	37,000

Source: "Debt Rescheduling: What Does It Mean?" *Finance & Development* 20, no. 3 (Sept 1983): 26–29. World Bank, Debtor Reporting System and data compiled by IMF staff.

Notes: This table does not include some cases for which sufficient information was not available.

P = Paris Club Agreements   A = Aid Consortia Renegotiations

C = Commercial Bank Agreements   © = Under negotiation with commercial banks at the end of May 1983

[1] As of end-May, 1983.

[2] Estimates.

171

least in some cases, moratoriums or outright debt cancellation will be required to avoid crippling incipient development or unacceptable social and human costs.

Third, financial institutions must be reformed. Several proposals have been made, ranging from the establishment of a world central bank to creation of a Third World monetary fund.

Finally, a set of proposals has been put forward to address the basic problem of insufficient annual export earnings. Under this rubric are plans for commodity price stabilization (discussed in greater detail in Chapter 7), the levy of taxes on world trade or armaments production, and the annual issue of SDRs.

PROPOSALS FOR SUPPLEMENTARY FINANCING

Several proposals focus on increasing the access to and the size of financial resource flows. One plan would expand IMF resources for lending through increased member quotas. Greater IBRD financing could be achieved by shifting the gearing ratio (the ratio of loans to assets) from the present 1 : 1 to 2 : 1 or higher (private banks typically have gearing ratios of about 10 : 1). An IBRD energy fund could be established to provide loans for vital energy imports and to develop new domestic energy sources to reduce these imports. More cofinancing by the IBRD might encourage private lenders to ease terms and/or make new loans (see Chapter 4). The IDA could make more low-interest loans to the poorest countries (those with 1981 per capita incomes below $410). Other proposals would increase the capital of regional development banks, stipulate more direct bilateral aid from advanced industrial countries, and sell IMF gold holdings (100 million ounces).

The Brandt Commission report (Brandt et al. 1980) concentrates on supplementing financing measures. The commission argued that substantial resources need to be transferred to and within the developing countries to finance the following:

(1) Projects and programs to alleviate poverty and expand food production, especially in the least developed countries

(2) Exploration and development of energy and mineral resources

(3) Stabilization of the prices and earnings of commodity exports and expanded domestic processing of commodities. (Brandt et al. 1980, p. 254)

The various proposals for supplementary financing would help the objectives outlined by the Brandt Commission by providing more capital for the Third World. IMF lending generally carries lower interest costs than loans from the IBRD: 7.5 percent versus 11.5 percent. The IDA provides even cheaper financing – 2 to 4 percent – but its activities are confined to the poorest countries. Sale of IMF gold holdings (100 million ounces) would create a fund of some $30 to 40 billion for use by the IMF to increase lending or subsidize interest payments.

These proposals, however, are not panaceas. None deals fundamentally with the structural problems of debt overhang or insufficient export earnings. They would, to various degrees, provide cheaper financing than the private banks and ease the liquidity shortage created by the withdrawal of private resources. In most cases the methods for underwriting these proposals have been well articulated. However, it is unclear how or from whom regional development banks, which are generally far more under the control of Third World participants, would acquire additional capital. In any event, the AICs have strong reservations about virtually all of these proposals, which they fear will weaken the solvency of the international financial institutions. Several critics have pointed out that increased IMF lending probably would not increase the supply of lending capital. Private banks simply would use the opportunity to shift their more dubious and least prudent loans to the IMF. In other words, the IMF would bail out the banks, and taxpayers in the AICs would bear the costs.

DEBT RELIEF

Even if new resources are found, the problem of debt overhang must be addressed through debt relief or debt reorganization. Debt relief takes various forms, ranging from renegotiation and rescheduling of payments to a moratorium on, or even cancellation of, all or part of the debt. These measures are last-ditch attempts to forestall imminent default by a country in meeting its debt service.

For instance, Poland announced in December 1981 that it was unable to pay installments on its $26 billion debt to international creditors. (Although it is not a Third World country, Poland's case illustrates the process of debt relief.) In September 1982, following extensive negotiations, bankers agreed to reschedule the $3.4 billion ($2.3 billion in principal, $1.1 billion in interest) that was due in 1982. Of that total, $2.2 billion in principal and $366 million in interest would be postponed for four years. Of the remainder, $366 million in interest and $115 million in principal were paid, and another $366 million in interest was deposited into a special account for Poland to use in financing its essential imports (New York Times 1982).

Poland chose not to unilaterally cancel its debt, since default would risk access to future credits. (In fact, both the United States and the World Bank are forbidden to make loans to countries formally in default.) Yet Poland was unable to reduce imports enough to raise foreign exchange because such a cut would cripple domestic production and could spark political or social strife.

Default did not occur although Poland made no payments for an entire year. Default requires a formal declaration by a debtor bank or individual, and banks are hesitant to do this because it throws them into a particularly bad light with bank examiners and stockholders. In such cases, banks usually resort to debt moratorium and rescheduling.

Rescheduling may take several forms. There may be a secret meeting between representatives of the debtor country and the banks. Frequently the negotiations are directed by the IMF and usually follow prior agreement by the debtor to an IMF stabilization program. Rescheduling may provide a mix of additional loans, new capital through grants or lower interest payments, a change in the timing of repayments, and cancellation of part of the debt.

Third World countries usually find rescheduling to be embarrassing, painful, lengthy, and costly. The debtor is stigmatized, although the banks and multilateral lending agencies often are equally culpable. More seriously, UNCTAD has recommended that the rescheduling process should provide debt consolidation, grace periods, and adequate terms for amortization. Lending agents have resisted, arguing that any easing would encourage countries to borrow excessively.

Another alternative is "conditional repayment." Under this arrangement installments fall due only in those years when the economic performance of the debtor country is strong (Helleiner 1979). This approach has already been employed under the Lomé Convention, which stipulates that loans for commodity price stabilization are repayable only when the price and earnings on exports are in excess of the averages in the preceding four years.*

While reschedulings and moratoriums may postpone debt service payments on part or all outstanding loans and provide breathing space until the world economy improves, some economic analysts think they only postpone the day of reckoning. Debt restructuring may make repayment seem more manageable, but some economies burdened by a sizable debt overhang lack the capacity ever to catch up. Bangladesh was in this situation in 1972. Future prospects were so bleak that several European countries canceled Bangladesh's debt.

RECOMMENDATIONS FOR INSTITUTIONAL REFORM

Proposals for institutional reform try to solve some of the underlying structural problems of the international debt economy. An international central bank could be set up as the lender of last resort to the national central banks and

---

*Another approach involves repayment of loans in the debtor's currency. This method also has precedent. The Pan American Health Organization uses this technique to operate a highly effective revolving fund for purchase of vaccines. The U.S. PL-480 commodity sales also authorize this form of relief.

to supervise international lending. A second set of proposals would increase Third World representation in international financial organizations. Some observers think that a larger voice for the developing countries in the IMF and the World Bank is improbable, and advocate a new monetary fund – controlled by the Third World – similar to the International Fund for Agricultural Development (IFAD). Another proposal would establish a Third World debt forum so that debtor countries could articulate their joint concerns and develop collective strategies.

One of the more far-reaching recommendations was made by Felix Rohatyn (1983). His proposal would stretch out Third World debt by having either an agency of an existing institution – the World Bank or IMF – or a new, specially constituted organization accept responsibility for Third World loans and refinance them as long-term, low-interest bonds issued by the institution itself. In effect, the new agency would become a substitute creditor. The banks would suffer a loss of income that would have to be written off. However, those losses would be offset to some extent by more secure loan portfolios. Actual losses would be distributed between bank shareholders and taxpayers.

Another proposal would create an agency, underwritten by the industrial nations, that would assume a portion of the present outstanding debt at face value. The agency would reschedule debt maturities in line with each country's payment capacity. Those debts could then be marketed to third parties. The private banks would then have marketable debts and the debtor countries would have more convenient payment schedules. As a quid pro quo, banks would have to keep their trade credit lines open at precrisis levels. Hopeless cases would be written off (Bogdanowicz-Bindert 1983).

Peter Leslie, general manager of Barclay's Bank, has recommended formation of a rediscounting facility. He maintains that such a facility is necessary because commercial banks will be unwilling to continue lending under present conditions, and no existing agency is anxious to acquire the commercial banks' shaky portfolios. Under this plan the commercial banks would shift responsibility for outstanding loans to the central banks of their respective countries. Leslie insists that this is feasible because it could stimulate world recovery and thereby promote the AICs' national interests (Leslie 1983).

These proposals share a common drawback. They are resisted by AICs and by the MNIs: the World Bank and the IMF. The multinational lenders have avoided or minimized involvement as intermediaries. Meanwhile, it is not clear how a new international central bank could provide sufficient liquidity, quite apart from the mechanics of gaining accord on its establishment. The AICs already oppose increasing Third World voting strength in the IMF and World Bank, arguing that it would undermine institutional creditability in the world capital markets where funds must be raised. The proposal for a Third World Bank has also foundered on the reef of raising funds; the truth, however unsavory, is that any sizable capitalization must come from the AICs.

TRADE-RELATED PROPOSALS

Trade-related proposals generally link debt servicing with the Third World nation's capacity to earn foreign exchange through exports. A proposal by Bailey et al. (1983) would create a new financial instrument called exchange participation notes. These notes would be issued by debtor countries to their creditors and would replace existing payment schedules with entitlement to a portion, perhaps 1 percent, of national foreign-exchange earnings. The creditor would be repaid either faster or slower than the original terms, depending on the level of trade. The proposal avoids the pitfalls of tied loans. By limiting repayment to a portion of exports, it ensures that a sufficient amount of foreign exchange remains for essential imports.

Another proposal is for the IMF to issue enough annual SDRs to equal targeted growth for world trade. This would provide the liquidity needed for real growth, which countries had to borrow privately during the 1970s. Moreover, in contrast with the ultimately restrictive impact caused by oscillating cycles of excessive lending and no lending that characterizes private banks' policies, these SDRs would be predictable and would stimulate world trade. The major drawback of this proposal has been the unwillingness of industrialized creditor nations to accept SDRs in lieu of goods and cash, and to accept an implied inflationary pressure on their economies.

A further proposal would appropriate income from world seabed resources for international development. The bulk of undersea resources are not owned by any single nation; they represent the international commonwealth. Hence, there is an appropriateness in assigning these resources for international purposes, such as economic development or debt relief. One major problem with this proposal is that initially the income would be quite limited (about $1,500 million in the first three years). Furthermore, dividing the earnings equitably means negotiating a formula among nations with widely divergent interests. That, in fact, is the single largest factor undermining all tax-related proposals. There is no existing mechanism to force losers in these schemes to participate, and there is no apparent disposition by these nations to pay such taxes voluntarily.

INTERNATIONAL TAXATION

Proposals for international taxation would channel an annual flow of resources into development loans that would not have to be repaid and, unlike development grants, would not depend on the whims and political approval of the industrial nations. Relatively low rates of taxation would raise rather large sums. For example, total aid to the Third World in 1980 was under $20 billion. That sum could have been raised by a 5 percent tax on arms production. A

10 percent reduction in arms exports would provide all the funding require
by IDA for the poorest developing nations. Clearly, an added benefit from such
taxation would be a disincentive on arms production and export.

A proposed tax on world trade would be heavily resisted by trading nations. However, it might win support from domestic industries threatened by
exports. Moreover, if it were applied on all traded goods, there would be no
appreciable distortional effect, except for nations that perennially run trade surpluses. A 1 percent tax on world imports would yield $20 billion.

Table 10.2 examines the impact of three proposals: a sales tax on world
trade, a tax on world arms production, and a tax on arms exports. The tax on
trade would be borne most heavily by the industrial nations of Western Europe
and Japan; the United States would pay 14 percent and the oil exporters 10
percent. A tax on military expenditures would fall most heavily on the United
States and the Soviet Union, followed by Western Europe. Japan would pay
relatively little. A tax on military exports would fall most heavily on the United
States, followed by the USSR and Western Europe.

A PACKAGE SOLUTION?

Whatever the merits of any specific proposal, it is obvious that Third World
debt is Hydra-headed. Only a comprehensive package will get at the problem.
One such plan was designed for Brazil (Perkins and Selvaggio 1984). Under
this scheme Brazil would declare a moratorium of two to five years on all debt
service, principal and interest. This would give the Brazilian economy enough

TABLE 10.2.   Incidence of International Taxation Proposals (percent)

Tax Base	Industrial Capitalist World			Middle East	Third World Oil Importers	Socialist World	
	USA	Europe	Japan			COMECON	China
World trade	14	43	8	10	18	7	1
Military expenditures	23	17	2	7	6	37	8
Military exports	33	26	1	1	4	34	1

Note: Rows may not total 100 due to rounding.
Sources: International Monetary Fund 1982; U.S. Arms Control and Disarmament Agency
1980.

time to grow to meet its obligations. When repayments resumed, they would be tied to national export earnings. Instead of paying half its export earnings (as the World Bank reported for 1982), Brazil would assign only, say, 10 percent of its larger profits to pay off its debt. Furthermore, the private banks would suspend flexible interest rates and use the fixed rate charged in 1971. That would not be an easy pill for the banks to swallow, but the plan would serve their long-term interests, since guaranteed smaller profits are preferable to default. Meanwhile, Brazil would adopt a set of policies sharply different from those recommended by the IMF. The domestic economy would be primed rather than deflated, and taxes would be raised to control the country's $25 billion internal debt. Finally, Brazil should build its trade with other Latin countries by entering into clearing agreements. Such countertrade may be the hidden door that will allow developing countries to escape the "debt trap."

SUMMARY

Debt problems will not be resolved easily. By 1984 bankers were at last willing to recognize publicly that the debt crisis would last the rest of the decade and would require dramatic actions to resolve (*Wall Street Journal* 1984). The critical concern, however, was how to achieve a degree of economic recovery without destroying the economies of the Third World. For the Third World the pressures to default were looming increasingly large, in spite of the potential danger implied for the stability of the world banking system.

A related issue was that any moratorium on debt repayment could cause substantial harm to the banks, which were highly leveraged and whose loans were often 20 times as large as their capital. By 1982 the exposure of 12 of the 13 major U.S. banks in Latin America was over 100 percent of their total capital. A major default would cut deeply into their capital and reduce their lending abilities, with possible contractionary consequences (Cline 1983).

By mid-1982 the incentive for a number of Latin nations to default was high because interest payments loomed large in relation to new borrowing and even exceeded it for the major Latin borrowers. For 1983 the World Bank (1984) reported that for all developing countries more money was paid out in interest and principal than was received in new loans. Thus, the developing countries were transferring more money to the industrial capitalist countries than they received from them. The incentive to default was growing.

What was standing in the way of the Third World default? The main factor was the perceived consequences of the defaulting country's trade. Cline (1983, p. 89) noted, "A defaulting country would risk isolating itself economically from the rest of the world. At best it would forfeit the opportunity to borrow at some future date when foreign capital might be extremely vital to it, because of an export collapse, for example." Lack of credit for trade would mean that developing countries would have to pay cash for imports, and since very few had sufficient reserves, they would be unable to import what they needed to feed their citizens and fuel their factories. An added peril cited by Cline was the danger of reprisals, such as trade embargoes and seizure of resources. Two countries that did repudiate their debts, Cuba in 1961 and North Korea in 1974, faced difficulty in borrowing on U.S. financial markets, though not in European markets.

Third World countries appear to be facing a Hobson's choice. They can either accept the medicine of the IMF, deflate their economies, suffer destruction of their economies, and experience severe reductions in the living standards of their poorest citizens and political instability, or they can default on their debts and risk trade reprisals from the United States and other creditor nations. With Third World debt at over $800 billion, with servicing costs outpacing new loans, and with little hope for an early economic recovery, the situation appears bleak at least for the remainder of the 1980s.

What can the Third World do to gain release from the jaws of debt? There is no simple solution. Yet in order to preserve the gains of the 1970s, it seems that one approach offers the best chance of success in the 1980s and beyond. This involves a four-part strategy.

First, there would be a moratorium on prior debt for the most debt-ridden countries. They would pay no interest or principal for between three and five years, depending on their circumstances. This step is not without precedent. In 1978 Great Britain canceled the debts of 17 of the poorest Third World countries. The official term used was "retrospective terms adjustment," and the total debt to the British government was an estimated $2.5 billion.

Second, this breathing space would be used to revive domestic economies and reflate domestic demand, particularly for wage goods consumed by the poor. This would have to be financed by major tax reforms and closure of avenues of corruption and capital flight. Without the millstone of debt, these nations could eventually begin to import goods from the industrial world, which in turn would buy their exports and thereby raise domestic incomes.

Third, in order to deal with reduced availability of capital to finance trade flows, Third World nations would actively pursue countertrade. This would allow them to get by the difficulties surrounding disruption of their trade during the moratorium, to develop new markets, and to build South-South trade. (The mechanics of this approach are explained in Chapter 11.)

Finally, at the end of the moratorium and when interest payments resume, loans would be repaid at reduced interest rates, and the U.S. monetary authorities would actively work to keep the U.S. interest rate down. (See Silk 1984 for a discussion of a May 1984 conference to discuss this option.) Yet in order to do this, the United States must cut its military spending, which is programmed to increase from $275 billion in 1984 to $397 billion by 1987 (*Defense Monitor* 1983). A sharp reduction in this expenditure not only would free funds for economic development and reduce international tensions, it would also allow reduction in the U.S. interest rate and stimulate world economic recovery.

11

BARTER INDUSTRIALIZATION:
A PATH
TO ECONOMIC INDEPENDENCE

The developing nations lack the political and economic power to make the structures of the present international economic order heed their interests. In order to acquire power, the Third World may have to create autonomous institutions and instruments. One possible route is to make virtue of necessity and create systems of countertrade.

These systems can take a variety of forms. Six types have emerged to account for a growing, though indeterminate, share of world trade (some estimates range as high as 25 percent, although the IMF projects a figure of only 1 percent). Counterpurchase, buyback, investment performance agreements, compensation arrangements, clearing agreements, and economic cooperation agreements have one thing in common: they are barter or quasi-barter arrangements. That is, the seller delivers technology, finished goods, or equipment to the buyer and contractually agrees to purchase goods from the buyer that are of equal or greater value than the products he is selling.

Historically, countertrade has been associated with East-West agreements.* However, it is often overlooked that in the aftermath of World War II, Japan and the nations of Western Europe lacked foreign exchange and improvised various forms of barter. Their limited cash reserves were used to import American goods, while trade with other countries was handled through clearing arrangements or barter. Now the Europeans need barter not to finance imports but to stimulate exports. That is, with the drying up of private financing and the reduction in concessional aid, Third World countries are turning to counter-

---

*Immediately following its revolution in 1917, Russia needed grain, but lacked the cash to but it. Armand Hammer, chairman of Occidental Petroleum, cabled Lenin offering to exchange grain for furs. In 1983 Hammer negotiated a similar deal, exchanging oil exploration services and equipment for future delivery of crude oil from China.

trade to finance vital imports. Countertrade also offers a way to sidestep trade restrictions in the markets of the AICs on the growing array of products manufactured in the Third World.

HOW COUNTERTRADE HELPS THIRD WORLD ECONOMIES

Countertrade can help in several ways. First, it conserves scarce foreign exchange. When Japan agrees to finance an aluminum smelter in Brazil in exchange for fixed quantities of finished aluminum after the factory is operating, Brazil acquires a vital industry for its development efforts without dipping into its exchange reserves or adding to its external debt.

Second, developing nations have a greater probability of avoiding balance-of-trade deficits. Imports are offset by exports of equivalent or greater value. Thus, Colombia was able to obtain Spanish trolley buses to alleviate its urban transportation problems by directly swapping Colombian coffee, thus avoiding the need to sell enough coffee on a depressed world market to finance the sale.

Third, countertrade can open up new markets. MNCs are willing to barter because their marketing expertise can locate new buyers. General Motors for instance, had little difficulty reselling the alumina obtained from Jamaica in exchange for vehicles. Coca Cola, General Electric, International Harvester, Levi Strauss, Citibank, and many other MNCs engage in countertrade and have set up their own countertrade departments.

Fourth, countertrade can upgrade manufacturing capacity. Third World nations can exchange raw materials or unprocessed commodities for plants and equipment, and thus improve their technological base. For instance, Canada agreed to provide Mexico with the technology for processing petrochemicals, pulping wood, and mining coal in return for oil.

Fifth, export prices can be kept profitable. This occurs when exchange takes place at ratios greater than the world market price would support. Added costs may be borne by the seller, inflating the price of the original sale while maintaining the price of the counterpurchased goods. One example of this was Uruguay's exchange of meat, rice, and wheat for $50 million of Iranian oil in 1982.

Finally, restrictive tariff and nontariff barriers can be leapfrogged. This can occur through exchanging goods at nominal values higher than prevailing market prices (thus avoiding claims of dumping). Or the Third World nation can use the legal apparatus of its industrial partner, thereby transferring any legal burden to the importing firm.

As countertrade has become a vital concern, many Third World countries – including Ecuador, Indonesia, Malaysia and Brazil – have established special government agencies to expand it. Countertrade is particularly useful as a way to control variations in import capacity and fluctuating demand for exports. An OECD study found that Tunisia and Sri Lanka had more success in balancing the flow of imports and exports through barter than through regular multilateral trade. The same study, however, suggested that larger countries, such as India and Egypt, found multilateral trade to be more stable (OECD 1970).

SUPPLIER MOTIVATIONS

Countertrade also holds certain advantages for the supplier, particularly in a situation of growing competition for world markets and resurgent nationalism. MNCs see countertrade as a way to obtain a long-term, reliable supply of raw materials, component parts, or finished products at a stable price. This is particularly important for purposes of strategic planning. Second, countertrade may be the only way for a firm to enter a particular market. By concluding a countertrade agreement, an MNC may gain an edge over its competitors by demonstrating a willingness to accommodate the needs of a developing country to conserve foreign exchange, and thus get its foot in the door and pave the way for future sales. Finally, the risks of countertrade can be partially offset by potential tax breaks. A transaction in goods rather than cash permits underestimating the value of the sales, thereby reducing the tax or tariff liability of the company.

Although risks do exist, companies have found that they must accommodate themselves to this form of business or be excluded from a vital and growing area of international trade (Welt 1982). Because countertrade is advantageous to both buyers and sellers, exporters and importers, its role has expanded. According to the *Economist,* it accounted for one-quarter of the world's trade in 1982.

FORMS OF COUNTERTRADE AND BARTER

As noted previously, there are various forms of countertrade. These are summarized in Table 11.1.

Counterpurchase

This mechanism allows developing countries to soften the impact of deteriorating terms of trade and the shortage of foreign capital that accompany the current debt crisis. Primary producers can trade their undervalued goods for high-priced manufactured products. By compelling the industrialized nations to accept payment in commodities, developing countries may circumvent the inequities of the international trading system and achieve better control over their markets and higher net return on their exports.

TABLE 11.1. Barter-Based Trade and Investment Agreements

Type	How It Operates	Example
Counterpurchase	A set of parallel sales agreements in which the supplier sells a product and orders unrelated products to offset the buyer's cost	Colombia asks equipment suppliers to buy its coffee; the Spanish government company ENSA sells buses to Colombia and purchases an equivalent value of coffee
Buyback or compensation agreements	Under an agreement separate from the sale of a factory, the supplier agrees to purchase or accept as partial payment the plant's output for a specified period	China awarded a $500 million contract to Italy's Tecnotrade to expand its mines and modernize its railroad, with partial payment to be in the form of coal
Investment performance requirements	Government approval of foreign investment proposal is made contingent upon forcing investors' commitment to export	U.S.-owned Brink's Inc. was permitted to purchase a Canadian truck body firm on condition that 80 percent of the factory's output be exported
Clearing agreements	An exchange of products between two governments to achieve an agreed-upon value of trade	India and the USSR have an agreement for balanced trade between them
Economic cooperation agreements	Long-term agreements between two countries involving exchange of raw materials for technology	Mexico will exchange oil for a range of advanced industrial technologies from Canada

Source: Prepared by author.

Counterpurchase agreements are more sophisticated and flexible than forms of precapitalist barter. Arrangements are split into two separate transactions: the original sale and the counterpurchase of products to offset or partially balance the original sale. This separation of transactions permits the use of various intermediaries, such as banks and MNCs, to find buyers for commodities such as Jamaican bauxite, Malaysian rubber, or Colombian coffee.

Three examples illustrate the forms that counterpurchase agreements can take. In 1982 Colombia found that its debt service was just over one-sixth of

India is using an investment buyback to exploit its vast marine wealth. Eleven Indian firms chartered vessels from Japan, the Republic of Korea, and Taiwan. The Indian partner receives 15 percent of the value of each catch; the foreign partner, 85 percent. All operating and marketing responsibilities are borne by the foreign partner. Under this scheme the Indian partner is able to purchase one vessel every 18 months. In three to four years the entire fleet will be "Indianized," with the added advantage that during this time the partner acquires experience in marketing the catch in foreign countries (Pellay 1984).

Investment buybacks do pose risks for the supplying company. After all, a potential competitor is being created that may use the brand name or transfer the technology to third parties. When production begins, the output may flood existing markets – this has already occurred with bulk chemical buybacks from Eastern Europe. Despite these dangers, however, firms are willing to use this device to secure major sales when there is industrial slack in the AICs. The OECD estimated that investment buybacks totaled between $30 and $35 billion between 1969 and 1979 (Welt 1982).

Investment Performance Requirements

The investment performance requirement (IPR) is another form of countertrade. Under the IPR, approval of investment proposals is tied to commitments by the foreign investor to export. The IPR gives the host country an instrument to influence or control where production will be manufactured and sold, thereby shaping MNC policies to reflect national needs and provide greater equity of return. For example, Canada introduced an IPR on an investment by the U.S.-owned Brinks Inc. Brinks was permitted to purchase a Quebec truck-body manufacturing firm if it would purchase all of its armored truck bodies from Canada and export 80 percent of the plant's output.

Bilateral Clearing Agreements

Two countries wishing to trade with each other without expending foreign currency can employ bilateral clearing agreements. Each party agrees to exchange a set value of goods over an interval of time, usually a year. Accounts are kept in a mutually specified currency, and the balance of trade is monitored to assure compliance. If an imbalance occurs, the creditor will seek to increase its imports. If the accounts cannot be brought into parity, the net importer may sell its credit at a discount to a third party, often a trading house. This system, called switch trading, was popular following World War II, when most European countries were short of foreign exchange.

Economic Cooperation Agreements

These are long-term agreements, usually covering 10 to 15 years. They typically stipulate exchange of technology for raw materials. Thus, the Canadian government has agreed to supply Mexico with advanced technology for processing wood, food, and petrochemicals and for developing new oil and natural gas fields. Equipment for an electric power grid and a telecommunications system are included in the package. In return, the Mexicans will ship oil to Canada. Mexico has similar agreements with Spain and Japan and a separate South-South deal with Brazil that includes mutual exchange of minerals and technology.

ADVANTAGES OF BARTER-BASED INDUSTRIALIZATION

In the postwar era trade has grown under a multilateral clearing system. For example, country A sells a commodity to a firm in country B, then takes its profits and buys goods from country C. This process can pass through the alphabet several times before a product produced in country B is finally imported by a firm in country A. If there is no clearance – country B's exports do not equal its imports – then country B is left with a balance-of-trade deficit that has to be offset by capital transfers through either loans or foreign investment. Barter agreements, which were common prior to the nineteenth century, use determinate clearing: no products are imported unless products of equal value are exported.

Since the mid-1970s most Third World countries have faced two types of problems: those arising from an inability to sell enough commodities at a profitable price and those related to debt overload. By directly linking a nation's imports to its exports, barter-based industrialization avoids both kinds of problems. On the one hand, the pressure to find new buyers for commodities falls on the exporters of manufactured goods from the AICs, if they want to increase their business in the Third World. On the other hand, barter reduces the level of trade deficits that require financing through capital transfers. Barter-based industrialization also avoids the pitfall of borrowing to finance new production capacity for goods that may never be sold because of trade barriers in the AICs' markets. Under the barter system MNCs run interference for Third World exports, thereby increasing market access.

Perhaps most important, barter-based industrialization may promote complementary Third World industrialization. This will happen where countries use countertrade to create new markets for each other's products. This occurred in Malaysia's trade with Burma (see Box 13).

A further advantage of barter-based industrialization is that it permits countries and industries to plan their production years in advance and to improve their profitability and efficiency because a substantial section of the potential market is secure. The Eastern European countries have used barter for years as a means of stabilizing their production and anticipating demands. In addition, barter-based industrialization is especially valuable during the initial years of production, when levels of productivity tend to be low and costs high. Under normal conditions new forms have minimal access to world markets.

THE PROBLEMS OF COUNTERTRADE AND BARTER-BASED INDUSTRIALIZATION

Barter-based industrialization does have drawbacks. Its most pesistent critic is GATT. The primary argument is that barter shields industries from market competition, and thus does not produce true development. Moreover, barter agreements result in products being purchased from inefficient producers and inevitably increase costs for consumers and the rate of inflation. GATT argues that when barter distorts the patterns of world trade away from the more efficient producers, it reduces world prosperity. Barter requires careful planning and may entail higher risks. The industrial nations are concerned that barter, which represents a retreat from multilateralism, will undermine the growth of world trade (Huh 1983).

MNC AND BANKING INTEREST IN COUNTERTRADE

Despite the theoretical arguments against barter, a number of MNCs and banks are actively pursuing countertrade. General Motors, for example, formed a subsidiary (Motors Trading Corporation) to negotiate barter agreements with foreign governments, to purchase goods from participating countries, and to arrange financing where necessary. One agreement involved the exchange of automobiles for alumina ore from Jamaica. Similarly, General Electric Trading Co. was established in March 1982, with offices in 30 countries. GE had barter sales of about $100 million in 1982, with a target ceiling of $2 billion for 1987. Finally, Northrop Corp., which sells aircraft, had to adapt to the demand for barter sales. In 1975 the firm sold Switzerland F-5 fighter airplanes, but in order to complete the sale, Northrop had to assist Switzerland with its exports. The company prepared a survey of Swiss goods for export and, through its network of salespeople in 80 countries, helped Switzerland sell an added $209 million worth of products overseas, including a deal for Swiss elevators in Egypt. In 1983 Northrop was busy developing an export program for Turkey to enable it to buy Northrop fighters. When barter works, one hand washes the other:

the country receives a needed product, service, or technology, and a corporation can maintain production and profit levels (*Business Week* 1982).

Banks also serve as intermediaries in these arrangements. They are able to use their international information networks to assist customers in locating and identifying buyers for countertrade sales. Citibank has a department devoted to countertrade. From the bank's point of view, investments are often more bankable, particularly in the Third World, if suppliers have contracted to purchase part of the project's output, thereby generating a stream of earnings to ensure repayment.

CONCLUSION

Barter-based industrialization may be a desperate response to a desperate situation. Thurow (1983) has commented that the Third World countries will be able to meet their debts only by exporting more products. That imperative runs into the stone wall of market restrictions in the AICs. How, for example, can Brazil pay its debts if it can't sell its steel? Thurow's solution: "If I were Brazil, I would fill a ship with steel and send it to one of my European creditors – together with the comment that if they wanted to be sensible and sell the steel in Europe they could have their money back."

In an important sense, barter-based industrialization is related to Gandhi's concept of "Swadeshi" and E. F. Schumacher's notion of "small is beautiful." Gandhi believed that India's economy was penetrated and dominated by British colonial interests so that it no longer served or reflected domestic needs.

> Free trade for a country which has become industrial, whose population can and does live in cities, whose people do not mind preying upon other nations and therefore, sustaining the biggest navy to protect their unnatural commerce may be economically sound. . . . Free trade may be good for England which dumps down her manufactures among helpless people and wishes her wants supplied from outside at the cheapest rate. But free trade has ruined India's peasantry in that it has all but destroyed her cottage industry. Moreover, no new trade can compete with foreign trade without protection . . . Germany developed her sugar industry by a system of bounties. (Gandhi 1967, p. 46)

Gandhi maintained that "If not an article of commerce had been brought from outside India, she would be today a land flowing with milk and honey" (1967, p. 4). The concept of Swadeshi is based upon finding domestic sources of supply: ". . . It would be your duty and mine to find neighbors who can supply our wants, and to teach them where they do not know how to proceed . . ." (1967, p. 5). Some may argue that Swadeshi is merely autarky by another name: the total exclusion of foreign products. Others may reply that it is not the total exclusion of foreign products but, rather, preference for domestic ones where such are available.

Clearly, such notions contradict the concepts of comparative advantage and free trade. Yet, the evidence is mounting that when a country such as Chile (between 1974 and 1983) opens its economy to foreign imports, the result is not prosperity but the destruction of domestic industrial capacity. Moreover, the overseas borrowing to import technologies and factories that characterized the 1970s may have rapidly expanded the range of domestic production, but it also bred its own form of economic destabilization.

A new basis of industrialization must be found. However, the hope that the Third World might turn to agricultural exports to develop its economy has long been bankrupt. Apart from the chronic instability of commodity prices, agricultural prices seldom keep pace with rising costs of industrial products. Meanwhile, the Third World's share in agricultural trade dropped from 40 percent in 1961–63 to 30 percent in 1971–72. Over two-thirds of the benefits of recent increases in the prices of export agriculture have accrued to the industrial countries, which have a capital-intensive agricultural base.

One of the most disturbing aspects of reliance on exports is that the largest beneficiaries from export sales are seldom the farmers who grow the crops. Instead, the foreign earnings are used to import luxury items for the wealthy, usually urban, classes. For example, Senegalese peasants are forced by taxation to concentrate on production of peanuts for export to Europe. A sizable portion of the foreign exchange is used to import wheat flour for production of French bread for urban dwellers (Lappe and Collins 1977).

Finally, export-oriented agriculture appears to require import-intensive technologies. Heavy use of chemical fertilizers and pesticides is necessary to boost production. The unfortunate by-product is that a large part of what is exported will be used to pay the import bill.

Ironically, it is food production that best illustrates the benefits that a barter-based industrial strategy can reap. In barter-trade economies, agricultural production would be primarily oriented toward meeting domestic food needs. Investment and income would flow toward the food production sector, raising the quality of rural life and closing the gap between the living standards of rich and poor. Lappe and Collins (1977) argued:

> With food self reliance . . . *trade becomes an organic outgrowth of development not the fragile hinge on which basic survival hangs.* Only after food production has been diversified and people are feeding themselves can trade play a positive role. . . . A country simply cannot hold out for just prices for its exports if it is desperate for foreign exchange with which to import food. Once basic needs are met, however, trade can become a healthy extension

of domestic need rather than being determined strictly by foreign demand.
(p. 24, emphasis added)

Data from China and Brazil indicate some of the possible benefits from this
reorientation. China focuses its agricultural investment on production of domestic food crops. Famine is no longer cyclical, and food imports are strictly
supplemental. Brazil, on the other hand, has pursued an export-oriented strategy. While prices for coffee and soybeans bob up and down on world markets,
the country is now heavily dependent on imports to feed itself.

Countertrade offers one avenue out of the lacunae of trade-debt crises that
have steadily worsened since the 1960s. It may be the only way that countries
poor and short of markets for exports can obtain vital imports. It is not a panacea. Substantial problems remain, and each country adapts a variety of policies
to its unique circumstances. Countertrade industrialization will not avoid the
need for tax reform that will make the rich pay their fair share and will give governments the financial base to pay for the social overhead expenses required
by industrialization. Countertrade also will not resolve problems of misapplication of resources or inefficiency and corruption in financing investment programs. It will not stop the wholesale waste of the world's resources in a dangerous arms race.

However, countertrade may help reorient the trade-debt system and permit
nations to exercise prudence in management of foreign trade and finance without causing excessive sacrifice by their populations. It may also provide a possible escape from the web of restrictions that cut off access to industrial markets.
It may also provide better leverage in obtaining a fairer share of the world's
wealth. If the developing nations succeed in expanding their economies, a more
lasting basis for truly free trade and economic prosperity will exist.

BIBLIOGRAPHY

INTRODUCTION

World Bank. 1981. *World Development Report.* Washington, D.C.: World Bank.

CHAPTER 1

Angell, J. W. 1929. *The Recovery of Germany.* New Haven: Yale University Press.

Block, Fred. 1977. *The Origins of the International Economic Order.* Berkeley: University of California Press.

Brown, William A. 1940. *The Gold Standard Reinterpreted; 1914-1934.* 2 vols. New York: National Bureau of Economic Research.

Knight, M., and J. Salop. 1977. "The New International Monetary System." *Finance and Development,* June, pp. 19-22.

Rodríguez, Rita M., and E. Eugene Carter. 1979. *International Financial Management,* 2nd ed. Englewood Cliffs, N.J.: Prentice-Hall.

Storey, Christopher. 1981. "The Chaotic Decade Since 15 August 1971: A Survey of the Wreckage." *International Currency Review* 13, no. 4: 5-12.

Yeager, L. B. 1976. *International Monetary Relations: Theory, History and Policy,* 2nd ed. New York: Harper and Row.

CHAPTER 2

Atkinson, Caroline, and James Rowe. 1982. "Problems in International Lending." *Washington Post,* Mar. 14, pp. G1-2.

Baran, Paul. 1956. *The Political Economy of Growth.* New York: Monthly Review Press.

Barnet, R., and Ronald Müller. 1974. *Global Reach.* New York: Harper.

Block, F. 1979. *The Origins of International Economic Disorder.* Berkeley: University of California Press.

Bolles, Lynn. 1982. "Kitchens Hit by Priorities." In Jerome Nash and P. Fernandez, eds., *Women, Men and the International Division of Labor.* New York: SUNY Press.

Frank, André Gunder. 1980. *Crisis in the World Economy.* New York: Holmes and Meier.

Girling, Robert H. 1982. "The Contradictions of Educational Reform." Paper presented to Stanford University Conference on International Education, Oct.

_____. 1973. "Dependence and Persistent Income Inequality." In F. Bonilla and R. Girling, *Structures of Dependency.* Stanford, Calif.: Institute of Political Studies.

Girling, Robert H., and Sherry Keith. 1977. *The Employment Crisis.* Geneva: International Labour Organisation.

Graham, P. A. 1982. "Risk in International Banking." *Journal of the Institute of Banking,* June.

Griffin, Keith. 1970. "Foreign Capital, Domestic Savings and Economic Development." *Bulletin of the Oxford Institute of Economics and Statistics* 32, no. 2 (May): 99.

Hackett, John. 1982. *The Third World War,* 2nd ed. New York: Berkeley Books.

Helleiner, G. K. 1979. "Relief and Reform in Third World Debt." *World Development* 7, no. 2: 113-24.

Hope, Nicolas. 1982. "Loan Capital in Development Finance: The Role of Banks and Some Implications for Managing Debt." Washington, D.C.: World Bank. Mimeographed.

Janarain, I. 1976. *Trade and Development.* Georgetown: University of Guyana Press.

Latin American Regional Report (London). 1982. "Mexico and Central America." Oct. 29.

Lever, Harold. 1982. "International Banking's House of Cards." *New York Times,* Sept. 24, p. 25.

Lewis, Arthur. 1954. "Economic Development with Unlimited Supplies of Labor." *The Manchester School,* Apr.

McMullen, Neil. 1979. "Historical Perspectives on Developing Nations' Debt." In L. G. Frank and M. J. Seiber, eds., *Developing Country Debt.* New York: Pergamon.

Mendelsohn, M. S. 1981. *The Outlook for International Bank Lending.* New York: Group of Thirty.

New York Times. 1982a. "Banks Ease Polish Interest Payments." Sept. 15, p. D1.
_____. 1982b. "International Banking's House of Cards." Sept. 24, p. A27.

O'Brien, Richard. 1981. *Private Bank Lending to Developing Countries.* World Bank Staff Working Paper no. 482. Washington, D.C.: World Bank.

Payer, Cheryl. 1982. *The World Bank.* New York: Monthly Review Press.
_____. *The Debt Trap: The IMF and the Third World.* New York: Monthly Review Press.

Pearson, Lester. 1969. *Partners in Development.* New York: Pall Mall Press.

President's Export Council. 1980. *The Export Imperative,* vol. I. Washington, D.C.: U.S. Government Printing Office.

Roberts, D. 1981. "The LDC Debt Burden." Federal Reserve Bank of New York, *Quarterly Review,* Summer.

Robischek, Walter. 1980. "Some Reflections About External Public Debt Management," pp. 1-22. Mimeographed.

Sampson, Anthony. 1981. *The Money Lenders.* New York: Viking.

Schmidt, Benecio. 1973. "Dependency and the Multinational Corporation." In Frank Bonilla and Robert H. Girling, eds., *Structures of Dependency.* Stanford, Calif.: Institute of Political Studies.

Seiber, M. J. 1982. *International Borrowing by Developing Countries.* New York: Pergamon Press.

Wall Street Journal. 1981. "High Interest Rates Place Fresh Strain on Developing Nations; Banks Concerned." Feb. 10, p. 1.

Washington Post. 1982. "Big Banks' Problem Loans Grow 63% so Far This Year." Oct. 28, p. C8.

World Bank. 1981a. 1982. *World Development Report.* Washington, D.C.: World Bank.
_____. 1981b, 1984. *World Debt Tables.* Washington, D.C.: World Bank.

CHAPTER 3

American Bankers Association. 1981. *The Future of Development Banking Abroad.* New York: American Bankers Association.

Bartlett, S. 1981. "Transnational Banking: A Case of Transfer Parking with Money." In Robin Murray, ed., *Multinationals Beyond the Market.* Brighton, Sussex: Harvester Press.

Baster, A. J. S. 1935. *The International Banks.* London: King.

Brittain, Alfred III. 1981. "The Drive into Worldwide Banking." *Euromoney*, Oct., pp. 60-81.

Cameron, Juan. 1980. "What the Bankers Did to Poland." *Fortune*, Sept. 22, pp. 125-26.

Cline, William. 1983. "External Debt and Global Financial Stability." Testimony before U.S. Senate Foreign Relations Committee, Jan. 19. Mimeographed.

Davis, Stephen. 1979. *The Management Function in International Banking.* New York: John Wiley and Sons.

De Vries, Rimer. 1983. Testimony before the U.S. House of Representatives Subcommittee on International Economic Policy, Jan. 19.

Gisselquist, David. 1981. *The Political Economics of International Bank Lending.* New York: Praeger.

Graham, P. A. 1982. "Risk in International Banking." *Journal of the Institute of Banking,* June.

Griffith-Jones, Stephany. 1983. "The Growth of Transnational Finance: Implications for National Development." In Dianna Tussie, ed., *Latin America in the World Economy.* New York: St. Martin's.

————. 1980. "The Growth of Multinational Banking, the Eurocurrency Market and Their Effects on Developing Countries." *Journal of Development Studies* 16, no. 2 (Jan.): 204-23.

International Monetary Fund. 1982. *Annual Report.* Washington, D.C.: IMF.

Jenkes, Leland H. 1927. *Migration of British Capital to 1875.* New York: Alfred Knopf.

Lewis, Cleona. 1938. *America's Stake in International Investment.* Washington, D.C.: Brookings Institution.

Magdoff, Harry. 1969. *The Age of Imperialism.* New York: Monthly Review Press.

Matheison, J. A. 1982. *U.S. Trade with the Third World: The American Stake.* Muscatine, Iowa: The Starkey Foundation.

McMullen, Neil. 1979. "Historical Perspectives on Developing Nations' Debt." In L. G. Frank and M. J. Seiber, eds., *Developing Country Debt.* New York: Pergamon.

Mendelsohn, M. S. 1981. *The Outlook for International Bank Lending.* New York: Group of Thirty.

New York Times. 1982. "International Banking's House of Cards." Sept. 24, p. D27.

O'Brien, Richard. 1981. *Private Bank Lending to Developing Countries.* World Bank Staff Working Paper no. 482. Washington, D.C.: World Bank.

Porzecanski, A. 1981. "The International Role of U.S. Commercial Banks: Past and Future." *Journal of Banking and Finance* 5, no. 1 (Mar.): 5-16.

Rey, Nicholas, and John Niehuss. 1982. Testimony before U.S. House Committee on Banking, Finance and Urban Affairs. June 22. Mimeographed.

Rodríguez, Rita, and E. Eugene Carter. 1979. *International Financial Management*, 2nd ed. Englewood Cliffs, N.J.: Prentice-Hall.

Sampson, Anthony. 1981. *The Money Lenders*. New York: Viking.

Sandburg, Michael. 1981. "The Need to Be a Global Bank." *Euromoney,* Oct., pp. 56-58.

Sarmet, Marcel. 1981. "Recent Trends in International Project Lending." *The Banker,* Oct., pp. 123-25.

Sherman, Howard. 1977. *The New Gnomes*. Washington, D.C.: Transnational Institute.

Stallings, Barbara. 1978. "Peru and the U.S. Banks: Privatization of Financial Relations. . . ." In Richard Fagan, ed., *U.S. Foreign Policy and Latin America*. Palo Alto, Calif.: Stanford University Press.

Taillon, Roger. 1983. "Where the Banks Put Their Bad Debts." *Euromoney,* May, pp. 161-62.

Thorn, P., et al. 1979. *Who Owns What in World Banking, 1977-1978*. London: Bankers' Research Unit.

Triffin, Robert. 1964. *The Evolution of the IMF System: Historical Reappraisal and Future Perspectives*. Princeton Studies in International Finance no. 12. Princeton, N.J.: International Finance sec., dept. of Economics, Princeton University.

United Nations. 1955. *Foreign Capital in Latin America*. New York: United Nations.

Washington Post. 1982. "Problems in International Lending: Are the Banks Heading for Trouble?" Mar. 15, p. D1.

Wolff, R. 1971. "The Foreign Expansion of U.S. Banks." *Monthly Review*, May, pp. 17-30.

World Bank. 1984. *World Debt Tables*. Washington, D.C.: World Bank.

CHAPTER 4

Ayers, Robert. 1983. *Banking on the Poor*. Cambridge, Mass.: MIT Press.

Balassa, Bela. 1981. *Structural Adjustment Policies in Developing Economies*. World Bank Staff Working Paper no. 464. Washington, D.C.: World Bank.

DeWitt, R. Peter. 1977. *The Inter-American Development Bank and Political Influence*. New York: Praeger.

Economist. 1982. "A Bank for All Seasons: A Survey of the World Bank." *The Economist*, Sept. 4, pp. 1-36.

Felton, John. 1982. "U.S. Role in the World Bank Faces New Test." *Congressional Quarterly*, Feb. 27, pp. 451-56.

Fishlow, A. 1972. "Brazilian Size Distribution of Income." *American Economic Review*, May.

Girling, Robert. 1973. "Dependence and Persistent Income Inequality." In Frank Bonilla and Robert Girling, *Structures of Dependency*. Stanford, Calif: Institute of Political Studies.

Hayter, Teresa. 1971. *Aid as Imperialism*. London: Penguin.

Hurni, Bettina S. 1980. *The Lending Policy of the World Bank in the 1970's*. Boulder, Colo.: Westview.

Inter-American Development Bank. 1984. *Annual Report 1983*. Washington, D.C.: Inter-American Development Bank.

Jamaica, National Planning Agency. 1982. *Structural Adjustment of the Jamaican Economy. 1982-1987*. Kingston: Government Printing Office.

Knight, Peter. 1983. *Economic Reform in Socialist Countries: The Experiences of China, Hungary, Romania and Yugoslavia*. World Bank Staff Paper no. 579. Washington, D.C.: World Bank.

Lappé, Frances Moore, et al. 1980. *Aid as Obstacle: Twenty Questions About Our Foreign Aid and the Hungry*. San Francisco: Institute for Food and Development Policy.

Lewis, Jerry. 1981. "The Trouble with the World Bank." *Wall Street Journal*, Sept. 18, p. 30.

Mason, E. S., and R. E. Asher. 1973. *The World Bank Since Bretton Woods*. Washington, D.C.: Brookings Institution.

New York Times. 1982. Oct. 10, pp. F1, F28.

Payer, Cheryl, 1983. "Tanzania and the World Bank." *Third World Quarterly*, Oct., pp. 791-813.

———. 1982. *The World Bank*. New York: Monthly Review Press.

Political Structure of the New Protectionism. 1981. World Bank Staff Working Paper. Washington, D.C.: World Bank.

Rothberg, E. H. 1975. *The World Bank: A Financial Appraisal*. Washington, D.C.: World Bank.

Stern, Ernest. 1982. "1983, 1984 and Beyond." *The Bank's World*, Nov., pp. 2-4.

United States House of Representatives, Committee on Banking, Finance and Urban Affairs. 1982. *The Future of Multinational Development Banks*. Washington, D.C.: U.S. Government Printing Office.

United States Library of Congress. 1978. *Toward an Assessment of the Effectiveness of the World Bank and Inter-American Development Bank in Aiding the Poor*. Washington, D.C.: U.S. Government Printing Office.

United States Senate, Committee on Foreign Relations. 1981. *U.S. Contributions to Multilateral Development Banks and International Organizations*. Washington, D.C.: U.S. Government Printing Office.

United States Treasury. 1982. *U.S. Participation in the Multilateral Development Banks in the 1980s*. Washington, D.C.: U.S. Government Printing Office.

Williamson, John. 1982. "On the Proper Roles of the World Bank and I.M.F." Testimony before the Subcommittee on International Development Institutions, U.S. House of Representatives Committee on Banking, Finance and Urban Affairs. June 17.

World Bank. 1980a-1983a. *Annual Report*. Washington, D.C.: World Bank.

———. 1980b. *Cofinancing*. Washington, D.C.: World Bank.

———. 1980c-1983b. *World Development Report*. Washington, D.C.: World Bank.

———. 1982c. *Focus on Poverty*. Washington, D.C.: World Bank.

Wright, E. Peter. 1980. "World Bank Lending for Structural Adjustment." *Finance and Development*, Sept., pp. 20-23.

CHAPTER 5

Bello, Walden, and David Kinley. 1983. "The Rule of the IMF." *Multinational Monitor*, July, pp. 11-14.

Brandt, Willy, et al. 1980. *North-South: A Program for Survival*. Cambridge, Mass.: MIT Press.

Brau, Eduard. 1981. "The Consultation Process of the Fund." *Finance and Development*, Dec.

Carrizo, José. 1979. "Peru's Babies Are Dying." *New York Times*, Aug. 24, p. 25.

Coleman, Lewis. 1983. "Do IMF Prescriptions Make Sense?" *Institutional Investor*, Sept., pp. 141-62.

Connors, T. A. 1979. "The Apparent Effects of Recent IMF Stabilization Programs." International Finance Discussion Paper, Board of Governors, Federal Reserve System.

Council of Economic Advisors. 1973. *Economic Report of the President.* Washington, D.C.: U.S. Government Printing Office.

Dell, Sydney. 1981. *On Being Grandmotherly: The Evolution of IMF Conditionality*. Princeton Essays in International Finance no. 144. Princeton, N.J.: Princeton University Press.

Díaz-Alejandro, Carlos. 1981. "Southern Cone Stabilization Plans." In William Cline and Sidney Weintraub, eds., *Economic Stabilization in Developing Countries*. Washington, D.C.: Brookings Institution.

Diehl, Jackson. 1982. "Exxon, Others Find Projects Awry in Chile." *Washington Post*, Oct. 3, p. D2.

Economic Commission on Latin America. 1976. *Estudio económico de América Latina 1975*. Santiago, Chile: ECLA.

Economist. 1981. "Ministry Without Portfolio: International Monetary Fund." Sept. 26, pp. 2-35.

Feinberg, Richard. 1983. "The Standby Arrangements of the International Monetary Fund and Basic Needs." In Margaret Crahan, ed., *Human Rights and Basic Needs in the Americas*. Washington, D.C.: Georgetown University Press.

Girvan, Norman, and Richard Bernal. 1982. "The IMF and the Foreclosure of Development Options: The Case of Jamaica." *Monthly Review*, Feb.

Girvan, Norman, et al. 1980. "The IMG and the Third World: The Case of Jamaica 1974-1980." *Development Dialogue* no. 2.

Gisselquist, David. 1981. "IMF Primer." *Center for International Policy Report*, Jan., pp. 1-7.

Group of Twenty-four. 1984. Communiqué. Washington, D.C.: Group of Twenty-four.

Henzell, Perry. 1982. *Power Game*. Kingston, Jamaica: Ten A.

Hooke, A. W. 1981. *The International Monetary Fund: Its Evolution, Organization and Activities*. Washington, D.C.: IMF.

IMF. 1982. *International Financial Statistics Yearbook 1981*. Washington, D.C.: IMF.

Katseli, Louka T. 1981. "Devaluation: A Critical Appraisal of the IMF's Policy Prescriptions." *American Economic Review*, May, pp. 359-63.

Killick, Tony, ed. 1984. *The Quest for Economic Stabilization: The IMF and the Third World*. New York: St. Martin's.

Killick, Tony, and M. Chapman. "Much Ado About Nothing: Testing the Impact of IMF Stabilization Programs in Developing Countries." London: Overseas Development Institute. Mimeographed.

Kincaid, G. Russell. 1981. "Conditionality and the Use of Fund Resources: Jamaica." *Finance and Development*, June, 18-20.

Lappé, Frances Moore, et al. *Aid as Obstacle*. San Francisco: Institute for Food and Development Policy.

Multinational Monitor. 1982. "Exposing the IMF and World Bank." Oct.

National Advisory Council. 1981. *Annual Report to the President and the Congress 1980*. Washington, D.C.: U.S. Government Printing Office.

New York Times. 1984. "New Latin Debt Crisis." Mar. 11, p. D1.

Nowzad, Bahrain. 1981. *The IMF and Its Critics*. Princeton Essays in International Finance no. 146. Princeton, N.J.: Princeton University Press.

Payer, Cheryl. 1975. *The Debt Trap*. New York: Monthly Review Press.

Sharpley, Jennifer. 1981. "Economic Management and the IMF in Jamaica: 1972-1980." Paper presented at meeting of Development Research and Action Program, Bergen, Norway. Reprinted in Killick 1984.

United States Treasury. 1982. *U.S. Participation in the Multilateral Development Banks in the 1980s*. Washington, D.C.: U.S. Government Printing Office.

Villareal, René. 1980. "The IMF's Policies and Employment: The Latin American Experience." Paper presented at Sixth World Conference of Economists, Mexico City, Aug.

Washington Post. 1983. "Brazil Succeeds in Getting Most of Its Financing." Feb. 24, p. D-1.

Williamson, John. 1982. *The Lending Policies of the International Monetary Fund*. Washington, D.C.: Institute for International Economics.

CHAPTER 6

Datta-Chaudhuri, M. K. 1981. "Industrialization and Foreign Trade: The Development Experiences of South Korea and the Philippines." In Eddy Lee, ed., *Export-Led Industrialization and Development*. Geneva: International Labour Organisation.

Bressard, A. 1982. *RAMSES 1982: The State of the World Economy*. Cambridge, Mass.: Ballinger.

Krueger, Ann O. 1983. "The Effects of Trade Strategies on Growth." *Finance and Development*, June, pp. 6-8.

_____. 1978. *Foreign Trade Regimes and Economic Development*. Cambridge, Mass.: National Bureau for Economic Research.

Little, I. M. D. 1981. "The Experience and Causes of Rapid Labour Development in Korea, Taiwan Province, Hong Kong and Singapore and the Possibilities of Emulation." In Eddy Lee, ed., *Export-Led Industrialization and Development*. Geneva: International Labour Organisation.

Meier, Gerald. 1968. *The International Economics of Development: Theory and Policy*. New York: Harper and Row.

Michaely, Michael. 1975. *Foreign Trade Regimes and Economic Development*. New York: Columbia University Press.

Myint, H. 1958. "The Classical Theory of International Trade and the Underdeveloped Countries." *Economic Journal*, June, pp. 317-37.

Park, Yung Chul. 1981. "Export-Led Development: The Korean Experience 1960-78." In Eddy Lee, ed., *Export-Led Industrialization and Development*. Geneva: International Labour Organisation.

Smith, Adam. 1937. *An Inquiry into the Nature and Causes of the Wealth of Nations*. New York: Modern Library.

Smith, Sheila, and John Toye. 1979. "Three Stories About Trade and Poor Economies." *Journal of Development Studies*, Apr.

Sodersten, Bo. 1980. *International Economics*. New York: St. Martin's.

Todaro, Michael. 1981. *Economic Development and the Third World*, 2nd ed. New York: Longman's.

World Bank. 1982. *World Development Report*. Washington, D.C.: World Bank.

CHAPTER 7

Anjaria, S. J., et al. 1982. *Developments in International Trade Policy*. Washington, D.C.: IMF.

Baird, Peter, and Ed McCaughan. 1979. *Beyond the Border*. New York: NACLA.

Behrman, Jere. 1979. "International Commodity Agreements: An Evolution of the UNCTAD Integrated Commodity Program." In William Cline, ed., *Policy Alternatives for a New International Order*. New York: Praeger.

Bressard, A. 1982. *Ramses 1982: The State of the World Economy*. Cambridge, Mass.: Ballinger.

Brook, E., et al. 1978. *Commodity Price Stabilization and the Developing Countries*. World Bank Reprint no. 66. Washington, D.C.: World Bank.

Cline, William, ed. 1979. *Policy Alternatives for a New International Order*. New York: Praeger.

Frank, André Gunder. 1982. "Asia's Exclusive Models." *Far East Economic Review*, June 25.

Gkzakos, E. 1973. "Export Instability and Economic Growth: A Statistical Verification." *Economic Development and Cultural Change* no. 4: 670-78.

Golt, Sidney. 1974. *The GATT Negotiations, 1973-75. A Guide to the Issues*. London: British North America Committee.

Havrylyshyn, O., and Martin Wolf. 1981. *Trade Among Developing Countries*. World Bank Staff Working Paper no. 479. Washington, D.C.: World Bank.

Knudsen, O., and A. Parnes. 1975. *Trade Instability and Economic Development*. Cambridge, Mass.: Lexington Books.

Lohr, Steve. 1972. "Protectionism Imperils East Asia's Exports." *New York Times*, Dec. 9, p. D1.

Lord, M. J. 1980. "Commodity Export Instability and Growth in Latin American Economies." In W. C. Labys et al., *Commodity Markets and Latin American Development: A Modeling Approach*. Cambridge, Mass.: Ballinger.

MacBean, A. 1966. *Export Instability and Economic Development*. London: Allen and Unwin.

Morawetz, David. 1980. *Why the Emperor's New Clothes Are not Made in Colombia*. World Bank Staff Working Paper no. 368. Washington, D.C.: World Bank.

Moxon, R. W. 1974. "Offshore Production in Less Developed Countries." New York University Graduate School of Business, *Bulletin*, July.

NACLA. 1976. "Electronics: A Run for Their Money." *Latin America Report*, Jan.

Reidel, James. 1983. *Trade as an Example of Growth in Developing Countries: A Reappraisal*. World Bank Staff Working Paper no. 555. Washington, D.C.: World Bank.

Scheider, Steven, 1975. "The Paper Tiger Starts to Roar." *Berkeley Journal of Sociology*.

United Nations. 1978. *Transnational Corporations in World Development: A Re-examination*. New York: United Nations.

_____. 1969. *Restrictive Business Practices*. New York: United Nations.

UNCTAD. 1981. *Trade and Development Report 1981*. New York: UNCTAD.

_____. 1976. "An Integrated Commodity Programme." Geneva: UNCTAD.

Wilcynski, J. 1976. *Multinationals and East-West Relations*. Boulder, Colo.: Westview.

CHAPTER 8

Business America. 1981. "New Congress Sets Its International Agenda." Feb. 23, p. 11.

Dam, K. W. 1970. *The GATT, Law and International Economic Organization*. Chicago: University of Chicago Press.

Diebold, William. 1952. *The End of the ITO*. Princeton Essays in International Finance no. 16. Princeton: Princeton University Press.

Farnsworth, Clyde. 1984. "Effects of Cut in Steel Imports." *New York Times*, May 2, p. D2.

_____. 1982. "Trade Conference in Geneva Divided over Basic Issues." *New York Times*, Nov. 28, p. 1.

Golt, Sidney. 1974. *The GATT Negotiations, 1973-75: A Guide to the Issues*. London: British North America Committee.

Guest, I. 1982. "Tough Sell to Keep Doors of Trade Open." *Christian Science Monitor*, Oct. 18.

Hindley, B. 1980. "Voluntary Export Restraints and the GATT's Main Escape Clause." *World Economy* 3, no. 3 (Nov.): 313-41.

Hudec, Robert. 1975. *The GATT Legal System and World Trade Diplomacy*. New York: Praeger.

Kemper, Pia. 1980. *The Tokyo Round: Results and Implications for Developing Countries*. World Bank Staff Working Paper no. 372. Washington, D.C.: World Bank.

Krasner, Stephen. 1981. "Transforming International Regimes: What the Third World Wants and Why." *International Studies Quarterly* 25: 19-48.

MacBean, A. I., and P. N. Snowden. 1981. *International Institutions in Trade and Finance*. London: Allen and Unwin.

Meier, Gerald. 1973. *Problems of Trade Policy*. Oxford: Oxford University Press.

Monroe, Wilbur. 1975. *International Trade Policy in Transition*. Lexington, Mass.: D. C. Heath.

Perez, Lorenzo, ed. 1978. *Trade Policy Toward Developing Countries*. Washington, D.C.: AID.

Soderstein, Bo. 1980. *International Economics*. New York: St. Martin's.

Washington Post. 1982. "Geneva Negotiations on Trade May Fail." Nov. 10, p. D-9.

World Bank. 1983. *World Development Report 1983*. New York: Oxford University Press.

Yeats, Alexander. 1978. *Trade Barriers Facing Developing Countries*. Stockholm: Institute for International Economic Studies.

CHAPTER 9

Amin, Samir. 1977. "Self Reliance and the New International Economic Order." *Monthly Review*, July-Aug. pp. 1-21.

Bonilla, Frank, and Robert Girling. 1973. *Structures of Dependency*. Stanford, Calif.: Institute of Political Studies.

Brandt, Willy, et al. 1980. *North-South: A Program for Survival*. Cambridge, Mass.: MIT Press.

Clairmonte, Frederick. 1983. "Pointers to the Eighties: UNCTAD in Belgrade." *Raw Materials Report* 2, no. 3: 6-9.

Ezenwe, Uka. 1979. "UNCTAD V and the Prospects for the 1980s." *Intereconomics*, Mar/Apr., pp. 55-59.

Frank, André Gunde. 1980. *Crisis in the World Economy*. New York: Holmes and Meier.

Krueger, Anne O. 1983. "The Effects of Trade Strategies on Growth." *Finance and Development*, June, pp. 6-8.

_____. 1978. *Foreign Trade Regimes and Economic Development: Liberalization Attempts and Consequences*. Cambridge, Mass.: National Bureau for Economic Research.

Lee, Eddy, ed. 1981. *Export-Led Industrialization and Development*. Geneva: International Labour Organisation.

Magdoff, Harry. 1978. "The Limits of International Reform." *Monthly Review*, May, pp. 1-11.

Monroe, Wilbur F., and Walter Krause. 1977. "UNCTAD IV: An Appraisal." *Columbia Journal of World Business*, Summer, pp. 78-87.

Morbach, Reiner. 1979. "The Results of Manila." *Intereconomics*, July/Aug., pp. 163-67.

Sauvant, Karl P. 1982. *The Group of 77*. New York: Oceana.

Singer, Hans. "The New International Economic Order: An Overview." *Journal of Modern African Studies* 16, no. 4: 539-48.

South: The Third World Magazine. 1981. "UNCTAD Rocks the Boat." Oct., pp. 75-79.

Spero, Joan E. 1977. *The Politics of International Economic Relations.* New York: St. Martin's.

Ul-Haq, Mahbub. 1976. *The Third World and the International Economic Order.* Washington, D.C.: Overseas Development Council.

UNICEF. 1983. "The Impact of the World Recession on Children." New York: United Nations. Mimeographed.

United Nations. 1982. *Toward the New International Economic Order.* E.82.II.A.7. New York: United Nations.

United Nations Economic Commission on Latin America. 1950. *The Economic Development of Latin America and Its Principal Problems.* New York: United Nations.

Wohlmuth, Karl. 1977. "Transnational Corporations and International Economic Order." *Intereconomics* no. 9/10: 237-44.

CHAPTER 10

Bailey, N. A., et al. 1983. "Exchange Participation Notes: An Approach to the International Financial Crisis." In *The International Financial Crisis.* Washington, D.C.: Georgetown University.

Bogdanowicz-Bindert, C. 1983. "Debt: Beyond the Quick Fix." *Third World Quarterly* 5, no. 4 (Oct.): 828-38.

Brandt, Willy, et al. 1980. *North-South: A Program for Survival.* Cambridge, Mass.: MIT Press.

Brunner, Karl, et al. 1983. "International Debt, Insolvency and Illiquidity." *Economic Affairs,* Apr., 160-66.

Cline, William. 1983. *International Liquidity and the Stability of the World Economy.* Washington, D.C.: Institute for International Economics.

Cuddy, John. 1983. "Assessing Liquidity Requirements of Developing Countries, 1984-1986." *Third World Quarterly* 5, no. 4 (Oct.): 815-27.

Defense Monitor. 1983. "The Need for a Level Military Budget." 12, no. 2: 1-4.

Economist. 1983. "The International Debt Threat: A Way to Avoid a Crash." Apr. 30, pp. 11-24.

Gerowitz, Mark. 1984. "Banks' International Lending Decisions: What We Know, Implications for Future Research." Paper presented at World Bank Seminar on Debt and the Developing Countries, Washington, D.C., May.

Helleiner, G. K. 1979. "Relief and Reform in Third World Debt." *World Development,* 7, no. 2: 113-24.

International Monetary Fund. 1982. *Direction of Trade Statistics Yearbook.* Washington, D.C.: IMF.

Joshi, Vijay. 1981. *International Adjustment in the 1980s.* World Bank Staff Working Paper. Washington, D.C.: World Bank.

Leslie, Peter. 1983. "Techniques of Rescheduling: The Latest Lessons." *The Banker,* Apr., pp. 22-30.

Finance and Development. 1983. "Debt Rescheduling: What Does It Mean?" 20, no. 3 (Sept.): 26-29.

New York Times. 1982. "Banks Ease Polish Interest Payments." Sept. 15, p. D1.

Overseas Development. 1978. "New Move on Debts." July, p. 1.

Perkins, P., and Kathy Selvaggio. 1984. "Untying the IMF Knot." *Multinational Monitor*, Feb., pp. 18-22.

Quirk, William J. 1983. "The Big Bank Bailout." *New Republic*, Feb. 21, pp. 17-21.

Rohatyn, Felix. 1983. "A Plan for Stretching out Global Debt." *Business Week*, Feb. 28, pp. 15, 18.

Rowan, Hobart. 1983. "IMF, World Bank Meet amid a Funding Crisis." *Washington Post*, Sept. 25, pp. H1, H9-10.

Samuelson, Robert. 1983. "Debt Burden Endangers Recovery." *Los Angeles Times*, Oct. 3, pt. II, p. 5.

Seiber, M. J. 1979. *Developing Country Debt*. London: Pergamon Press.

Silk, Leonard. 1984. "Capping Rates in Debt Crisis." *New York Times*, May 9.

Sjaastad, Larry A. 1983. "The International Debt Quagmire: To Whom Do We Owe It?" *The World Economy* 6, no. 3 (Sept.): 305-24.

U.S. Arms Control and Disarmament Agency. 1980. *World Military Expenditures and Arms Transfers*. Washington, D.C.: The Agency.

Vaubel, Roland. 1983. "The Moral Hazard of IMF Lending." *The World Economy* 6, no. 3 (Sept.): 291-303.

Wall Street Journal. 1984. "Banks Pressured to Give Sizable Breaks on LDC Loans." Mar. 12.

Williams, John. 1983. *IMF Conditionality*. Cambridge, Mass.: Institute for International Economics/MIT Press.

Wionczek, M. 1979. "Possible Solutions to the External Public Debt Problem of Developing Countries: Final Report." *World Development* 7: 211-24.

World Bank. 1984. *World Debt Tables*. Washington, D.C.: World Bank.

CHAPTER 11

Birley, Rupert. 1983. "Can't Pay? Will Pay, but in Sultantas." *Euromoney*, May, pp. 187-90.

Business Week. 1982. "New Restrictions on World Trade." July 19, pp. 118-22.

Far Eastern Economic Review. 1983. "Going Under the Counter." Jan. 27, pp. 49-53.

Feinberg, Richard. 1982. *Subsidizing Success: The Export-Import Bank in the U.S. Economy*. Cambridge: Cambridge University Press.

Freivalds, John. 1982. "Barter Is Back: Creative Finance for Cash Poor Export Markets." *Agribusiness Worldwide*, Aug./Sept., pp. 25-30.

Gandhi, M. K. 1967. *The Gospel of Swadeshi*. Bombay: Bhatiga Vidya Bhavan.

Huh, Kyung Mo. 1983. "Countertrade: Trade Without Cash?" *Finance and Development*, Dec., pp. 14-16.

Lappé, Frances Moore, and Joseph Collins. 1977. *World Hunger*. San Francisco: Institute for Food and Development Policy.

OECD. 1970. *The Developmental Impact of Barter in Developing Countries*. Paris: OECD.

Pellay, Stephen. 1984. "India's Linked Trade.'" *Development Forum Business Edition*, Feb. 16, pp. 1-2.

Segal, Jeffrey. 1983. "Malaysia Changes Its Tune on Swap Shopping Deals." *Far Eastern Economic Review*, Jan. 6, pp. 1-2.

Thurow, Lester. 1983. "A Faltering Locomotive." *Newsweek*, June 6, p. 82.

Verzariu, P. 1978. *East-West Countertrade Practices: A Guide for Business*. Washington, D.C.: U.S. Department of Commerce.

Welt, Leo. 1982. *Countertrade: Business Practices for Today's World Markets*. New York: American Management Association.

GLOSSARY

Absorptive capacity: the ability of a country to utilize foreign private investment or loans in a productive manner

Advanced industrial countries: the now advanced capitalist countries of Western Europe, Japan, North America, and Australia

Balance of payments: a summary statement of a nation's financial transactions with the rest of the world

Balance of trade: the net value of trade in goods over a year, that is, exports minus imports – if exports exceed imports, the trade balance is "favorable"; if imports exceed exports, it is "unfavorable"

Barter: exchange of goods and services directly for other goods and services without use of a financial medium of exchange

Bilateral aid: loans or grants based on direct arrangement between two countries

Capital account: the portion of the balance of payments that shows the volume of private foreign investment and public grants and loans that flow to a country over a year

Cofinancing: joint financing of a development project by a private bank or multinational corporation and a multilateral development bank

Comparative advantage: country X has a comparative advantage over country Y if, in producing a given commodity, it can do so at a relatively lower opportunity cost (in terms of alternative commodities that could be produced) than country Y

Debt: the amount of public and publicly guaranteed loans that has been disbursed, net of canceled commitments and repayments (in common usage this term usually excludes private, unguaranteed, and short-term debt.

Debt service: the sum of interest payments and principal repayments on external public and publicly guaranteed debt

Devaluation: the lowering of the official exchange rate between one currency and the currencies of the rest of the world

Economic development: the process of improving the quality of people's lives; three important aspects are reduction of poverty, increase in employment opportunities, and creation of conditions conducive to self-esteem through improved institutions – health, education, and governmental

Economic system: the organizational and institutional structure of an economy, which includes the nature of resource ownership and control – such as capitalism, market socialism, command socialism, and mixed systems.

Extended fund facility: credits provided by the IMF, beginning in 1974, to meet the needs of countries in special balance-of-payments difficulty over a period beyond the normal one-year standby loan, and up to three years

Export processing zone: a free-trade area where imported goods enter duty-free and are processed for export by local labor

Export promotion: government efforts to expand a country's volume of exports through providing export incentives to producers

GATT: an international body set up in 1947 to explore means of reducing tariffs

Gross domestic product: the total output of goods and services produced by a country's economy – that is, within its borders by both residents and non-residents

Group of Ten (G-10): the group of 10 industrial capitalist countries that dominates the policy making of the IMF: Belgium, Canada, France, Italy, Japan, the Netherlands, Sweden, the United Kingdom, the United States, West Germany, and Switzerland (an associate IMF member).

Group of 77: a loose coalition of over 100 countries (originally 77) formed at UNCTAD to express and further their collective interests; it was instrumental in the formulation of the NIEO, a wide-ranging set of proposals for reform of trade and commodity agreements and restructuring of the international monetary order

Import substitution: the deliberate effort to promote domestic industry by replacing imported manufactures, such as appliances, shoes, and steel, with local substitutes

Internal rate of return: the return, in terms of added production or improved social welfare, from the capital investment in a project or infrastructure over the lifetime of the investment, expressed as an annualized percentage of total costs

Investment performance requirement: a condition established at the time of a foreign investment – for example, that a specified percentage of the output will be exported

Loans: the transfer of funds from one economic unit to another, such as from a private bank to a government, that must be repaid with interest (a gift of money or technical assistance does not have to be repaid)

Multilateral development bank: one of the international development banks – such as the World Bank, Inter-American Development Bank, African Development Bank – that acquires its funding from a group of nations for lending to its members

Multilateral trade negotiations: a series of negotiations among the world's nations under GATT and UNCTAD that have been aimed at reducing tariffs and other trade restrictions

Multinational corporation: a corporation with headquarters in one country and branch offices in other countries

New International Economic Order: the wide-ranging set of proposals for reform of the world's trade and financial systems, including proposals for regulation of multinational corporations, transfer of technology, and economic aid

Newly industrialized country: any of the handful of developing countries that have managed to substantially industrialize their economies during the period since 1960: Brazil, Taiwan, Singapore, South Korea, Cuba

Orderly marketing agreement: a collusive arrangement between (mainly industrial) nations to share the international market and regulate their exports accordingly

Quota: a physical limitation on the quantity of any item that may be imported into a country – for instance, so many tons of steel

Second World: the economically advanced socialist countries – the USSR and Eastern Europe

Special drawing rights: a form of international financial asset created by the IMF, often referred to as "paper gold," for use in settling international accounts

Structural adjustment loan: a highly conditioned loan from the IMF to a country that grants access to IMF resources on the condition that regular performance criteria are met (the conditions are termed a "stabilization program")

Tariff: a fixed percentage tax assessed on the value of an imported commodity, levied at the point of entry

Terms of trade: the ratio of a country's average export price to its average import price

Third World: the approximately 120 developing countries of Asia, Africa, the Middle East, and Latin America, characterized by low levels of living and economic dependence on the advanced industrial countries of the First and Second Worlds.

UNCTAD: a U.N. body established in 1964 to promote international trade, with central focus on the problems of the Third World.

Voluntary export restraint: an agreement between trading nations to restrict their exports to a certain market – for example, Japan, beginning in 1983, agreed to restrict its exports of automobiles to the U.S. market.

INDEX

ABOUT THE AUTHOR

Robert Henriques Girling is a Jamaican-born economist. He was graduated from the University of California and received an M.A. from the University of Essex, England, in economics and a Ph.D. from Stanford University. He was employed as an economic planner by the government of Jamaica. Dr. Girling has taught at the Federal University of Minas Gerais in Brazil and at the University of the West Indies. He is presently a professor of management at California State University, Sonoma, and serves as consultant to several international organizations. He is co-editor of *Structures of Dependency* and author of various articles on management and economic development.